PIERRE FRANEY'S KITCHEN

PIERRE FRANEY'S KITCHEN

BY PIERRE FRANEY
WITH
RICHARD FLASTE

Photographs by Arnold Rosenberg

Designed by Marjorie Anderson

Times
BOOKS

Published by TIMES BOOKS, a division of
Quadrangle/The New York Times Book Co., Inc.
Three Park Avenue, New York, N.Y. 10016

Published simultaneously in Canada by
Fitzhenry & Whiteside, Ltd., Toronto

Library of Congress Catalog Card Number: 82-50044

ISBN 0-8129-1023-0

Manufactured in the United States of America

For Claudia, Diane, Jacques, Becky and Jordan

ACKNOWLEDGEMENTS

This book is a compendium of my own preferences, but it would not have been possible to write it without the help of some wise friends. Although he did not directly work on this book, Craig Claiborne, my colleague at *The New York Times,* has, of course, had a pervasive influence on it; I have worked in his kitchen, using his equipment, nearly as often as in my own. My gratitude, too, goes to the expert staffs at the two Dean & Deluca stores (one in East Hampton, the other in Manhattan) and at the Bridge Kitchenware Corporation in Manhattan who have frequently allowed me to borrow equipment for demonstration or testing when mine was worn to the point of inadequacy and who have moved me in the direction of some possibilities for equipment that might not have occured to me otherwise. And then there is Joan Whitman, a diligent editor and friend of many years, who brought to this book her own special intelligence and insights.

Pierre Franey

CONTENTS

INTRODUCTION

This is not a consumer catalogue. True, it is intended to be a guide, but more than that, too. It is a personal book about kitchen equipment and food and my experiences with both, growing out of a half-century of cooking for a living. I find myself working on it at a time when my life is somewhat more comfortable than it has been in other years, and I am aware that not every reader of this book can rush out and duplicate my kitchen and its equipment. Nor should every reader: a lot depends on how closely one's proclivities in the kitchen resemble mine. I think, for example, if I did more Chinese cooking I would have acquired by now a great deal more than my simple wok and Chinese strainer.

I am also profoundly aware that, despite the emphasis on the importance of equipment in this book, good cooks can prepare fine food under the worst of conditions.

In my mind's eye I can still vividly see the one furnished room on West 75th Street in New York City I occupied in 1940 when I was a newcomer to the United States. There was a two-burner stove. I had a black iron frying pan, an iron Dutch oven and a two-quart kettle. I had brought with me from my home in France a good paring knife, a chef's knife and a whisk. I also had the trussing needle my brother had fashioned out of copper. There was a French pepper mill, too, and a vegetable peeler. And that was about it.

But I had already spent time as a cook in Paris and New York and I knew how to prepare food inexpensively and well. I made every manner of casserole in that Dutch oven. There was tripes à la mode de Caen — tripe was very inexpensive

then. And how I loved chicken au pot, simple boiled chicken (even then, at home and cooking alone, I always trussed my chickens, using my brother's needle). Of course, I made beef stew and rabbit stew. If I were fortunate enough to be entertaining a young woman, I might splurge on steak au poivre, seared magnificently in my old iron frying pan.

Even now there are times when I find myself with relatively little good equipment on hand. I travel much of the time giving demonstrations. On one trip, all I had with me were an electric skillet, a small convection oven (one of those electric ovens that are light enough to be portable and that use the principle of blown hot air to cook food), a two-burner electric stove, a food processor, a few pots, four good knives and not much more. In other words, it was nothing like my kitchen at home (although a lot better than my place on West 75th Street). For that demonstration I prepared a chocolate mousse, an apple tart, an orange soufflé, a cold salmon mousse, chicken curry — and I could have done a great deal more than that.

Yet in both of these instances — when I was on 75th Street and when I was on the road — I was truly just making do. Give any good cook a heat source and a vessel to hold food in and he will figure out how to make satisfying meals. But give that same good cook the kind of equipment described in this book and his horizons will become extraordinarily wide. The sauces he couldn't do before can now be done. The baking that required specific molds becomes a possibility. Dishes that were enormously intricate when done for the home without modern machinery — I'm thinking of the likes of fish quenelles — are now easily within reach.

And for the beginning cook, the best of equipment provides the best of starts. A bad pot will burn a hollandaise sauce every time; a good pot can prevent that. A bad knife will make it hard to chop rapidly and precisely and is dangerous because it requires so much pressure that it may slip and inflict a wound. A fine knife pays for itself without doubt — most especially if one is a novice.

Good equipment can prevent the kind of frustration, anger and disappointment that will turn the new cook away from all the possibilities for creativity and satisfaction this avocation offers. And initial failure can force one to take refuge among the legions who cook little, and don't even admit to that, laughing nervously about their inabilities in the hopes of brushing them aside.

What I have tried to do in this book is present the pieces of equipment that really do matter to me. Everything here is something that I have used often and that I believe can expand the capacities of the home cook.

Although the use of the equipment is sometimes self-evident, often it is not. And occasionally there are tricks of the trade to be learned even for the simplest of devices. So the descriptions of the utensils, pans and machines are, where even remotely useful, accompanied by pictures showing them in action and describing the techniques that I prefer.

Much of the equipment is also accompanied by recipes. It is, of course, in most cases silly to provide a recipe to help illustrate the use of a knife. On the other hand I believe it makes a world of sense to provide recipes for certain pots, machines and other devices. Prepare that hollandaise just once in a slant-sided copper saucepan and you will understand immediately how protective a good pan can be.

Moreover, I have been appalled by some of the recipe books that accompany many of the devices sold for home use, and I hope that this book in some way will stand as an antidote to those. The recipes I offer are exactly those I use for my clay roasting pan and my ice cream machine and my food processor. They are for the most part simple: home cooking, I think, becomes burdensome if it is too complicated.

As I contemplated doing this book, I realized that it wasn't just good food that made me happy, or the preparation of it (as much as I do like the process), but that somehow the equipment itself had properties that gave me a sense of contentment. The knives I had on 75th Street are still with me in East Hampton, Long Island. Now, so many years later, when I reach for one of them I feel a sense of warmth, a sense of partnership long standing. More practically, I believe the longevity of these knives is solid evidence that it pays to have good equipment to start with, the best you can buy, although that is not always the same thing as the most expensive. Cast iron pans, for instance, are splendid additions to a kitchen but they are, even now, very inexpensive.

Unfortunately, I have been unable to include prices in this book. The rate of inflation in recent years makes specific prices useless and misleading, except perhaps as a guide for comparison. Yet that same comparison, along with a far truer guide to actual prices, can be gained by a brief visit to any of the many cooking equipment shops that have been bursting into prominence all around the country, or from a quick look at a mail-order catalogue.

Because so many specialty stores are now in existence I feel confident that virtually everything in this book can be bought or ordered through a store just about anywhere in the country. But for those rare instances where that may prove untrue, I have supplied in an appendix several reliable sources that sell much of what is included here.

Obviously, this book taken in its entirety represents what I believe to be the contents of a kitchen that is as complete as it need ever be. But I am often asked to simply name the basics for a capable home kitchen. What follows is a list that I hope will prove useful (all of the items listed are discussed in detail in this book except the toaster, corkscrew, timer and tea kettle whose virtues seem self evident, and I have no particular insight to add).

Two cast iron skillets, 6½ inches and 10 inches
Two black steel frying pans, 9½ inches and 12½ inches
12-inch heavy straight-sided skillet (sautoir) with cover
Stainless steel or heavy gauge aluminum saucepans in 1-, 2- and 3- quart capacities
7-inch nonstick frying pan
Four knives in carbon steel or high carbon stainless: 4-inch paring knife, 6-inch utility knife, 12-inch chef's knife, 9-inch serrated bread knife
Sharpening steel and sharpening stone
Three spatulas: in wood, metal and rubber (a scraper)
Two-pronged fork
Three long kitchen spoons, one in slotted metal, another in solid metal and a third in wood
Graduated measuring cups in glass and metal
Metal measuring spoons
Nest of mixing bowls
Can opener and beer can opener
Swivel vegetable scraper
Flour sifter
Multipurpose grater
Nutmeg grater
Two stainless steel strainers, one with coarse weave, one with fine weave
Colander
Tart pan
Tongs
Two wire whisks, one with stiff wires and the other more flexible
Hand-held electric mixer
Kitchen scissors
Tea kettle
Coffee pot
Toaster
Pastry brush
Pepper mill
Kitchen timer
Plastic chopping board
Large casserole
Corkscrew
Rolling pin and pastry blender
Food processor
Eight-quart kettle with cover
Soufflé dishes of 6-cup and 1¼-cup capacities
Trussing needle and kitchen twine
Oval and rectangular roasting pans
Ladle
Kitchen scale
Rapid-registering meat thermometer
Salad drier

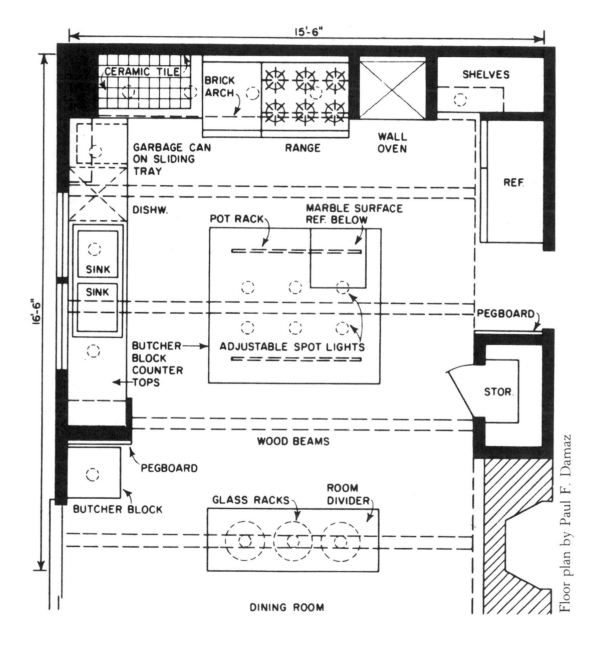

Floor plan by Paul F. Damaz

KITCHEN DESIGN

The route I took to East Hampton, Long Island, from Burgundy always seems direct enough to me when I think about it. It just sounds circuitous in the telling.

The days in Paris as an apprentice at the Drouant naturally led, step by step, to an accumulation of skills that ultimately brought me into contact with Henri Soulé, a maître d'hôtel with a sense of destiny. I would soon join him in New York to work at Le Restaurant du Pavillon at the 1939 World's Fair in Flushing. That led to my participation in the creation of his Le Pavillon in Manhattan, our way of keeping a magnificent World's Fair going. The inimitable Soulé was in charge of everything at Le Pavillon, including, it seemed, most of New York's society. My domain was smaller; over time I eventually took charge of his kitchen.

It was because of that association with Soulé that I came to reside permanently in New York, and it was also because of him that I became familiar — intimate, perhaps, is a better word — with East Hampton. In the weeks of summer when the Pavillon was closed, Soulé and I and much of the rest of the staff (many of whom are still in East Hampton or its environs to this day) would open what turned out to be the ill-fated Hedges restaurant. Anyone who wanted to show good faith (i.e., anyone who wanted to ensure that a desirable table at the Pavillon would still be available in the winter) was under some obligation in Soulé's mind to make the journey to East Hampton and the Hedges in the summer.

It was in those years, the early fifties, that I bought my beach house in East Hampton, a cottage on Gardiners Bay. Ten years later I bought what I call my house in the woods in East Hampton, with the intention of living there occasionally in the winter and renting it out in the summer when my family and I would stay in the cottage.

I remember walking into the house in the woods for the first time and looking at the kitchen. My heart sank. If I were ever to reside here permanently, I thought, the kitchen would have to go. This was no way for a man of food to live. It's not that it was terrible, mind you. Rather, it was typical, thoughtless.

The time did come, years after I had broken with the Pavillon and was setting up a steady relationship as a columnist with the new Living Section of *The New York Times* in 1976, when my wife and I decided that East Hampton should be our primary home. We would continue to use the cottage on the beach in the summer, but we would live continuously in the much more substantial house in the woods in the cooler seasons. I would need its kitchen for testing and creating recipes, as well as for the customary entertaining.

Fortunately, a man named Paul Damaz, a neighbor and a friend, was an architect of some considerable reputation who had helped many of my acquaintances from France design homes here. We both examined the kitchen, which was not enormous but large enough.

The entrance, strangely and inconveniently, was between the stove and the sink, so to enter the kitchen someone might actually walk right into the middle of the cook's concentration. The stove was of the standard electric variety, my objections to which I will describe later when I discuss the stove I ultimately bought. There was no "landing space" next to the stove, nowhere to put a hot pot just removed from the heat. There was little counter space. The refrigerator was small and silly, given what I require from a refrigerator. The kitchen was cut off from the dining room by a wall.

Standing there, beholding this barren design, Damaz and I were not despondent. In fact, we felt that sense of invigoration that beginnings often bring. We would gut the place and start over. "Well," Damaz said, "what shall we do?"

What we were going to do — and what I believe deeply is the right course for anyone who takes food seriously and is in a situation that allows the doing of it — was to create an organic whole. In my case, we would combine the kitchen, the dining room, a greenhouse and the outdoors. The kitchen would have two vistas: the exterior one opening directly through windows over the sink and through the glass sliding doors to the woods and a terrace which would serve as an outdoor dining area; and the interior one, the open view into the formal dining room.

The idea of a kitchen closed off, away from the dining area, strikes me as inappropriate in these days when there are rarely servants to run back and forth between kitchen and dining area. Now, far more often than not, it is the cook who is also the host, and a dividing wall unnecessarily removes the cook from guests or family.

Next to the terrace would be an herb garden within quick reach for that last-minute tarragon or dill or whatever. The greenhouse would be attached to the dining room to provide herbs and salad in the cold months.

Within the kitchen, there would have to be work space, but it needed to be attractive (I have always imagined that if I ever open another restaurant it will have a direct view from the dining room into the kitchen, just like this). The arrangement of the work areas and the tools, large and small, in the kitchen would have to satisfy my understanding of how a good cook moves. There should be no wasted steps, no jogging to the distant refrigerator for butter, or running around a table to get to it. The stove should not be, as it often is, some five strides away from the sink (think of the annoyance when you need to drain pasta).

A good kitchen needs plenty of space for chopping parsley and rolling dough — and for informally sitting down to a sandwich. There would be a responsive stove whose fire would be intense when necessary and gentle when necessary. There would be a refrigerator that could hold a great volume of food without hiding any of it. There would be a dishwasher, of course (a piece of equipment, incidentally, about which I have few opinions; I only ask that it work). Properly installed racks were needed to hold a great array of pots.

I wanted a pantry near the refrigerator and it had to be large enough never to be too crowded. It would, of course, be well organized. Everything, absolutely, in my kitchen must have its permanent place. Just as I do not wish to waste steps through poor organization, I want to avoid waste of time and the anger growing out of frustration that comes when a necessary item cannot be found.

The walls would be well used: spice racks, cabinets, peg board and shelving but none of it too high. In the speed and flow of cooking one doesn't want to climb stepladders.

The wastebasket would be placed on a sliding tray in a cabinet between the sink and the stove so that it could remain extended outward as I cooked and be hidden at other times.

The floor would be genuine terra cotta, which is remarkably easy to clean. The bricks, as part of the wall's decor, would be a special variety baked to high density; they are not porous and will not absorb grease or odors.

As I think the accompanying diagram of my kitchen shows, the entire design was, in the end, one of great simplicity, allowing me freedom of movement and ready access to everything I needed.

Although I was grateful to have some spaciousness, I believe most of the principles I espouse apply in some degree to small kitchens, too. Cooks working in small spaces still need capable equipment; they still need to be well-organized (perhaps even better organized because of the space limitations). And small kitchens, especially, should open to the dining room: The heat and isolation, the constrictions of a small kitchen walled away from the rest of the world, can make cooking something similar to serving a sentence.

The remainder of this chapter is devoted to the specific pieces of major equipment in my kitchen and why I chose them. Although it has been my intention to avoid brand names, here that aversion seems unwarranted. In my experience with this equipment, some brands have truly established themselves as superior to others. In some instances, the best sources for these pieces of equipment are the professional supply houses that abound in most cities.

The Gas Range

When home cooks get serious they start to cast covetous eyes on their neighbors' professional ranges. The restaurant range they usually buy, when they do decide to splurge, is a Garland. When I set up my own kitchen, I chose a Wolf.

The decision was relatively easy. I'd worked with both stoves in restaurants over the years, as well as every imaginable nonprofessional stove. I felt that if I were going to spend a lot of money on a range for my home I wanted it to be the sturdiest I could find; I wanted it to suffer abuse gladly. In my experience and that of others I've talked to, both the Wolf and the Garland proved to be good pieces of equipment, but the Garland is more bulky and less heavy. The relative heaviness of the Wolf gives me the sense of sturdiness I want, and so far that sense has not been betrayed.

Brands aside, there is a real question as to whether even serious cooks actually need a professional range. A friend of mine who knows a lot about food feels she cooks too infrequently to justify buying one. The puny flame that comes from her range, she says, is adequate as long as she puts her iron pan on it and lets it heat enough to get truly hot.

I can do without that inconvenience, though. And I suspect many others, even those who cook infrequently but want to do it well, would agree. The BTU's delivered by the flame of my Wolf (17,500) are about three times

greater than those of standard ranges. What that means is that for someone who cooks at high flame, as I do, the stove is not a source of frustration. It does what one wants it to do. And it can also be turned down to a soft heat as well (although I frequently use a heat-diffusion device called a Flame Tamer when very little heat is required, as in simmering a stock).

The one range I never would willingly use is an electric one. There is simply no real control. You can't lower the heat quickly or in subtle decrements and you can't raise it fast enough. You don't see the flame and thus miss an important visual clue about temperature. But an electric oven is marvelous (see the ensuing discussion).

In buying any professional range, an important decision revolves around the number of burners: four, six, eight. I have six, and even with the enormous amount of cooking I do, I rarely have all of them going at once. Simply for cooking, four is plenty. But what you find is that the six burners actually provide you with a good deal more maneuvering room. With just four burners, if you put a casserole and a sauté pan on the range you will run out of workspace. The difference in width is about 6 inches, 23 inches for four burners and 29 for six. The difference in price is not great. So I would recommend six burners if your kitchen can take a range that size.

Professional stoves are offered with many variations. I chose to have two ovens — I might be doing bread and pastry at the same time — rather than the storage area that the second oven might have been. Instead of a salamander broiler over the range, I have a long shelf. For me, it is important to have warm places to move food as it is done and to keep utensils that I need quickly. It turns out that the griddle my stove came with, off to the left

of the burners, is used very little for its original purpose. But I call it my landing space, the perfect area to drop a hot pot just as it is removed from the flame. Since it is always warm, I use it to proof my bread as well.

Electric Oven

Even for someone who makes his living in the constant company of pots, pans and soufflé dishes, as I do, the possession of a third oven may seem like excess, conspicuous consumption. Nevertheless, I can justify it.

My third oven is an electric Thermador. The reason I wanted it incorporated into the design for this kitchen is that I long ago learned that gas heat in a broiler is more drying than electric heat. The ideal stove would come with a gas range, which provides superb regulation of heat, and an electric oven, with its excellent broiling ability.

Incidentally, when I broil in this oven I leave the door ajar. The meat should be getting its heat directly from the electric element and less

so from the surrounding air, which, in effect, would be roasting it instead of broiling.

The electric oven has a number of other advantages over the gas ones in my Wolf. I like to be able to see a soufflé as it rises, viewing it through the glass in the door. And the oven is built into the wall at a height precisely measured to suit mine so that when I open it to baste a roast there is no stooping and no groping.

My experience with brands of electric ovens is not especially broad. I bought this one based on a stable reputation and several things that I knew it did well. Its heat recovery is very fast. When an oven door is opened for basting or other manipulations, the loss of heat is always considerable and a good oven should be able to recover quickly. The Thermador also has an interior exhaust fan. Since I roast at high heat, 425 degrees or so for a chicken, I could be filling my kitchen with smoke every time I open the oven. The fan prevents that.

A feature that came with this oven, a feature I never use, is a temperature probe. This bit of cleverness is intended to be plugged into a roast, with the oven's built-in thermostat set for a given temperature, and then the oven will turn itself off when the desired internal temperature is reached. I believe that if you start letting the oven do that kind of work you forget about the food that's in it, get lazy, forget to baste or to check it when it should be checked, and something that matters will inevitably be lost.

The oven is built into the red brick that sets the tone for my kitchen, but anyone contemplating this needs to remember that ordinary brick will not do. It is essential to get brick that is baked to high density to avoid porosity. Porous brick will absorb fumes and fats and be difficult to clean. What I wanted, and what I got, was brick that could be cleaned with a sponge.

Primary Refrigerator

I know quite a lot about bad refrigerators. There is one in my basement from the days before I renovated the kitchen. It's a noisy, little, inadequate piece of equipment. And the one at my beach house is no winner, either.

My primary refrigerator-freezer in my house in the woods is a Sub-Zero measuring 83 inches in height and 48 in width. The freezer is vertical to the left side of the refrigerator. Among the most important features I looked for in choosing this relatively expensive model was its ability to help me sensibly organize my stores so that I can find them quickly.

I like a refrigerator that is capacious and yet shallow at the same time. In deep refrigerators you can't find much toward the back, which is frustrating and wasteful because some forgotten food always spoils.

The Sub-Zero is only 16 inches deep, but it is high enough and wide enough to hold a great deal. There are three door shelves, each five inches deep, and six drawers at the bottom, two for meat, four for vegetables. The meat drawers are backed by a cooling element to keep them more thoroughly chilled than the others.

Obviously, in both refrigerator and freezer I expect a constant cold — 0 degrees for the freezer (necessary for ice cream and meat) and about 40 in the refrigerator. This freezer section has a fan that runs only while the door is closed to circulate the chill and inhibit moisture formation.

I am always careful not to overpack the refrigerator, which would diminish circulation and make the cooling uneven. And I never put anything in it, such as a hot stock or sauce, that will introduce steam into the unit, which would crystalize around the cooling elements, reducing their effectiveness. It would also temporarily raise the temperature in the refrigerator. When the temperature of food whipsaws from 40 to 50 or more the food deteriorates quickly.

The door has a handle that extends top to bottom so that it can be grasped anywhere, without fumbling, even if I am warily watching something on the range as I open the door. The door opens to my right. If it opened to the left, I would have to step around it and waste motion. And, of course, the refrigerator has to be relatively quiet, a silent, competent partner.

Auxiliary Refrigerator

While I really do think the good home cook does well to consider an extra oven, such as the electric one I described earlier, I'm not so sure about an extra refrigerator. My built-in auxil-

iary refrigerator has a permanently chilled slab of marble sitting on top of it. I mention it here not because it is essential but because for any very serious cook who does a great deal of baking this little refrigerator is at least worth knowing about.

It is a Delfield refrigerator, 36 inches high, whose original purpose was to serve in a sandwich shop. It never was intended to have an ordinary closed top to it. It comes with stainless steel containers that would nest in the open top to hold tuna fish, sliced tomatoes and so on, presenting the sandwich-maker with a supply of food kept constantly cool.

What I did was to put those inserts to other uses and replace them with a slab of marble, 24 inches square and ¾ inch thick, so that the same principle that keeps the sandwich man's food cool would keep my marble cool for rolling out dough.

Of course marble is naturally cool and that is why it is so much preferred over wood boards. It also will not warp or split the way wood can.

But in a kitchen made hot by intense periods of cooking or in warm seasons, even those natural cooling properties of marble give out.

This is particularly irksome in the production of any dough that requires a great deal of butter, such as puff pastry for napoleons or vol-au-vents. The butter begins to melt and you find yourself rolling dough that is too sticky to be manageable. The usual recourse is to flour the dough, which does make it stick less but begins to damage its texture.

To ensure cool marble, it is possible to try to find room in an ordinary refrigerator to chill it. Some people accomplish the same thing by storing their marble in the basement. Restaurant pastry chefs keep their marble constantly chilled with the help of refrigeration coils. On a smaller scale, that is precisely what I did at home.

Certainly, if this contraption did nothing more than keep marble cool, it would be wasteful in space and energy. But the fact is the interior of the refrigerator does not go unused while it is cooling my marble. The refrigerator is the height of my worktable and it is built into it. The worktable is directly behind me as I stand at the range. So whether I am cooking or preparing to cook, this little refrigerator is accessible without my taking so much as a single step to get to it. I use it to store the things I need all the time: butter, cream and eggs, as well as ingredients for the particular dish at hand.

Pot Racks

The only error I admit to in my kitchen is the height of my pot racks, 83 inches off the floor. They should have been a trifle higher. I knew that for sure when Roger Fessaguet, the chef, who is about two inches taller than I am,

came to visit and repeatedly banged his head into my pots while working with me in the kitchen.

To be candid, the fault is mine entirely, and I mean to rectify it one day. Paul Damaz, friend and architect referred to earlier in this chapter, had insisted that the racks should be higher, and to this day he walks into the kitchen and regrets his capitulation.

The rest of the rack design I left to him, and it is all exemplary. He knew that the racks had to be custom-built as part of a larger design. So when the kitchen was constructed, beams were hidden above the plaster of the ceiling with the specific intention of supporting pot racks in precisely the spots where they ultimately would be.

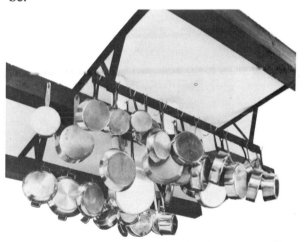

The two racks themselves are strips of black steel five feet long, one running parallel to the near edge of the my worktable and one running parallel to the far edge. The idea was to have an uncluttered array of pots and not the jumble some racks present. The ones along the near edge of the worktable are those that I reach for most, as I spin away from the range, grab a pot, and spin back. The ones along the far edge are those I need less often. Between the racks is a thick decorative wood ceiling beam, one of eight that reach from my kitchen through the dining area. This one is not merely decorative, however, in that I use it to hang the pots with handles too long for one of the steel racks. It is higher than the racks, and hooks have been placed firmly in it to support enormous copper saucepans, for instance.

The hooks on the steel racks are movable, which gives great flexibility. Each steel rack is supported by a triangle of steel screwed into a steel beam that is in turn screwed into a hidden wood beam above the plaster. Usually, thirty-six pots and pans hang from this arrangement of wood and steel, some of them substantial in weight, and I have never noticed so much as a quiver.

In addition to permitting easy access to the pots, the racks were designed to guide light. Over my work space there are six 75-watt floodlights. Three are placed in each of the channels formed between the pots. The result is bright light focused directly on the work area and no glare in my eyes, because the pots act as lamp shades in effect. And thanks to this arrangement, there is always an attractive soft glow on the pots as they hang there awaiting their turn on the flame.

It is the image of these lovely hanging pots, more than anything else I think, that makes the kitchen, as viewed from the dining room, a handsome thing to look at.

The Greenhouse

I have never regretted winter because I am devoted to skiing. I miss my garden, of course, but I make up for its loss with a greenhouse that extends out from my dining room, although in my mind's eye it extends directly out of my kitchen. I hurry from the stove or the worktable into the greenhouse for the fresh herbs that are at the core of my cooking. The basil leaves are there to be placed around fish. The basil and thyme are there as a team to be mixed with butter and cream and Parmesan cheese for pasta. I also have parsley in the greenhouse, along with a little bay tree, for its bay leaves.

Gardening writers always talk about the many attractions of a greenhouse, but for the cook it is the availability of these fresh plants that takes away many of winter's penalties. Fresh herbs in a spaghetti primavera will certainly make all those trucked-in vegetables immeasurably better. Fresh rosemary brings springtime to lamb chops.

Because of the greenhouse, I find myself in December already looking forward to fresh vegetables from the garden. By January, I start lettuce from seed (Bibb and Boston). In a month, that means, there will be young leaves for salad. In the summer, lettuce leaves are taken for granted; in February, when I have guests for dinner and walk into the greenhouse for those newborn leaves the familiar Bibb has become a treasure.

I also start leeks in January and transplant them to the garden after the last frost. In February, the eggplant, tomato and pepper plants are begun. The tomatoes will be transplanted to the garden last, not until the end of May or early June when they are very strong.

So what the greenhouse has done for me is both real and psychological. It provides some fresh herbs and some vegetables most of the time when the garden is out of commission. But by giving me a headstart on the growing season, it also allows me the great luxury of feeling that the period in which many fresh foods will be absent is brief and inconsequential.

The major shortcomings of greenhouses are

their cost and the space they require. But, obviously, it is not the greenhouse that does the growing; it's the sun. And if I did not have the space I have now I would certainly look for other ways to grow herbs indoors and to start some vegetables, and I urge anyone who enjoys cooking to try. A bright windowsill can do much of what a greenhouse can. In addition to the plants I've mentioned, savory, chives, rosemary, oregano, chervil and mint do well indoors, even simply on a windowsill.

Over the years, I've learned what will work and what won't. For a long time, I was rather disheartened with my tarragon experience. It seemed to me it was a hardy enough plant and ought to survive in a greenhouse, but the plant always failed. It was with great relief that I learned from Linda Yang, a gardening writer, that tarragon fails for virtually everybody.

KNIVES & RELATED TOOLS

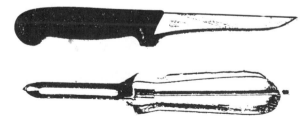

The knife problem has pretty well been solved. The invention of high-carbon stainless steel has eliminated the dilemma most good cooks confronted in earlier years whenever they wished to buy a knife. There was ordinary carbon steel, which produced a fine cutting edge, an edge that could be maintained easily with frequent honing. However, if not dried meticulously, it invariably discolored and even deteriorated through rusting. So carbon steel proved to be an excellent material but a bit of a nuisance. At the same time, there was also stainless steel, durable as could be. It did not tarnish or rust. But, lamentably, it didn't take an edge very well and was nearly impossible to resharpen once it dulled. Finally a compromise was found, an alloy called high-carbon stainless steel. It will not sharpen as well as ordinary carbon steel but its edge is quite sharp enough to suit anyone's needs. And it does resist discoloration and rust — you can wash it without the sense that it is likely to oxidize itself into oblivion.

That said, I don't want to dismiss the carbon steel knife altogether. It is much less expensive than the newer alloy, and any cook with some aspirations but a limited budget would do well to consider whether he is willing to put up with the maintenance problems of carbon steel for the sake of significant savings.

Whatever metal is chosen, the next most important consideration is the construction of the knife. There are several clues to sturdiness. For one thing, good knives for home use have conspicuous riveting running completely through the handle and its tang, which is the metal extension of the blade that reaches into the handle.

The best knives, at least those that are intended for heavy use such as the chef's knife discussed in this section, have a full tang: the metal runs the length of the handle rather than stopping midway.

The handle should be comfortable, too. I prefer those with knobs at the top to allow a firmer grip, but I stay away from those with grips that are too elaborate. The knife should also feel well-balanced so that it can be tightly controlled.

How many knives do you need? To start with, two for sure. A really good chef's knife is the workhorse of the kitchen. A good paring knife will do a lot of the chores a chef's knife is too big to handle. After that, I think the utility knife is the best acquisition, as the description of it in the ensuing pages will make clear. Then, your own experience with cooking will tell you just how badly you need a knife for boning or for filleting or for opening clams. Even with just two knives, however, everyone should purchase a sharpening steel. The reason will be documented in the discussions on the steel and the sharpening stone. For now, let me say that there is no point in shopping seriously for a good knife if that knife is going to be permitted to deteriorate.

As for brand names, there are so many manufacturers of good knives these days that I'm not sure how valuable a name is. I am familiar with — and generally pleased by — Henckel, Wusthof and Hoffritz. Sabatier, one of the best known of all knife-makers, has become a name leased to many different factories, whose work is of varying quality, some very good, some not.

CHEF'S KNIFE

The most versatile, frequently used and important knife in the kitchen is known as a chef's knife. Those cooks who struggle along without a good one are so seriously handicapped by its absence that cooking is far more onerous than it need be.

The knife's most daunting characteristic is its size, which is probably why it is excluded from some kitchens. The most useful chef's knife is 10 or 12 inches in length — a frightening implement that apppears to those not familiar with it to be more a weapon than a cooking tool.

If you look at it closely, however, you'll see that it is merely a larger version of the little paring knife, and is thus part of a series of knives (the utility knife is in between) that are all essentially the same except for size. Each has a sharp point and gently rounded blade.

The main job of the chef's knife is to chop and slice. Many cooks these days rely on their food processors for these chores. But while the machines are very fast, they always result in a significant cleanup job afterward. Learning to wield a chef's knife well, to move the hands rapidly without fear of losing your fingers, will ultimately save a great deal of time. Chopping parsley can't even be done adequately in a food processor, which tends to do a bruising job. (Some cooks use scissors, I know, but that is too slow and inefficient for me.)

To chop the likes of parsley, the handle is gripped with one hand and the tips of the fingers of the other hand rest on the spine of the pointed end of the blade. The knife is then rapidly rocked over the parsley, with most of the cutting taking place toward the middle of the blade. Some cooks don't hold the handle at all, gripping the spine of the blade at each end with the fingertips and rocking the knife. The control you have, once you are good at it, is marvelous. A recipe will say coarsely chopped or finely chopped and you can do either with the absolute sense of knowing what you're about. A machine would tend to run away with the whole operation.

For slicing, the handle is grasped near its base, so the thumb can rest on the side of the blade to steady it. I also use my chef's knife as a cleaver to go through bone. But I am extremely careful to strike the bone near the handle of the knife, where the blade is thickest and where no chopping or slicing is done.

A knife used as frequently as this one needs to be sturdy enough to survive ordinary use as well as a fall or two, and all the caveats about sturdiness in the introduction to this section apply especially here. A well constructed chef's knife, with a full tang running through its handle, will (thank goodness!) tend to fall handle first if it is accidentally dropped.

1. *Cut the stems off the parsley and gather the leaves into a compact ball.* **2.** *Hold the parsley with one hand, fingers curved under so the knife can slide up and down the knuckles. Grasp the knife with the other hand and slice the parsley, moving your hand back as you go to serve as a guide.*

3. *Grasp the handle and the wide portion of the knife blade with one hand. Press the fingertips of the other hand on the pointed end of the knife, using that end as a pivot.* **4.** *Quickly move the handle up and down and back and forth over the parsley in a rocking motion.*

PARING KNIFE

To a significant extent, cooking is a matter of control — making your tools do exactly what you want them to. And nowhere is control more important than in the use of the paring knife, a tool that is often called upon to do the most delicate kinds of work. When I find one that has just the weight and balance I want, a knife that has a grip that feels molded to my hand, I never give it up. (Testimony to that is the knife I've used almost every day since the 1930s.)

Paring knives, with blades ranging from 2 to 3¾ inches, are the smallest in a series of similarly shaped knives. The largest is the chef's knife, with a blade that can be 10 inches or longer. Somewhere between it and the paring knife is the utility knife. With all three, the blade, for most of its length, is flat and then, with a graceful arc, ends in a sharp point. The reason for the shape is that it facilitates chopping, which is done with an action initiated at the tip in a rocking motion and followed by a quick slide forward.

The paring knife is useful for chopping such things as shallots and very small onions. Its pointed tip comes into play when you want to take the eyes out of a potato, and its whole blade is at work when you're separating the leaves of a cauliflower from its stem and its flowerets from the core.

But the moment when control is everything is in the preparation of a garnish. If, for instance, you intend to decorate a fish dish with champignons tournés — mushroom caps bearing a spiral design — you'll need to learn to use a paring knife like an artist working on an etching.

For such very intricate work, the blade itself, not the handle, is clasped, with the thumb positioned along the side of the blade, almost at its tip. For other chores, the hand is largely on the handle, the thumb at the base of the blade. At the point where the blade emerges from the handle it should be wide enough to allow a purchase for the thumb.

A frequent use for a paring knife — especially for those cooks who follow recipes of my devising — is in removing the skin from tomatoes. Typically, recipes tell you to drop the tomato into boiling water for 10 seconds, and then lift them out and, with the paring knife, strip away the skin. Actually, depending on the condition of the tomato, it is sometimes safer to allow the tomato to stay in the water another couple of seconds or so.

Another use is for removing the skins of fruits, such as apples. What you want to do — and I find it quite an enjoyable little chore — is to remove the skin in a long spiraling strip. This can be done with surprising speed once you are practiced at it.

1. *To flavor a leg of lamb, cut six or eight slits about ½ inch deep and insert slivers of garlic. Use just the tip of the paring knife.* **2.** *Put a tomato in boiling water for about 10 seconds. Then grasp the skin with the paring knife and your thumb and pull the skin off.*

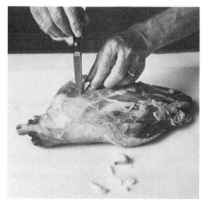 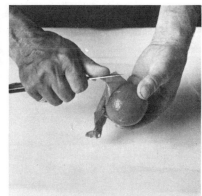

3. *Peel round fruit, in this case an apple, by cutting off about one inch of peel in one piece. This lets you follow the contour of the fruit.* **4.** *Use your paring knife to cut broccoli into flowerets, peel the stems and then cut a cross in each stem so that it will cook as quickly as the floweret.*

5. *To hull a strawberry, push the tip of your paring knife in at an angle and run it around the stem, pulling out a conical shaped piece with the stem.*

UTILITY KNIFE

There is one knife — it is often called a utility knife — that seems to exist in limbo. It has the same basic shape as the indispensable chef's knife and as the small paring knife. But, with its blade of about 6 inches, it is smaller than the former and larger than the latter.

It seems so unspecific in name and size, it could be mistaken for the kind of tool that can be used for many chores but isn't especially good at anything in particular.

That impression would be wrong. A primary use for this knife — and if it could do nothing else this would be enough — is in the carving of a chicken. Suddenly, its properties seem very specific: It has just the right degree of rigidity (a boning knife is too firm, a filleting knife too flexible), and it is the perfect length and weight for negotiating the contours of a chicken (a chef's knife is clumsily large).

When I carve a roasted chicken, I begin by pulling the leg and thigh away from the body and cut them free as one piece. I split them away from each other at the joint. I then cut off the wings. In order to have the breast meat come away neatly once work is begun on it, I cut down at an angle just at the end of the breastbone, but not through the back. To carve the breast, I take the point of the utility knife and work it along the ridge of the breastbone, cleaving close to the bone, all the way from that initial horizontal incision. With the knife and a fork, I gently pull the white meat away from the bone. I then do the same on the other side of the breastbone.

The knife is also invaluable in cutting up a raw chicken, but in that job it needs to be accompanied by a larger, heavier utensil that will be brought into play whenever bone is to be cut.

So one could simply call this a chicken knife and be done with it, were it not for the fact that it is too versatile to be categorized so easily. It is my most important knife in slicing and chopping onions, although for chopping finely the job is finished by the chef's knife. It is also used in many other slicing jobs, such as in the preparation of vegetables for a soup. The usefulness of this knife reminds me of the fait-tout saucepan (see page 92) in that its versatility is proved by how often you reach for it. In making an apple charlotte (recipe, page 196), for instance, I use my utility knife constantly, shaping the bread for the lining and slicing the apples.

As with every other knife, this one, too, ought to be the best you can afford. A fine knife will outlast most other possessions, giving good service, in some instances, for generations.

To cut up chicken for sautés or frying:

1. *With your utility knife, cut off the bony wing tips and discard.*
2. *Pull out the wing and cut through at the first joint. Repeat with the other wing.*

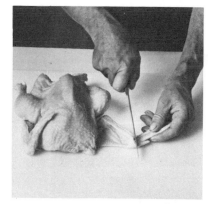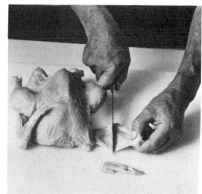

3. *Turn the chicken on its breast and slit the skin where the thigh joins the body. Pull the leg out to the side to crack the joint, then cut around the thigh from the backbone down and through the joint.* **4.** *Pull the leg away from the body and cut through to release the thigh from the backbone.*

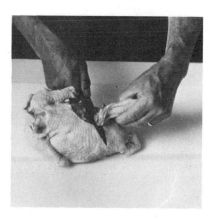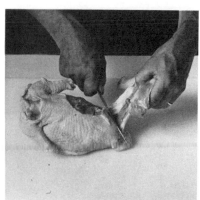

5. *Turn the bird around and slit the skin and remove the other leg in the same manner.* **6.** *Turn the chicken on its side and grasp the wing, pulling it forward slightly to reveal the ball joint where it is joined to the body. Cut through the joint.*

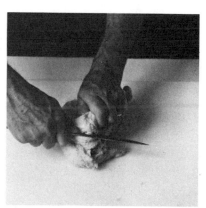

7. *Pull up on the wing and cut a straight line from the wing to the breast bone, taking a small piece of breast meat with the wing.* **8.** *Turn the chicken around and on its other side. Remove the other wing by cutting from the breast bone back to the wing joint.*

9. *Cut through the ball joint that joins the wing to the body.*
10. *Grasp the wing and joint and pull it up with one hand while releasing the wing from the breast bone with your utility knife.*

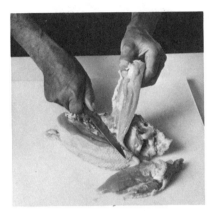 

11. *Using a chef's knife, cut the rest of the breast from the backbone.*
12. *Cut the breast in half with the chef's knife, cutting through the breast bone.*

13. *Place the leg skin side down and look for the small piece of yellow fat over the joint. Cut through that joint to sever the leg from the thigh. Repeat with the other leg.*
14. *You will have 2 breast pieces, 2 wings with slice of breast attached, 2 drumsticks, 2 thighs, 2 wing pieces. Use the backbone for stock.*

To carve a roast chicken:

1. *Lay the chicken on its side and put a two-pronged fork into the flesh of the thigh. Pull the leg and thigh away from the body and slice through with your utility knife to release it.* **2.** *Cut through the joint where the leg meets the thigh. Turn the chicken over and repeat with the other leg.*

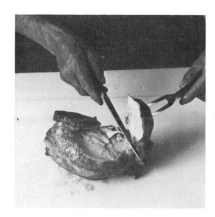 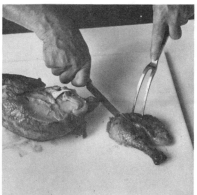

3. *Put the chicken on its back and insert the fork in the breast to steady it. Cut off the wings on both sides.*
4. *Slice down at an angle just at the end of the breast bone, but do not cut through the backbone.*

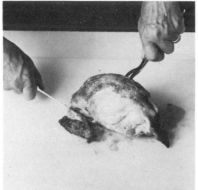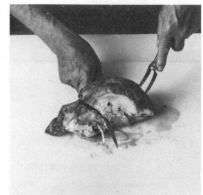

5. *Starting at that point, cut down along one side of the breast bone, releasing the large piece of breast meat. Turn the chicken and repeat on the other side.* **6.** *Cut off the wishbone and remove the small piece of meat surrounding it. Use the chicken carcass for soup.*

FILLETING KNIFE

The filleting knife is meant to negotiate a delicate course — the obstacles presented by the flesh and bones of a flatfish, for instance — and so it is slender and somewhat flexible. A good one gives you such an awareness of the fish at the knife's edge that it is as if your own sense of touch were extended right through the steel. A filleting knife also has a very sharp point so that it can neatly pierce the skin of a raw fish.

Filleting can be done at the fish store quite expertly. But cooks who allow the shop to do the work pay more than simply the tip for the service: A fish filleted much in advance of being cooked will certainly dry out. And when fish is bought already filleted in the supermarket, the head and bones are nowhere to be seen, perhaps having been discarded. That's a considerable waste, I think. By doing the work at home and saving those parts, a cook gets a good start on fish stock, which is uncomplicated and fast to make.

Every decent fisherman knows how to fillet. My son has often returned from a fishing trip loaded down with bluefish too numerous to count, set himself up somewhere in the back of the house and cleaned and filleted them all with remarkable speed. But the nonfisherman needs to know that the filleting of a fish is not so easy as it looks, requiring practice and the thorough familiarity with a fish's form that experience brings.

Before starting the job, think of what needs to be accomplished. You want to remove the side of the fish intact, an area from below its gill to above its tail. So you begin by making an incision behind the gill that reaches the bone but does not go through it. Then, using the tip of the knife, cut all the way along the top ridge of the fish. Still using the point of the knife, gently make repeated incisions behind the fillet as you peel it from the bone with your free hand. It reminds me of trying to remove an adhesive bandage without hurting the patient. The procedure is the same with a round fish, except the knife follows the curved bone.

Most kitchen tools are not restricted to the uses for which they were designed, and that is true of the filleting knife. When it isn't coping with fish, a fine filleting knife is a terrific small slicer. Because its 7-inch blade is slender, such a knife will produce extremely thin slices of breast of chicken for a salad, for instance. An ordinary 10-inch slicing knife would feel cumbersome confronting a kiwi fruit, but the filleting knife is perfect for slicing kiwi for a tart.

More than many another knife, the filleting knife should be stainless because so much of its time is spent in moisture.

1. *To fillet a flatfish such as sole or flounder, cut at an angle down to the bone between the head and the body. The fin stays with the head.* **2.** *Hold the head with one hand and insert just the tip of your knife under the skin near the head.*

 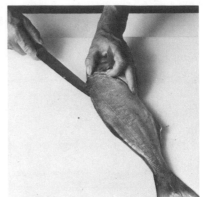

3. *Push the knife away from you and run the tip around the perimeter of the fish, leaving the tail on. Your knife will run along the top of the dorsal bone.* **4.** *Open up the fish and cut along the bone from tail to head, just down to the skin without cutting through.*

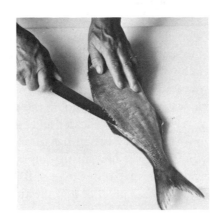 

5. *Hold the fillet in one hand and pull up on it as you go along. Use a gentle scraping motion with your knife to release the fillet. Turn the fish over and cut the fillet from the other side.* **6.** *Place one fillet skin side down and grasp the tail with one hand. Insert your knife between the skin and the flesh.*

 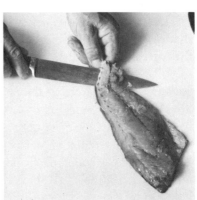

7. *Still holding the tail, push your knife in a gentle sawing motion along the flesh to release it from the skin.* **8.** *When the skin has been removed from both fillets, make a v-shaped cut at the head end of each fillet to remove the small bone there.*

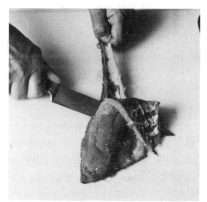 

FISH STOCK

3 pounds fish bones (may include head of fish with gills removed)
2 cups coarsely chopped celery
2 cups thinly sliced onions
1 whole clove garlic, unpeeled, sliced in half
2 cups chopped, well-washed green part of leeks
3 sprigs fresh thyme, or 1½ teaspoons dried
1 bay leaf
2 quarts water
1 cup dry white wine
¼ teaspoon peppercorns
   Salt to taste

1. Run the bones under cold running water.
2. Place bones in a kettle and add the remaining ingredients. Bring to the boil and simmer about 20 minutes. Strain.
3. Return the strained stock to the kettle and reduce by half.
   Yield: 4 to 6 cups.

SERRATED KNIFE

There are two serrated slicing knives in my kitchen, each with a specific purpose. The smaller has a 9-inch blade and a more pronounced serration than its 12-inch relative. That jagged blade gives the knife bite so that it can work just as a saw would. It's employed in my kitchen primarily as a bread knife, deftly biting through the brittle crust without shattering it and without squeezing the bread out of shape. The best way to slice a long, thin loaf of bread, incidentally, is on the bias so that you produce larger, handsomer slices.

Although these slicing knives are sometimes called bread knives, their uses are broader than the name indicates. They are excellent for slicing tomatoes, without any significant loss of juice or shape. They're fine in dealing with fruits, such as lemons, too. And they are almost essential for slicing a cake into layers.

If this knife were used in slicing meat, however, it would tend to tear it. That's why the other knife, the 12-inch meat-slicing serrated knife, has a gentler serration. Such knives are suitable for turkey, roast beef, ham and so on. But be careful in approaching anything terribly delicate, such as smoked salmon. With the likes of salmon one is much better off with the smooth precision of the slicing knife described in the preceding discussion.

One strong reason to consider buying a serrated slicing knife for meat is that it requires none of the honing with a sharpening steel that is so necessary with other knives. The high-carbon stainless steel serrated knife will hold its edge forever, or so it seems to me. I've had that 12-inch slicer for four years — and never touched a sharpening steel to it.

1. *My 9-inch serrated knife is used primarily as a bread knife because it cuts through the crust without shattering it.* **2.** *To get large slices, cut the bread on the bias, holding the knife at an angle to the cutting board.*

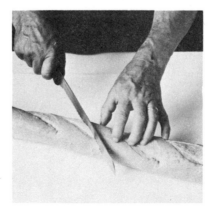

BONING KNIFE

Most legs of lamb sold in this country come with an extraneous bone, the hipbone, which takes up space, makes the roast harder to carve and contributes virtually nothing of value. And, if that isn't irritating enough, there is the fat: thick armorlike coats of it, when all anyone in his right mind would want is a thin layer.

For the extraneous bone and fat on legs of lamb — as well as for certain cuts of veal and for large chickens — a boning knife is a useful tool. If you know an especially good and willing butcher and use him all the time, the need for such a knife is less, but it still exists.

A good butcher will also, on request, slice down the length of a roast and remove the bone efficiently so that the meat can be stuffed, rolled closed and tied. But it is more satisfying to do the boning yourself because it allows you to understand intimately how the meat is laid out and to stuff it more thoroughly, if stuffing is your intention.

And by doing the job yourself, you leave your options open. After getting home, for instance, you might decide that instead of stuffed leg of lamb, a simple broiled lamb with rosemary is in order. The trick then is to butterfly it (boning the lamb and then flattening the meat by cutting away at the base of any protusions and folding them back, slicing at the seams so to speak, until the protrusions are level.

The boning knife has a thin, rigid blade of 5 or 6 inches in length. It is rigid because vigorous butcher work would snap a slender knife. By the same token, that rigidity prohibits the knife's effective use in boning anything fragile, a squab, for example, or even fish, because it does not allow you to feel the blade's progress the way a thin knife would, and you might end up cutting into the flesh.

The knives designed in Europe and those in the United States often differ in the shape of their handles. The American ones have a straight, blocky handle; the European ones a molded grip I prefer.

1. *A leg of lamb as it comes from the butcher has the large hipbone (at the bottom left of the picture), which should be removed so that the lamb is easy to carve and cooks evenly.*
2. *To remove the bone, follow its contour with the tip of your boning knife, grasping the bone with your free hand.*

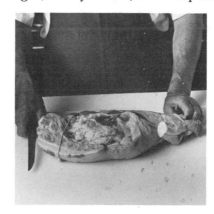

3. *Pull up on the bone and cut deeper as you go along. Always keep the knife blade against the bone so you don't cut the flesh.* **4.** *Pull up on the bone and release it from the leg. Save the bone to cook with the meat because it gives added flavor.*

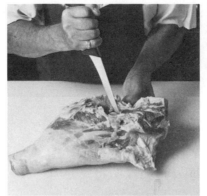

5. *Turn the lamb over and slice off the heavy layer of fat. Leave only a thin layer, about ⅛ inch, to flavor the meat and keep it from drying out.* **6.** *The trimmed leg of lamb ready to be seasoned for roasting.*

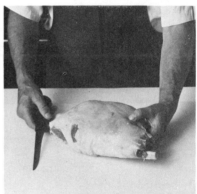

BROILED LEG OF LAMB WITH HERBS

1 7- to 8-pound leg of lamb,
   boned
   Salt and freshly ground
   pepper to taste
1 tablespoon finely
   chopped garlic
1 tablespoon crushed
   rosemary
2 teaspoons chopped dry
   basil
¼ cup olive oil
4 tablespoons lemon juice
3 tablespoons wine vinegar
4 tablespoons melted
   butter

1. Trim excess fat from the lamb and cut its sinews in such a way as to allow it to lie as flat as possible. Remove any conspicuous sinews that might make the lamb tougher.
2. Place the lamb in a shallow pan and rub it with salt, pepper, garlic, rosemary and basil. Mix the oil, lemon juice and vinegar and pour the mixture over the lamb. Cover tightly with plastic wrap and allow to marinate for 4 to 6 hours, turning the lamb every 2 hours.
3. Preheat the broiler for 10 minutes. Place the lamb in the broiler, 4 to 5 inches from the flame, and cook for 10 to 15 minutes on each side, basting occasionally with the marinade. Most cooks prefer the lamb seared on the outside, pink on the inside (about 140 degrees).
4. Remove to a warm plate and brush with butter. To serve, slice thinly on the bias.

Yield: 6 to 8 servings.

ROAST LEG OF LAMB

1 6- to 7-pound leg of lamb
6 cloves garlic, slivered
1 tablespoon oil
   Salt and freshly ground
   pepper to taste
1 medium onion, cut in half
   crosswise
¾ cup water

1. Preheat the oven to 400 degrees.
2. Prepare the lamb for roasting by cutting away the hipbone and excess fat.
3. With a paring knife make small incisions in meat and insert garlic slivers.
4. Rub the lamb with oil and place it in the pan, fat side down, along with onion and the hipbone (with most of its fat removed). Sprinkle meat with salt and pepper.
5. Roast the lamb on the floor of the oven (or lowest rack, if in an electric oven), basting every 15 to 20 minutes. Turn fat side up after ½ hour. After 1 hour total cooking time, remove all liquid from the pan and pour water into the pan.
6. Continue roasting for 15 minutes. The internal temperature should reach at least 140 degrees (for rare).
7. Remove from the oven and place the bone under the roast to serve as a rack in the pan, then let rest for 20 minutes as dripping juices enrich the gravy. Carve and serve with pan gravy.

Yield: 6 to 8 servings.

CLEAVERS

Because preparation is such a preponderant part of cooking, chefs of the Western world developed an elaborate system of knives. The Chinese, whose cuisine is also extremely reliant on preparation, arrived at the same place by a different route.

For the Chinese, a few basic cleavers do all the work, and they do it well because cleavers are capable of great precision. A Chinese cook can wield a cleaver with the dexterity of a French cook using a chef's knife. (The French have always used a cleaver, too, but it is larger and almost exclusively a butchering tool.)

Since Chinese cleavers are almost as readily available in the West these days as are standard knives, the home cook has a chance to see which implement suits his needs and his hand best. In my own kitchen, I find that one large Chinese cleaver and one French one are all I ever use.

Cleavers come in several sizes and shapes. The specialized ones aren't terribly useful to me because of my preference for Western knives. But the large cleaver is a marvelous tool for splitting ribs or cutting through chicken bones, and I sometimes find myself using it for slicing as well.

Heavy cleavers are valuable as mashers and tenderizers. They can be used to flatten a bit of veal by striking it with the side of the blade.

To hold a cleaver for most tasks, one extends the thumb and index finger out onto either side of the blade and then wraps the remaining fingers around the stubby wooden handle. Slicing is done in more or less the same fashion as that employed with a chef's knife, with the vegetable or meat steadied by the fingertips of one hand so as to expose only fingernails to the cutting edge of the blade. The knuckle of the middle finger should act as guide for the blade. The cutting edge should be at a slight angle to the surface, with the weight of the blade doing most of the work as it is lifted from the cutting board only a fraction of an inch with each motion. A bonus provided by cleavers is that their broad blades can be used to carry food from chopping block to pot.

1. *Holding the cleaver with thumb and forefinger on the blade, slice the thickest part of the flank steak into pieces about 2 inches wide. Hold the blade at a slight angle so you slice on the bias.* **2.** *Lay the end piece of steak flat and hold it with the palm while slicing through parallel to the board.*

3. *Stack a few slices and slice down with the cleaver into thin strips about ¼ inch wide.* **4.** *A cleaver can also be used to julienne vegetables, just as you would with a chef's knife.*

BEEF WITH ASPARAGUS

1 pound flank steak
2 tablespoons dark soy sauce
2 cups vegetable oil
4 teaspoons cornstarch
18 asparagus spears
1 teaspoon sugar
1 teaspoon salt
¼ teaspoon monosodium glutamate, optional
3 tablespoons dry sherry or shao hsing wine
3 tablespoons chicken broth

1. Place the beef on a flat surface and, using a sharp knife or cleaver, cut it against the grain into slices about 2 inches wide. (This is easier to do if the meat is partly frozen.) Slice each piece of flank steak horizontally into two or three pieces. Stack the slices and cut into ¼-inch strips.
2. Combine the beef with the soy sauce, 1 tablespoon of the oil and the cornstarch. Work the mixture with the fingers and set aside.
3. Cut off the tough ends of the asparagus, then scrape with a swivel-bladed peeler, leaving the tips intact. Rinse well. Drop the asparagus into boiling water to cover and simmer about ½ to 1 minute, depending on the age and size of the asparagus. Drain and immediately run under cold running water to chill. Cut the asparagus on the bias into 1-inch lengths, and put the pieces into a bowl of cold water until all are cut up. Drain.
4. Heat the remaining oil in a wok or skillet and when it is warm add the beef, stirring to separate the slices. (If the oil is hot the meat will stick together in a lump.) Cook no more than 20 or 30 seconds. Drain in a sieve-lined bowl to catch the drippings and discard all but 2 to 3 tablespoons of the oil.
5. Combine the sugar, salt and monosodium glutamate and set aside.
6. Heat the 2 to 3 tablespoons of reserved oil in the pan, and when it is almost smoking add the asparagus pieces. Sprinkle with the sugar mixture and cook, stirring, about 10 seconds. Add the beef and stir to blend. Add the wine and broth and cook 1 minute or less, stirring, until the sauce is almost absorbed in the beef.
Yield: 4 to 8 servings.

CARVING FORK

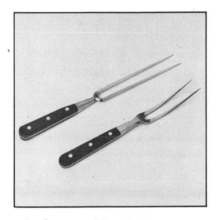

There are nuances in using almost every kitchen tool. The simple carving fork illustrates the point. Generally this fork comes in two designs. There is a curved fork (I prefer one about 10½ inches long) and a straight one (12½ inches in length is sensible).

The most important trick to learn in the use of a fork for carving is one that defies the common thinking: I rarely pierce a roast with the prongs. It seems foolish to make holes in a roast that will drain the very juices whose existence you went to such pains to ensure. What I do instead is position the prongs horizontally and press down on the meat so the prongs are holding it firm. One can apply this pressure with either the straight or the curved fork, but the curved one is better suited to this purpose, holding a roast as if it were a robot's cupped hand. There are indeed times when it makes sense to pierce meat, however. But the meat must be the kind that is supposed to be well cooked, such as a pot roast. You pierce the meat to hold it firm during carving and also to test it for doneness. It is sufficiently done only when the fork can be withdrawn with little or no resistance.

Either design works well in manipulating a steak on a grilling rack. (But, again, take care not to pierce the meat.) What the fork can do is slide between the rods of a grill and pop the steak free rather than scraping it free as a spatula would.

In purchasing a fork, there are several characteristics to look for. Stainless steel is the best material since it requires a minimum of care. The fork, like a good knife, should be solidly riveted at the handle and the tang, which is the metal extension of the fork that runs into the handle. The tang should be full. For reasons of sanitation, you want the fork to be fashioned smoothly so that there are no seams that can catch food and make it difficult to clean.

1. *To carve a roast, use a two-pronged fork to steady the meat while you slice it. But do not pierce the flesh because the juices will run out. Just rest the tines on the roast with firm pressure.*

SLICING KNIFE

Somewhere along the way — and I don't profess to know precisely when — man decided he liked the taste and look of thinly sliced meat. Ripping and tearing wouldn't do anymore. He needed knives, good knives that were sharp and slender. Over the years, as materials and designs have been refined, slicing knives have evolved into admirable precision instruments.

It is, however, still possible to ignore all those years of evolution. To achieve something that resembles a Cro-Magnon assault on a piece of meat, just choose the wrong knife.

In slicing, a principle to keep in mind is that the thinner the slice must be, the thinner the blade required. For working on prosciutto or smoked salmon (or salmon cured in other ways, such as the silken gravlax of Scandinavia), where thinness is crucial to taste and texture, you want a blade of 12 or 14 inches in length that is only about 1/16th of an inch thick. The technique in slicing anything that calls for such precision is to use tightly controlled short thrusts of the wrist, with very little arm motion. With salmon and other smoked or cured fish, the object is to cut on a bias, cleaving close to the skin without slicing through, shaving the fish from the skin, as it were. When the slices required are thicker than for salmon or prosciutto, the blade need not be as thin (although I still prefer one that is) and the slicing motion can be more free-swinging.

An exceptionally thin knife is, of course, quite flexible — too flexible for carving, which is a combination of slicing meat and cutting through joints. So to carve a large fowl, it's helpful to have two knives, a slender slicing knife and one that is about the same length or a little shorter but more rigid. That second knife is sometimes called a carving knife, but I've found that knives designated for other purposes, filleting for example, can frequently serve the purpose as well.

An interesting and relatively new design in slicing knives employs small hollowed-out ovals along its sides. This is not a serration; the cutting edge of the blade remains flat. The ovals diminish the friction that is especially noticeable in the slicing of moist meat such as rare roast beef.

Some slicing knives have pointed tips, others are rounded. The points serve as prongs that enable the cook to move a slice of meat deftly. But they are certainly not a necessity, and many cooks would, with some justification, just as soon avoid another potential hazard in the kitchen. I use both designs interchangeably.

GRAVLAX (Salt- and sugar-cured salmon)

2 **bunches fresh dill**
1 **4-pound section of fresh salmon, preferably cut from the center of the fish**
¼ **cup kosher salt**
¼ **cup sugar**
1 **teaspoon coarsely ground fresh pepper**
2 **tablespoons Cognac Mustard-dill sauce (see following recipe)**

1. Cut off and discard any very tough stems from the dill. Rinse the dill and pat it dry.
2. Bone the salmon section or have it boned. There should be two fillets of equal size and weight. Do not rinse the fish but pat it dry with paper toweling.
3. Combine the salt, sugar and pepper. Rub this mixture into the pink flesh of the salmon.
4. Spread one third of the dill over the bottom of a flat dish. Add one of the salmon pieces, skin side down. Sprinkle on Cognac. Cover this with another third of the dill. Add the remaining piece of salmon, placing it sandwich-fashion over the dill, skin side up. Cover with the remaining dill and place a plate on top. Add a sizable weight and let stand in a very cool place or in the refrigerator for 48 hours. Turn the "sandwich" every 12 hours, always covering with the plate and weighting it down.
5. Using a thin-bladed slicing knife, slice thinly on the bias like smoked salmon. Serve with Mustard-dill sauce.
   Yield: 12 to 20 servings.

MUSTARD-DILL SAUCE

½ **cup Dijon mustard**
2 **teaspoons dry mustard**
6 **tablespoons sugar**
¼ **cup white wine vinegar**
⅓ **cup vegetable oil**
⅓ **cup light olive oil**
½ **cup chopped fresh dill**
 Salt to taste

1. Combine the prepared mustard, dry mustard and sugar in a mixing bowl.
2. Using a wire whisk, stir in the vinegar. Gradually add the oils, stirring rapidly with the whisk. Add the dill and salt. Taste and correct the flavors by gradually adding more sugar, vinegar or salt.
   Yield: About 1½ cups.

SHARPENING STEEL & STONES

At a buffet in a restaurant of elegance and aspirations I remember watching a poor fellow try to slice roast beef as the impatient crowd pushed its way toward him. This young man had to suffer in public as the victim of at least two apparent mistakes: The roast beef was too rare for easy slicing and, in any case, the blade was almost certainly not sharp enough. As a result the meat was squashed and torn rather than sliced.

It is inefficient — and sometimes embarrassing— to allow a knife to grow dull. Moreover, a dull blade is more dangerous than a sharp one. It requires greater force and so it is more likely that its user will slip and cut himself.

Keeping a sharp edge on a good knife is not difficult, but diligence and the proper tools are required. Ignore those little slotted devices intended to hang on the inside of cabinet doors. When you draw a knife through one of those it tends to take away too much of the steel and shorten a knife's life.

The classic tool and the most effective over the long run is known as a sharpening steel — a ridged steel rod with a wooden handle. One 16 inches long is adequate for most home uses.

To use the steel, hold it pointed up in one hand, poise the knife blade's base near the tip of the steel, then draw the knife downward while sliding it toward you so that each action manages to run the whole length of the knife.

While working I use my steel frequently. I invariably turn to it before each chore. And if the job is a big one, I might use the steel five to ten times before I'm done.

I can't stress too strongly the need to use the steel often. I have met many home cooks who simply refuse to do it. Somehow this chore seems to cross the border between rational expenditure of time and lunacy. But these people are wrong. They almost always end up muttering about how bad the workmanship is even in expensive knives, blaming the manufacturer for their own negligence.

A knife under heavy use or one that has been neglected will require more than just the sharpening steel. A stone made of silicone carbide, with two abrasive surfaces, a coarse side and a smooth side, is invaluable in the home kitchen, especially when a knife has become battered after being dropped or carelessly used.

The most useful size is 7 or 8 inches in length and 2 inches in width. The coarse side is necessary for an extraordinarily dull blade or one that has been nicked. The smoother side follows the use of the coarse abrasion or can be employed alone on a knife that isn't terribly dull but needs some work. The stone should be oiled or moistened with water to diminish the friction.

In addition to the traditional stones, a new kind, one with fragments of diamond embedded in it, is available now. It is very good but much more expensive than the common variety.

1. *Use the sharpening stone when your knife is neglected and very dull. Place the thickest part of the knife on the stone and hold it lightly with one hand. Pull the knife toward you at a slight angle, ending at the tip.* **2.** *Turn the knife over and repeat, pulling the knife toward you.*

3. *If the knife has a dent or a nick in the blade, sharpen it first on the coarse side of the stone, then finish it on the smooth side.*

GRATERS

Grating and shredding are often such small jobs — a couple of teaspoons of Parmesan, a dusting of nutmeg, a hint of lemon rind — that the best equipped cook would feel foolish hauling out a food processor every time. So it's good that the old-fashioned, nonmechanical graters haven't been relegated to museum cases yet.

Some simple graters are intended to do lots of different jobs, others are highly specialized. In each case the purpose is very specific: to take a solid food and reduce it to countless minute particles that will release its flavor evenly into the surrounding flavors.

The grater I'm fondest of has the most limited of uses. It's the nutmeg grater, a small metal tool with a curved rasping surface and a lidded storage pocket on top. The pocket is charming, of course, but mostly it's extraordinarily functional. Nutmeg is a seed the size of a large marble that comes from the nutmeg tree, which is native to the Moluccan Islands but widely cultivated elsewhere. To produce enough ground nutmeg to top a custard you use only a bit of the seed; the remainder drops neatly into the storage pocket so you know just where to find it the next time around. (Whole nutmeg retains its flavor far longer than the often stale preground product.)

If you were going to have only one grater in the house, the classic, pedestrian multipurpose kind makes the most sense. This type usually has fine puncture holes on one side that work like sandpaper on a piece of nutmeg, and it also has the equivalent of coarser sandpaper for cheese or for bread crumbs. Then there are the holes that act as teams of small blades to do shredding. The smallest of these is good for lemon peel, the larger ones for vegetables. Some multipurpose graters also have a slit for making potato slices.

What you have to be wary of with these graters is poor workmanship. A very good one can be inexpensive but still made of rigid, durable steel, and it will not give you the feeling that it's about to collapse under pressure.

A marvelous tool is the Mouli rotary grater (there are other brands, but those others I've seen are less sturdy). It's a hand-held device with a container into which you drop a piece of hard cheese, which is then forced down onto a hand-cranked drum. As you crank the drum, slivers of cheese an inch long cascade out, the ideal texture and shape for Parmesan to be tossed with pasta. It also does an admirable job with carrots and many nuts, such as almonds and walnuts.

1. *Put a sheet of wax paper under a four-sided grater and rub a lemon or orange over the small holes to obtain grated peel, called zest.* **2.** *To grate hard cheese like Parmesan or Gruyère, use the rotary grater, which gives you long, thin strands of cheese.*

 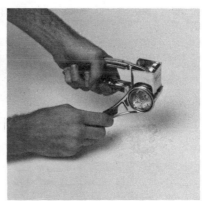

3. *A nutmeg grater that holds the seed in the top is easy to use when you need just a sprinkling of fresh nutmeg, as for pâté or on top of a custard.*

LASAGNE WITH TOMATO SAUCE AND RICOTTA

1 tablespoon olive oil
1 clove garlic, finely minced
½ pound ground lean pork
½ cup dry white wine
3 cups tomato sauce (see following recipe)
  Salt and freshly ground pepper to taste
12 lasagne noodles
2 cups ricotta cheese
¼ cup hot water
1 cup grated Parmesan cheese
¼ cup melted butter

1. Preheat the oven to 375 degrees.
2. Heat the oil in a skillet and add the garlic and pork. Cook, stirring, until pork turns white. Add the wine and bring to a boil over high heat. Cook, stirring, until wine evaporates. Add the tomato sauce, salt and pepper to taste.
3. Bring a large quantity of salted water to a boil and add the lasagne noodles, one at a time. Cook until almost tender. Add a quart of cold water to the pot. Drain and spread the noodles on a damp cloth.
4. Lightly grease a lasagne pan measuring approximately 13x8x2 inches. Add a layer of noodles.
5. Beat the ricotta with the hot water to make it spreadable. Spread about one third of the ricotta over the lasagne. Spread a layer of the tomato sauce over this and sprinkle with about ¼ cup of the Parmesan cheese. Continue making layers, ending with a layer of noodles sprinkled with a final quarter of the cheese. Pour the melted butter over all and bake for 15 to 20 minutes, or until the lasagne is piping hot and bubbling throughout.
   Yield: 4 to 6 servings.

TOMATO SAUCE

⅓ cup olive oil
4 tablespoons butter
2 cups chopped onion
2 tablespoons chopped garlic
2 tablespoons finely chopped fresh parsley
1 tablespoon finely chopped fresh basil, or 1 teaspoon dried
6 sprigs fresh thyme, or 1 teaspoon dried
1 teaspoon sugar
1 whole clove
5 cups chopped tomatoes
  Salt and pepper to taste

1. Heat the oil and 2 tablespoons of butter in a heavy casserole and add the onion, garlic, parsley, basil, thyme, sugar and clove. Cook, stirring, until the mixture is almost dry but still moist, about 5 minutes.
2. Add the tomatoes, salt and pepper and bring to the boil. Partly cover and simmer for ½ hour.
3. Put the mixture through a food mill, pushing through as much of the vegetable solids as possible. Stir in the remaining butter and bring to the boil.
   Yield: About 3 cups.

VEGETABLE PEELER

In 1939, when I was laboring as a young chef in New York, I returned to France for a short visit with family and friends. I happened to bring with me a slender American-designed gadget, the swivel-action vegetable peeler. By the time I left France to return to this country, I had accumulated so many requests for the little tool that I felt as if I were its representative abroad.

My friends wanted to be sure that I would return with an armload soon. As it happened, I never did. The war arrived, and years later, when I could go back, it seemed trivial to worry about the broken promise of an armload of vegetable peelers.

Nevertheless, even now that swivel-action peeler — or one just like it, actually — resides in my kitchen as a small testimony to American ingenuity. The reason I prefer it to other peelers is that the swiveling allows it to move with the contours of a potato or carrot far better than a stationary peeler or a knife.

I use it to peel asparagus, too. Too few cooks realize this job needs to be done and they end up with stringy asparagus. The fibrous base of the asparagus should be cut away and the remaining stalk should be peeled by grasping the tip in one hand and pushing the peeler away from it. If you did it in the other direction, the danger is that you would knock the tip right off.

The French do now have a swiveling peeler, too, but it is wider and less easy to use and store. The American peelers, which come in carbon steel or stainless (the carbon holds a better edge but rusts) are always very inexpensive, a great bargain when you look at how prices have climbed in recent years.

1. *Using a utility knife, cut off and discard the white, woody ends of the asparagus.* **2.** *Hold the tip of the asparagus with one hand and push the vegetable peeler away from you down the length of the stalk. Keep turning the stalk so that all the stringy skin is removed.*

MANDOLINE

The mandoline is a peculiar looking implement — something like a washboard on an easel stand. It got its name — or so one story goes — when an Italian chef described the rapid slicing motion as similar to strumming. To use it, the cook slides a vegetable down along the cutting surface until it strikes the desired blade.

It can produce a slice of potato 1/16th of an inch thick or ½ inch thick or any minuscule variation between the two. And it will deliver each slice rapidly at exactly the chosen thickness. That's a significant virtue in the preparation of a dish such as pommes Anna, the potato pie that relies for its texture and its color on the uniformity of its ⅛-inch-thick slices. When you are cutting zucchini for spaghetti primavera (see recipe, page 65), you intentionally try for different shapes to provide a variety of textures, and the flexibility of a mandoline allows you to get many different kinds of effects.

In addition to the straight slicing of vegetables, the mandoline has a number of other capabilities. Hidden on an axle beneath the machine are two rows of blades, one with ⅜-inch separations and the other with ⅛-inch spaces. The turn of a crank brings these blades above the cutting surface of the mandoline. And with them you can quickly produce julienne of zucchini or carrots or shoestring potatoes. The wider-spaced blades are for french fries. There is also a rippled blade for cutting ridges on a sliced beet or cucumber. This blade is indispensable for pommes gaufrettes — slices of potato that have an intricate waffle design.

I want to temper all this enthusiasm with a warning. The mandoline is not a toy. It takes a while to learn to use it properly. And the mandoline can be dangerous. If you start out with that Italian chef's simile in mind and strum rapidly, you will probably cut yourself. Until you're very skilled at this, use cautious downward strokes, being sure to hold the potato with the tips of your fingers so that your fingernails and not your skin are exposed to the blades. Or hold the vegetable with a cloth.

Better yet, when you purchase a mandoline, also buy the protective shield designed for it. This is a device that slides over the surface of the mandoline, holding the potato or other vegetable against the blades and your hand away from them. Unfortunately, it adds significantly to the price. The mandoline — and I know of only one that I can recommend wholeheartedly — is made in France by Bron.

1. *For pommes gaufrettes, push the peeled potato against the fluted blade, then give it a turn and do it again. This gives the potato slices a waffle effect.* **2.** *To julienne a long vegetable such as zucchini, push the trimmed vegetable lengthwise over the julienne slicing blade.*

ZUCCHINI JULIENNE WITH PESTO

⅓ cup (tightly packed)
   fresh basil leaves
¼ cup plus 1 tablespoon
   virgin olive oil
2 tablespoons pine nuts
2 tablespoons freshly
   grated Parmesan cheese
2 cloves garlic, halved
4 medium zucchini (about
   1¼ pounds), trimmed and
   cut into julienne strips
1 teaspoon salt
⅛ teaspoon freshly ground
   pepper

1. Combine basil, the ¼ cup oil, pine nuts, cheese and garlic in blender or food processor with metal blade. Process, turning machine on and off, until basil and nuts are coarsely chopped.
2. Heat the 1 tablespoon oil in a large skillet over medium-high heat. Add zucchini; stir-fry until heated through but still crisp, about 3 minutes. Season with salt and pepper.
3. Stir in the pesto sauce and mix well. Transfer to a heated platter; serve immediately.
   Yield: 6 to 8 servings.

CUCUMBER AND DILL SALAD

1 pound cucumbers
2 tablespoons white
   vinegar
   Salt and freshly ground
   pepper to taste
1 tablespoon sugar
2 tablespoons chopped dill

1. Cut the cucumber into even slices of about 1/16th of an inch. The total should be about 4 cups. (Such thin slicing is most adequately done with a mandoline, but, with practice, it can also be done with a chef's knife.)
2. Combine all the ingredients, tossing them gently with hands or spatula, and let stand at least an hour before serving.
   Yield: 6 servings as appetizer or as side dish for cold seafood.

FRENCH-FRY CUTTER

I find them irresistible, these little french-fry cutters. But the truth is that when I am preparing french fries seriously, I almost always do it by hand, with a chef's knife, falling back on tradition and habit and forgetting about these little machines. And then as soon as one strikes my eye (various ones have come and gone in my kitchen), I try it and I'm taken by it all over again.

The kind of french-fry cutters I like best are those that force the potato through gratelike blades, providing long, graceful fries. (Food processors can be equipped with a french-fry cutter, but the fries are not nearly so handsome as these.) The way the one pictured here differs in design from other similar machines is that the plunging is a two-step movement. As the slicing begins, the handle's arm grasps a hook and pulls the potato forward. When it is most of the way through, the arm is disengaged from that hook and moved to a further one to complete the action. The result is that the slicing is done with somewhat less force than it is in other machines.

This machine, by Westmark, is a combination of plastic and cast aluminum and steel. It seems sturdy enough, and it has suction cups on its base to secure it to the countertop.

Its most serious disadvantage is that it will not slice large potatoes. (The best potatoes for french fries, incidentally, are the driest: Idaho or Maine russet potatoes.)

The large ones will either have to be shaped to fit or else you will have to take up the traditional tool for french fry cutting, the chef's knife. The slow but sure method with such a knife is to flatten the potato's surface, slicing at either end and slicing a bit of potato from the sides so that it takes on a boxlike shape. Cut it lengthwise into ¼-inch layers and then cut those layers into ¼-inch-wide strips. The trick is to produce the longest french fries you can.

1. *Peel the potatoes and square them off, if desired. Using a utility or a chef's knife, cut them into ¼-inch slices.* **2.** *Stack the slices and cut them into ¼-inch strips.*

3. *Or peel the potatoes and push each one through the french-fry cutter.* **4.** *Put enough potatoes in the deep-fry basket to fill it halfway and lower them into oil heated to 330 degrees. The fat should bubble briskly. When potatoes have begun to blister but not yet turned brown, remove them from the oil. Rest the basket on its bracket until ready for the final cooking.*

FRENCH FRIES

2 pounds Idaho potatoes
Vegetable oil sufficient
in quantity to fill fryer
halfway
Kosher salt to taste

1. Peel the potatoes, placing them in a bowl of cold water as you go along to preserve their color. The potatoes can be sliced by machine or, of course, by hand. To do it by hand, cut off both ends and create sides so that the potato is flattened all around and becomes easier to handle. Cut ¼-inch slices lengthwise and then cut each slice into ¼-inch strips.
2. In a large mixing bowl, wash the slices to remove the starch. Place them in a colander and pat dry with towels. Put potatoes into fryer's basket.
3. Pour oil into deep fryer and bring to 330 degrees (determined by a deep fat thermometer). Stir it occasionally as it heats to help equalize the temperature. Lower the potatoes into the oil. Cook for 4 to 5 minutes to remove potatoes' moisture. Shake the basket occasionally. The basket should never be filled more than half way. If there is too large a quantity of potatoes for the oil, it will cool too quickly or might bubble over. When potatoes have begun to blister but have not yet turned brown remove from the oil and hang the basket on bracket. If desired, this step could be done hours ahead of time, with potatoes stored in a cool place, covered with paper toweling.
4. Raise the temperature of the oil to 360 degrees. Return potatoes to the oil, shaking constantly; potatoes will brown quickly, in a minute or less. Drain and pour from basket onto tray layered with paper toweling. Sprinkle with kosher salt.
   Yield: 4 servings.

CLAM KNIFE

In the age-old combat between carnivore and bivalve, I have had a measure of success, and at least part of the credit for it should go to a variety of knives specifically designed to open clams and oysters.

To be well armed in these battles you need three knives — one for cherrystone clams, another for littlenecks and a third for oysters (which I will deal with in the next discussion). For oysters, you also need a kitchen towel, neatly folded and placed in one hand where it will hold the shellfish and protect you if the knife-wielding hand slips. The towel should be damp to increase its grip.

Shellfish all open more easily if chilled first. But the approach to the different bivalves does vary in the specifics.

To take on a cherrystone clam, which is large and has a heavy shell, I use a rigid, blunt knife with a stainless blade of about 3½ inches in length, whose rounded tip is designed to minimize damage to the meat of the clam.

The clam is opened by cupping the shell in one hand. Place the knife edge between the lips of the shell (often the less rounded side of the clam is best) and, with the fingers, squeeze sharply inward against the back of the blade. If you get inside the clam just slightly, twist the knife to force the shell apart, then run the knife around the edge to the hinge of the clam, severing the muscle from the upper shell.

Once the shell is open, a usual next step in this country is to sever the muscle beneath the clam. The clam will be more succulent, however, if you defer that cutting until just before you eat it.

Littlenecks are more fragile than cherrystones and require a narrower blade that will slide between the shell halves without breaking them as the heavier blade might. The tip, which is more pointed than on the other knife, is useful in giving you tight control for cutting the muscle.

1. *Cup the clam in the palm of one hand, hinge facing out. Hold the knife parallel and insert it next to the hinge, pressing the blade with your fingers so that it goes in about ¼ inch.* **2.** *Turn the knife up and toward you to pry open the shell.*

3. *Run the tip of the knife around the shell, holding the tip up just to loosen the clam from the upper shell without tearing the meat. Run the tip of the knife under the clam on the bottom shell. Save the clam liquor if called for in the recipe.*

STUFFED CLAMS BOURGUIGNONNE

24 **littleneck clams**
¼ **pound soft butter cut into chunks**
1 **tablespoon finely chopped garlic**
3 **tablespoons chopped parsley**
1 **tablespoon chopped fresh basil (if available)**
2 **tablespoons fresh bread crumbs**
Salt and pepper to taste
2 **tablespoons grated Parmesan cheese**
1 **tablespoon Pernod**

1. Preheat the broiler.
2. Using a clam knife, open each of the clams and leave them on the half shell. Discard the top shells.
3. In a small mixing bowl, use a rubber spatula to bind butter with garlic, parsley, basil, bread crumbs, salt and pepper. Place about a teaspoon of the butter mixture on each clam. Arrange in a gratin pan and sprinkle with cheese.
4. Place pan in broiler, close to flame, and remove it when butter is bubbling; be careful not to overcook. It should take no more than two minutes. Place on top of range at high heat. Add Pernod to the pan. It will flame briefly. Remove from range at once and serve.

Yield: 4 to 6 servings.

OYSTER KNIFE

Oysters are like clams in that they are more easily opened when chilled. But even with the best of preparation, some of them will hang on to dear life with the strength of a super creature. The opening of an oyster takes practiced skill, a certain amount of strength and a good deal of caution. Always hold the shell with a towel protecting your hand. Injuries can be serious. And don't get your ego too involved in the job. There is no disgrace in giving up on an especially difficult opponent.

An oyster is not entered with the edge of the blade as a clam is, but with the point, which is thrust between the shells under the small lip that protrudes at the hinge.

There are many designs for opening oysters. Most commonly you will see a stubby knife with a blade like an arrowhead and a shield at the base of the handle. The shield is intended to halt the blade's progress so you won't stab yourself if you thrust too hard. I laud the idea and would not quarrel with anyone who wanted to opt for such a cautious design. But I don't much care for it because the blade seems too wide and prone to breaking the shell.

I prefer a longer (about 2 inches in length), narrower, pointed blade tapered on both sides. The fact that it has this double taper is not a problem since at no time do you grasp the knife blade itself as you would in forcing a clam knife sideways between shells. It should have a rounded handle that allows for an easy, quick twist of the knife once it penetrates the shell. Using this knife, you do have to practice to avoid letting the knife go too far. A punctured oyster deflates like a tire with a nail in it.

1. *Hold the oyster with a towel because the shell is sharp and the knife pointed. Push the tip of the knife into the rounded lip next to the hinge.* **2.** *Run the tip of the knife around the shell, loosening the oyster from the top shell without puncturing it.*

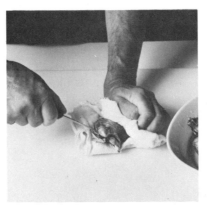

3. *Cut the muscle on the bottom shell near the hinge, but don't loosen the whole oyster if serving them on the half shell. They will stay plump longer. For dishes that call for the whole oyster and the liquor, hold the oyster over a bowl and run your knife under the oyster to loosen it, reserving the liquor.*

OYSTERS ROCKEFELLER

2 cups rock salt
12 oysters on the half shell
6 tablespoons butter
½ cup finely chopped green onion
1 cup chopped loose leaf spinach
½ cup finely chopped parsley
½ cup fincly chopped watercress
⅓ cup finely chopped basil
1 teaspoon finely chopped garlic
  Salt and freshly ground pepper to taste
  Dash Tabasco sauce
2 tablespoons Pernod
2 tablespoons grated Parmesan cheese

1. Preheat the broiler.
2. Spread rock salt along the bottom of a gratin pan to a depth of about ⅓ inch. Arrange the oysters, shell down, on the salt.
3. Melt the butter in a shallow skillet. Add onion and then spinach, parsley, watercress, basil, garlic, salt, pepper and Tabasco and stir with a wooden spatula as it bubbles for about 5 minutes. During the last minute of cooking stir in the Pernod.
4. Place a tablespoon of the sauce on each oyster and sprinkle each with Parmesan.
6. Place oysters as close to the flame as possible for 5 minutes.
   Yield: 4 to 6 servings.

TRUSSING NEEDLE

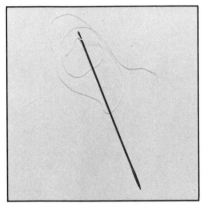

When I was a 14-year-old apprentice some decades ago at the Drouant in Paris, I was allowed to have only three tools: a paring knife, a vegetable peeler and a trussing needle. They were the standard beginners' tools not only because they were rudimentary but also because they would prove indispensable as time went on.

I still consider all three indispensable, even though one — the trussing needle — appears not to have found its way into very many home kitchens. I think its failure to do so is because the virtues of trussing poultry are not widely understood. In addition, trussing often seems to be too complicated and many cooks feel too harried to take the time. But, believe me, trussing is worth the effort.

To make the point to a skeptical visitor, I cooked two chickens, one untrussed so that its limbs were left to flop this way and that, and the other tightly trussed, its limbs sewed to its body and its openings at both ends sewed closed with loose skin.

The result was that the two chickens emerged from the oven in very different fashion. Not only did the untrussed one look gawky, but also it had cooked unevenly. The heat had moved through it like some erratic hot wind coursing through valleys and mountains and caves. Parts of the chicken were undercooked; other parts were dry. The skin at the base of the legs was so brittle that it burst when it was touched. But the trussed chicken had the symmetrical look that I have come to think of as beautiful, and it had cooked uniformly, browning evenly.

There are other advantages to trussing, too: It is helpful for containing stuffing in the cavities, and, because the bird is made into such a tight unit, it is easier to manipulate in the oven.

The method I use for trussing is of my own devising (although, for all I know someone else may have devised a similar method). It requires tying only one knot instead of the two usually needed and thus is faster than other methods.

You will need a trussing needle about 8 inches long for squab or Rock Cornish hens, 10½ for chicken and 14 for turkey, and some sturdy twine, the kind that is sold as kitchen twine in cookware stores. A single chicken requires about a yard of twine, but to ensure that you will not pull the cord all the way through as you tighten it, it's a good idea to begin with more than is actually needed.

When you first try trussing you will probably feel awkward, perhaps a little anxious, and slow. But persevere. After you've done it successfully several times, the whole procedure will take no more than about a minute.

1. *Put the bird on its back and bend the wings under.* **2.** *Thread a long trussing needle with kitchen twine. Grasp the legs and pull them back. Push the needle through the skin on one side of the tail cavity and out through the joint of the opposite leg. Leave enough string to tie a knot.*

 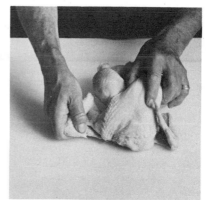

3. *Turn the bird on its breast. Bring the needle back and push it through the middle of the wing.* **4.** *Then push the needle through the neck skin, pinning it to the backbone, and out through the other wing.*

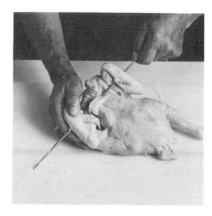 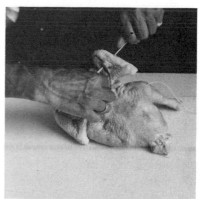

5. *Turn the bird over, pull the legs back, and push the needle through the leg joint and out through the skin on the other side.* **6.** *Press the legs down and push the needle through the skin under the breast bone. Pull it out the other side.*

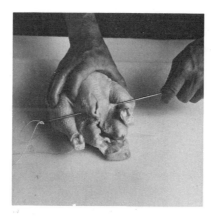 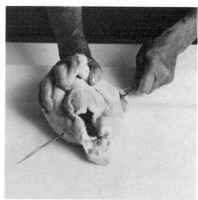

7. *Turn the bird on its side and pull the string tight. Tie a double knot.*
8. *The trussed chicken ready for cooking.*

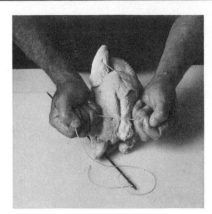 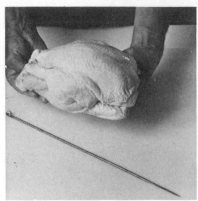

CHICKEN AU POT

1 **3-pound chicken, cleaned and trussed**
2 **whole cloves**
1 **onion (about ¼ pound), peeled**
4 **carrots, cut into 2-inch pieces**
4 **stalks celery, peeled and cut into 2-inch pieces**
1 **clove garlic**
1 **bay leaf**
½ **teaspoon thyme**
3 **sprigs parsley**
6 **peppercorns**
½ **cup converted rice**

1. Place the trussed chicken in an enameled iron casserole or deep, heavy saucepan, along with neck and gizzard. Cover chicken with water (about 10 cups).
2. Stick one clove in each end of the onion and drop into pot.
3. Place remaining ingredients except rice in the pot and bring to a simmer, uncovered. Skim fat and scum occasionally. After 20 minutes, add the rice. Simmer uncovered another 20 minutes. Untruss the chicken, carve and serve surrounded by vegetables. Yield: 4 servings.

CORNISH GAME HENS GRAND MÈRE (Roast game hens with potatoes and mushrooms)

4 Rock Cornish game hens about 1 pound each
4 tablespoons butter
12 very small peeled white onions
½ pound potatoes
½ pound mushrooms, about 8
Salt and freshly ground pepper to taste
¼ cup water
4 tablespoons chopped fresh parsley

1. Preheat the oven to 425 degrees.
2. Rub the game hens inside and out with salt and pepper. Truss them and place them breast side down in a buttered, heatproof, oval baking dish. Dot with 2 tablespoons of butter. Scatter the gizzards and necks around the hens. Reserve the livers. Add the onions and place the dish on a low flame on top of the stove to get the baking dish hot. Place in the oven and bake 20 minutes.
3. Meanwhile, peel the potatoes and cut them into ½-inch cubes. Drop them into cold water in a saucepan. Bring to the boil.
4. As the potatoes come to the boil, rinse the mushrooms and pat dry. Cut them into quarters and set aside.
5. When the potatoes reach the boil, drain them. Heat remaining 2 tablespoons of butter in a skillet and add the potatoes. Cook, shaking the skillet and tossing the potatoes so that they brown evenly, about 5 minutes. When lightly brown, add the mushrooms and salt and pepper to taste. Cook about 10 minutes, tossing and shaking the skillet.
6. At this point the hens should have completed their first 20 minutes of cooking. Turn the hens on their backs. Sprinkle the livers with salt and pepper and add them to the baking dish. Continue baking about 10 minutes.
7. Scatter the potatoes and mushrooms around the hens and continue cooking about 15 minutes, basting often. Lift the hens and let the cavities drain before they are removed.
8. Add the water and parsley to the vegetables in the pan. Bring to the boil on top of the stove, stirring. Serve the mushrooms and potatoes and the pan sauce with the hens, either whole or cut up.
Yield: 4 to 8 servings.

CUTTING BOARDS

You do need some wood surfaces in the kitchen (see especially the butcher block table discussion that follows), but not for chopping and slicing. The development of polyethylene chopping boards has made the familiar wooden ones obsolete.

Wood's main virtue has always been that it is soft enough not to damage a knife's blade. But its disadvantages are many. Wood is porous, so it absorbs moisture. Thus it dries slowly and is prone to swelling, warping and cracking. To minimize those effects, one has to wash it gingerly, with a sponge and soap, never soaking it or putting it in the dishwasher. And you can't really be certain how clean the wood is afterward. It can retain odors. Bacterial colonies may lurk in the cracks and pores of the wood. Most of the restaurant chefs I know have switched from wood to plastic because they are concerned about sanitation and about the health inspector's visits.

Plastic avoids most of wood's faults while retaining its virtue. It is soft enough to avoid blunting a knife but it is not porous. It can be soaked in the sink or cleaned in a dishwasher. The plastic is usually embossed with small ridges that prevent food from sliding on its surface.

However, the lightweight plastic board may slide around; to prevent that, place a damp cloth under it. Also, be sure to keep it away from fire, and don't place hot pots on it.

There are a number of plastic boards available in a variety of sizes, and they all appear somewhat similar. Before choosing one you'll need to take a few factors into consideration. For most work, the 17 by 10 inch is a good working size, but you may have trouble storing one so large or finding the counter space for it. And it may not fit into your dishwasher, if you have one. So there's good reason to think in terms of a small cutting board, perhaps 8 by 14 inches, although you will find that the zucchini slices keep rolling off.

Another consideration in acquiring a chopping board is to look for one with a handle. The handle permits you to hold the board with one hand and scrape the chopped or sliced food from the board directly into whatever you're preparing. It also allows for the board to be hung.

The most annoying characteristic of plastic boards is that all of them (at least all that I've seen) are terrible for carving meat or anything else that releases a lot of liquid. For some reason they come with no trough to catch the juices. So don't discard that old-fashioned wooden carving board.

1. *To chop an onion (or a shallot or large clove of garlic), place it on the cutting board and cut it in half through the root end.* **2.** *Place the onion half cut side down and make parallel cuts close together all along the onion without cutting through the root end.*

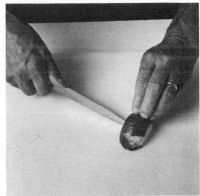

3. *Holding your utility knife with the blade parallel to the board, make several cuts up to but not through the root end.* **4.** *Slice down across the onion to achieve a fine slice.*

BUTCHER BLOCK

In the days when I worked in restaurants I would return home to my own kitchen each day, feeling that something important was missing there. Actually, lots of important things were missing, but I had one thing in mind, one thing that would give my kitchen the sense of meaning business. It was a butcher block for pounding meat.

Of course, I didn't need the butcher block at home in those days any more than I needed the other appurtenances of a well equipped kitchen. I did almost all my important cooking on the job. But still I would have felt better, more secure, if the butcher block were there in my own home.

Now I cook constantly at home. And one of the first things I made sure my new kitchen had was the butcher block I always yearned for. The reason has little to do with nostalgia — although the deeply worn butcher block tables were always in the kitchens of friends and relatives when I was growing up in France.

It happens that these tables are truly invaluable for certain tasks. If you have ever tried pounding a scaloppine of veal or a breast of chicken on an ordinary work surface you undoubtedly found that the surface bounced right back at you, requiring more effort and time than the proper surface would have.

Anyone pounding on a poor surface may well become frustrated and give up before the job is done correctly, before the veal or chicken or whatever is perfectly, uniformly thin so that it will cook evenly and to the proper tenderness.

My table is 34½ inches high and 18 inches square. Neither of those dimensions, however, is as important as the thickness of the solid block sitting on its sturdy legs. It is 1 foot of high-quality maple. It does not bounce back.

Having the table near me as I cook, I find more uses for it than simply employing it in the pounding of meat. It makes the cracking of bone easy and reminds me to do it. The reason you crack bone in making a stock or a demi-glace (which is a greatly reduced stock), is to release the protein that otherwise might be withheld from the liquid. I even do this in roasting pork or veal, cracking the exposed bone so that the protein will enrich the sauce prepared from the drippings.

Cleaning butcher block is something of a chore. Because it takes such a beating, fat gets pounded right into the wood's pores. To clean it I begin by scouring it with a sprinkling of salt and a wire block brush, which is a brush with short firm bristles (the salt prevents the fat from clogging the brush). Then I scrub it with a solution of bleach and water (about ½ cup of bleach to 2 cups of water).

SCISSORS

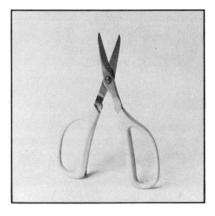

Because fins are so hard to deal with, it is terribly awkward to clean a fish without using a pair of scissors or shears. (Shears differ from scissors in that they look and feel more like a hedge clippers.) Recognizing that, some inexperienced cooks head straight to the sewing box and pull out scissors that are not up to the job. They fail to grip fins or tail, sliding off with every squeeze of the handles.

Unlike those for sewing and barbering, shears intended for fish or raw meat have a slight serration, which prevents them from sliding away. With shears designed for poultry, another factor can be helpful: One of the blades has a notch in the shape of a half moon about a quarter of an inch deep. The notch can grasp the bone of a chicken while the scissors clamp closed.

A number of companies have produced a multipurpose pair of scissors that will cause most cooks to smile. These scissors, usually about 8 inches long with a serrated blade for meat and fish and a small notch for bones, also have an area between the handles for opening jars and one for bottle caps. There is a screwdriver-like protrusion on one handle intended to pry open a box lid, and a flattened area, which is a little hammer. But I have the feeling it's not as useful as it wants to appear (certainly not much of a screwdriver, for instance).

Although at one time or another I have used all the scissors described here, I looked around my kitchen as I was preparing to work on this book and noticed that I had exactly two pair. One is the ordinary tool for cutting paper. The other is the little Chinese scissors pictured here. They are simply marvelous for cutting fins, even though they have no serration. Those two tools seem to be sufficient. I admire poultry shears, but have never used them much because I prefer the utility knife (see page 6).

Any good pair of scissors needs to be stainless steel so it won't rust or tarnish. Chrome-plated carbon steel often has the disheartening characteristic of shedding its chrome.

SMALL STOVE-SIDE UTENSILS

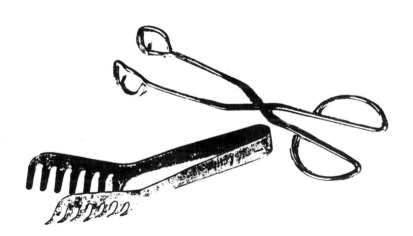

In the kitchen design discussion earlier in this book, I diligently pointed out how every major piece of equipment had to be in its place to diminish movement and frenzy during cooking. This is true of small pieces of equipment, too, the spatula, the spoon, the whisk that are required at once. How easily they can be lost or hidden behind larger tools!

All these utensils are, quite literally, extensions of the cook's hand. To reach for one and not find it fast results in the kind of frustration that borders on anger.

In my kitchen that frustration is largely avoided with the help of one of the plastic carousels that are quite common these days. It sits on my work space not far from the range and contains all those lifters, turners, beaters and the like in an orderly fashion. The carousel isn't absolutely necessary, of course, but a sense of organization is.

Another way you need to discipline yourself is in shopping for these utensils. Perhaps nowhere else in the realm of kitchen equipment is it possible to buy so much in the way of terrible utensils. There are spatulas that bend — and stay bent. There are plastic tools that melt on contact with hot food, adding an ingredient that is in no one's recipe.

So I urge you, in the consideration of each of the discussions that follow, not to take the easy way out with one of those dime-store utensils that hang everywhere, but to shop carefully for tools that will last. Don't be afraid to put some pressure on a ladle's handle before buying it to test its sturdiness.

The tools in this section don't have to be expensive to be worthy, however. Consider, for example, the wooden tools. They are marvelous aids in the kitchen and never cost more than a few dollars.

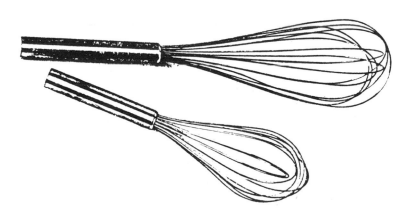

NARROW SPATULA

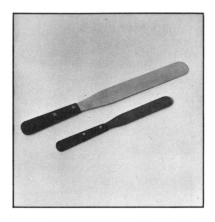

In the kitchen of a French restaurant, if the broiler chef calls for a spatula he most often means a narrow tool shaped more like a knife than the paddle-shaped implement commonly thought of as a spatula. It has a stubby handle and a long flat blade, sometimes serrated on one side, usually rounded at the end.

And it is a terribly important tool, the only spatula chefs typically carry with them on trips as part of their standard batterie. It is one of those tools, like the mandoline, that are somewhat alien in American kitchens, but once it has been introduced there the cook wonders how he could have lived without it all those years. It is used over the grill to turn small fillets of fish. It becomes an extension of the human hand as it reaches into the broiler to turn and lift a filet mignon. (A fork is faster in turning a steak, but it will pierce the meat and allow the juices to escape.)

This lifting and turning function requires high quality stainless steel. It needs to be flexible to slide under food, bending like a drawn bow, but then as the food is lifted the spatula needs to be rigid or else the steak will go tumbling ignominiously back into the pan as the blade of the spatula gives out.

Another reason for the flexibility is that these spatulas are superb decorating devices. I use mine, for instance, to place a wavelike effect on the surface of mashed potatoes (see recipe, page 77). Holding the spatula at the handle with one hand and on the blade with the other, I draw it across the surface, pressing down and releasing it rhythmically as I move it along to make the waves. If the purée has first been mixed with egg yolks, it can be dusted with grated cheese and then placed under the broiler, whence it will emerge as pommes mont d'or.

More frequently such spatulas are used to spread an icing on a cake or to smooth the butter cream between layers. The ones with serrated edges come in handy if you want to lend a ripple effect to the icing. But they are especially meant to be used to cut through layers of cake, like a bread knife.

The size spatula that makes the most sense to me is one with a blade of about 10 inches in length and about 1½ inches in width. It is a bit awkward for small cakes, however, and people who do a lot of baking may find they also need a spatula with a blade of about 7 inches in length.

The handle on one of these spatulas needs to fit your hand comfortably. I prefer the rounded ones to the flat. The handle will tend to come loose if it is not well fixed to the blade; a good clue to the sturdiness of the tool is if the handle is attached with two or three conspicuous rivets.

1. *A 10-inch flexible spatula is ideal for turning a crêpe quickly.* **2.** *It is also handy for smoothing the top of a soufflé or for frosting a cake.*

3. *A flexible spatula is used to level flour or sugar in a cup when you want an exact measurement.*
4. *The longer spatula with a rigid blade is best for turning pieces of chicken or meat so that it doesn't pierce the flesh as a fork would. Its shape allows you to maneuver in a crowded pan.*

RUBBER SPATULAS

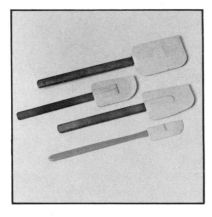

Granted, in the batterie de cuisine, rubber spatulas don't have much spark. One doesn't ordinarily carry on about them. Yet these spatulas are far more efficient than the hand at removing every bit of frosting from the edge of a bowl, and certainly better than the pastry corne. The corne, a device originally made from the hooves of animals, was an early crescent-shaped pastry tool that could slide along the side of a bowl to remove the batter adhering to it. The rubber spatula clings so tightly to the side of a bowl that there is nothing better as a scraper. In addition, the rubber heads on these spatulas — firm yet pliable — combine just the required qualities to stir and lift when folding in chocolate and beaten egg whites. I keep many at the ready for the sake of speed. I don't want to have to stop to wash the spatula I've been using for pastry when I have to tend to the mousse.

Different sizes help, too. There is a spatula with a very small head, no wider than an inch and 2½ inches long, which fits neatly into a jar of French mustard, for example. There is a large, firm one, almost 3 inches wide and 4½ inches long, that is required for batter. And there is what I think of as the standard size, 2 inches wide and 3½ inches long, for the likes of mayonnaise or mousse.

I have referred only to the rubber ones and not the plastic because I believe rubber to be far superior in that it is more pliable and clings to bowls better. Rubber nevertheless does have a drawback. Often, when I use one in a mixture that is too hot, the rubber degrades.

There are two kinds of handles: wood and plastic. I prefer the wooden ones, although each type has its advantages. Plastic does clean more thoroughly than wood, especially since it can be soaked, a treatment that is damaging to wood. But plastic breaks too easily, leaving you with only a stump of a spatula as it snaps. And it will melt if left too long on the edge of a pot.

1. *A rubber spatula is the best tool for pushing solids through a strainer because it will not damage the fine mesh.* **2.** *It is also the most effective for folding in egg whites. Use a figure-8 motion, pushing the spatula down in the center, up on the far side, down in the center and up on the side nearest you.*

CHOCOLATE MOUSSE

½ pound sweet chocolate
¼ pound bitter chocolate
6 large eggs, separated
¼ cup water
2 cups heavy cream
6 tablespoons sugar
Whipped cream for garnish

1. Cut the chocolate into ½-inch pieces and place in a small saucepan. Set the pan into water that is hot but not boiling. Let melt over low heat, stirring occasionally.
2. Put the yolks in a heavy saucepan — preferably a slant-sided fait tout — and add the water. Over very low heat, beat vigorously with a flexible wire whisk. A heat-diffusing device such as a Flame Tamer can be useful here in ensuring that eggs do not cook. Beat yolks until they thicken; the consistency of the sauce should be that of a thin custard such as a sabayon.
3. Remove from the heat and add the sauce to the melted chocolate, stirring it thoroughly with a rubber spatula.
4. Beat the cream with an electric mixer or whisk until stiff, adding 2 tablespoons of the sugar toward the end of the beating. Fold the cream into the chocolate mixture.
5. Using an electric mixer, beat the egg whites at medium speed until soft peaks start to form. Beat in remaining sugar, 1 tablespoon at a time, and continue beating, at high speed, until stiff. Be careful not to overbeat, which will cause the whites to break down. Fold the whites into the chocolate mixture with a large rubber spatula, quickly and thoroughly, turning the bowl all the while.
6. Using a rubber spatula, lift the mousse into a serving bowl and chill. Just before serving, garnish with whipped cream.
   Yield: 12 to 14 servings.

OTHER SPATULAS

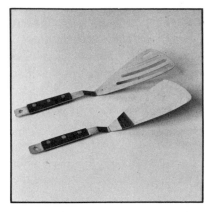

Are they spatulas or lifters and turners? I use the terms interchangeably. Purists won't call the metal paddle-shaped utensils I have in mind spatulas, reserving that term for the long, narrow tool in the preceding discussion. They're probably right but it all seems a bit precious to me. More important is the quality of these tools, and it is astonishing how bad they can be. I have seen them so poorly constructed that they have no spring to them. If you bend them they stay bent, believe it or not. The image that comes to mind is that of food splashing back into hot fat, as if it were on a slide.

Obviously, to find the good tool amid all the bad ones you have to know what you're looking for. A good spatula is sturdy and resilient, of course, and it should have a comfortable handle. I like wooden handles tightly riveted to the metal so that there are no crevices to collect food particles. The plastic handles I've come across look dismayingly fragile.

These utensils should also be well-designed. Generally speaking, the head should be at least 5 or 6 inches long. And the spatula should be made for specific purposes. No one spatula can do all jobs well. Because of this specificity of function, I don't think it is extravagant to have several metal lifters in the kitchen. One might be relatively stiff and heavy for lifting something like a veal roast stuffed with kidneys, when the trick is in not losing the kidneys along the way.

A squarish, slotted lifter allows you to pick up a hamburger while the fat drips away.

Perhaps most important is the flexible spatula that is rounded to fit the walls of a sauté pan so that it will slide under a fillet of sole, practically molding itself to the fish so that the flesh does not break.

1. *Slide the metal spatula under the fish fillet.* **2.** *As you turn the fillet over, hold it with your other hand so the flesh does not break.*

WIRE WHISKS

When the wire whisk came along, it revolutionized cooking. It could blend and beat better than an army of wooden spoons. Of course the whisk, as with any innovation, was resisted by some people, my grandmother among them. She would sit in her small kitchen in Burgundy, a bowl of mayonnaise between her knees, stirring laboriously with her favorite spoon for hours, when she could have been working for mere minutes with a whisk.

In many of today's kitchens, it seems to me, there are cooks who are also missing out on its benefits — but inadvertently. They may have a whisk that is so poorly made, for instance, that its wires lose their shape entirely when they come in contact with a sauce. Or they may have a good whisk, but only one. And the fact is that different whisks are designed to perform different functions.

The beating of egg whites requires a balloon-shaped (to fit the bowl) whipping whisk. The wires should be thin and there should be a lot of them, perhaps 12 looping over each other. This type of whisk has to be flexible so that its head whips forward with each flick of the wrist, creating a foam that incorporates the air and the egg whites.

Very often a whisk is used not for whipping, but for binding the ingredients of a mixture during cooking. A roux, for instance, which is a combination of flour and butter used as a base for many sauces, must be stirred constantly as it cooks. For such tasks, a relatively stiff whisk is employed with only 8 or so wires. But even with mixing whisks I like a little flexibility to increase the speed of the head.

A good tool saves time and energy only if it is used properly. In beating cream, for example, the springiness of the whisk and not the cook's arm should exert most of the force. With my elbow held slightly away from my body and my arm absolutely still, I start to beat, using only the smallest rotation of hand and wrist. It is important to do this with a rapid but comfortable cadence so as to get the job done without exhaustion. I find myself going at a rate of about 70 strokes a minute. When beating eggs, it is only toward the end when the whites must be flailed into stiffness, that I use my whole arm, along with wrist and hand, in revolutions around the entire bowl that are as rapid as I can make them.

Whisks come in many different sizes, and the size you use should be determined by the job at hand. A small whisk (10 inches) is useful for working in a shallow saucepan. A medium-size whisk (12 inches) is the right one for a deeper saucepan, and a longer whisk (14 inches) is necessary for a deep bowl. I like whisks that are made of stainless steel because they don't rust. And I much prefer whisks that have their wires soldered into the handles because I feel they are sturdier and easier to clean than the others.

1. *When blending or thickening a sauce, use a 10-inch wire whisk that will cover the entire bottom surface of the saucepan. Keep the whisk constantly moving in a figure-8 motion.* **2.** *A whisk is also useful when pushing solids, such as tomatoes, through a coarse strainer.*

3. *A flexible balloon whisk with many thin wires is essential for whipping egg whites. The important thing is to tip the bowl (preferably copper) and keep the whites around the whisk, not spread over the bowl. The motion should be a quick rotation of hand and wrist; the arm doesn't move.*

COLE SLAW

1   **whole egg**
1   **tablespoon Dijon mustard**
    Salt and pepper to taste
1   **teaspoon sugar**
3   **tablespoons white vinegar**
¾   **cup vegetable oil**
1   **teaspoon poppyseeds**
1   **medium carrot, grated (½ cup)**
1   **pound cabbage, shredded coarsely (6 cups)**

1. In a mixing bowl, blend egg, mustard, salt, pepper, sugar and vinegar. Add oil slowly, beating briskly with a small, flexible whisk. Mix in the poppyseeds.
2. Toss the carrot and cabbage with the sauce and taste to see whether additional salt and pepper are required.
   Yield: 6 to 8 servings.

FILLET OF SOLE MORNAY

¼ cup butter
6 fillets of sole, about 1½ pounds
Salt and freshly ground pepper to taste
¼ cup white wine
¼ cup flour
1 cup milk
1 cup cream
1 egg yolk
Freshly grated nutmeg
¾ cup grated Gruyère or Swiss cheese
2 tablespoons grated Parmesan cheese

1. Preheat the oven to 400 degrees.
2. Grease a gratin pan with 1 tablespoon of the butter. Place the fillet of sole in the pan, each piece folded in half. Sprinkle with salt and pepper to taste. Add wine. Bake for 10 minutes and remove from the oven.
3. Melt remaining butter in a saucepan. Add the flour and stir constantly with a stiff wire whisk until blended. Over low flame, add the milk, fish broth from baking dish and cream, blending vigorously with the whisk. Add the egg yolk and nutmeg, blending briefly. The sauce should be thick and smooth. Remove from the flame.
4. Add Gruyère and Swiss cheese and stir, tasting for seasoning.
5. Pour the sauce over the fish. Sprinkle with Parmesan and place under the broiler, about 4 inches from the flame, to brown.
Yield: 6 servings.

GRAND MARNIER SAUCE FOR FRUIT

3 egg yolks
⅓ cup sugar
3 tablespoons Grand Marnier
¾ cup heavy cream

1. Select a 1-quart mixing bowl that will rest snugly on top of a slightly larger saucepan. Add about 2 inches of water to the saucepan and bring it to the boil.
2. Put the yolks and sugar into the mixing bowl. Start beating vigorously with a flexible wire whisk, making certain that you scrape all around the inside bottom of the bowl to cover the entire rounded surface.
3. Sit the mixing bowl inside the saucepan (over but not in the water). Continue beating constantly and vigorously up to 10 minutes, or until the yolks are quite thick and pale yellow.
4. Remove the bowl from the saucepan and stir in the Grand Marnier. Scrape the mixture into a cold mixing bowl and put the bowl in the freezer temporarily. Do not allow it to freeze.
5. Whip the cream until stiff and fold it into the chilled sauce. Serve over fresh berries such as raspberries, strawberries, or blueberries or sliced fruit such as peaches or nectarines. This sauce is excellent over wedges of apple pie.
Yield: 4 servings.

WOODEN TOOLS

Wood is in many ways like cast iron: elemental, handsome, enduring. But unlike cast iron, wood remains — at least in some of its uses — irreplaceable.

So far nothing has come along that is nearly as good, for instance, as the wooden spatula. This tool, which is most often about a foot long and 2½ inches wide at its gently curving head, is often used as a turner, to flip chicken livers or sautéed chicken breasts. The way it is used to its greatest advantage, however, is in the preparation of sauces.

After you've sautéed those chicken breasts, what you might well find yourself doing is concocting a quick sauce. You'll deglaze the pan first by adding some wine or vinegar and by scraping the bottom of the pan to release the solids so they can be incorporated into the liquid. The tapered end of this spatula, held so that it is arched downward, scrapes the bottom without damaging it as a metal tool would, and without leaving behind a petroleum-derivative flavor as a plastic spatula might.

This wooden tool continues to be useful if you choose to thicken the sauce. Say you've decided to add cream and want to reduce it rapidly over a high flame. The important thing is to keep the cream from scorching; so you keep it moving, scraping the pan's bottom with the spatula as you did in the deglazing stage. I also use it to prepare custards such as crème anglaise.

And every kitchen since I don't know when has had a long wooden spoon in it, for stirring stock, for tasting, and for doing some of the same chores I usually assign to the wooden spatula.

Wood has many other uses, of course. I'd like to mention a couple of peculiar ones. Wooden pickle tongs are the most efficient tools for taking pickles out of jars. If you use your fingers, you will contaminate the liquid and the pickles will spoil more quickly than they otherwise would.

An olive spoon, with a bowl-shaped head designed to hold one olive at a time and with holes in the bowl to let the olive drain, serves the same purpose as the tongs. Wood does well with olives and pickles because it does not interact with acidic foods in any adverse way. That's why the little relish spoons that show up in delicatessen restaurants are also usually wooden.

In general, wooden implements ought to be made of hardwoods with close grains such as olive or boxwood, maple or beech. Olivewood is better looking and more expensive than the commonly seen beech, but I have no complaints with beechwood and I like its generally low price.

All of these tools require some common-sense care. Keep them away from the fire, which will blacken them. Soaking will soften them; so wash them rapidly by hand and dry them thoroughly.

1. *A wooden spatula is best for deglazing because it won't damage the surface of the pan and its squared end lets you cover a wide area quickly.* **2.** *In making custard or a crème anglaise, move the spatula all over the bottom of the pan in a figure-8 motion so that the custard doesn't stick.*

3. *To see if the custard is cooked, lift the spatula out and run your finger along its length. As soon as the custard does not run back together, remove it from the heat.* **4.** *The same spatula is useful for turning meats and chicken when incorporating flour to be sure the pieces are evenly coated.*

CRÈME ANGLAISE

⅔ cup sugar
6 egg yolks
½ teaspoon vanilla
2 cups warm milk
2 tablespoons rum, kirsch or Cognac

1. In a slant-sided fait-tout saucepan, mix the sugar and yolks with a wire whisk until it is lemon colored. Add the vanilla and blend well. Add the milk and blend.
2. Using a heat diffuser such as a Flame Tamer, cook the mixture at medium heat, swirling it and constantly scraping the bottom and sides of the pan with a wooden spatula to ensure even cooking. It is important to keep the mixture moving during the entire process. The mixture is done when it coats the spatula evenly (draw your index finger along the back of the spatula; if the mixture parts cleanly and stays parted the correct consistency has been reached). This occurs at about 185 degrees.
3. Pour the mixture through a fine-meshed strainer into a small mixing bowl. Cool somewhat at room temperature, stirring occasionally to maintain smoothness.
4. Add the rum, kirsch or Cognac and refrigerate.
5. To serve with meringues (see recipe, page 177) and ice cream (recipes appear on pages 222 to 225), place sauce on each plate and then place two meringues on top with a scoop of ice cream between them. If desired, drizzle chocolate sauce over the top.

Yield: About 3 cups.

Note: Crème anglaise is a basic sauce that can be served many other ways, too, with bread and butter pudding, for instance, or with floating islands or over some cakes (such as sponge).

SPOONS

The large metal spoons for stove-top cooking can be a help or a hindrance, depending on their design and on your knowledge about their possibilities. For instance, a large slotted or perforated spoon is almost a necessity in the making of poached eggs (a preparation that, for some reason, defies many cooks). To make these eggs, one simmers two or three inches of salted water laced with vinegar in a wide, straight-walled pan — preferably the sautoir discussed on page 88 — cracks an egg into it, and after a couple of minutes, when the egg is cooked but the yolk is still runny, one scoops the egg out with the slotted spoon. Try that with any other kind of spoon and the egg is likely to prove an elusive catch. Moreover, if you are cooking the eggs ahead of time to be briefly reheated and then sauced later, you will want to drop them gently into iced water to stop the cooking immediately. A spoon without slots will pour some boiling water into the cold water and ruin the operation.

This same spoon is, of course, fine for tasting beef in a stew and lifting vegetables from simmering water. It, like the spoons without slots, ought to feel comfortable in your hand and it ought to be sturdy. A rigid stainless steel is best.

That sturdiness is an especially important factor in the solid spoons, which may be used to transfer relatively heavy portions of food from one vessel to another. They also can be used for skimming soups and stocks, the job frequently reserved for ladles (see following discussion). Take one of these large spoons and glide its rim just under the surface of the liquid, edging the fat over toward the wall of the pot, and lift the fat out along with as little of the liquid as possible.

One of the most important uses for spoons is in basting. The technique I employ is to tip a roasting pan toward me so that the juices gather in one spot, and then I rapidly spoon out some of the juices and pour them over the roast. Basting should be done every 10 minutes or so. Because it is an annoyance, it is often neglected, to the great detriment of the roast. The standard oval spoon can be used for basting, but I much prefer a spoon design in which the head is positioned horizontally, so that the spoon is shaped something like a hammer, allowing for extraordinarily easy access to the corners of a pan.

Quenelles are also shaped best with spoons. A bowl of water must be at the ready to keep the spoons moist. After a fish mixture, for example, has been rendered smooth by a food processor, I scoop a portion of it into one spoon, round the top of that portion with the moistened spoon and then, with that same moistened spoon, scoop it free and drop it into a pan where it will be gently simmered. The final shape is a pleasant oval. This procedure can be done with spoons of any size, depending on the size of the quenelle desired.

1. *Use three spoons when shaping quenelles so that one can be kept moist in a bowl of water. Scoop out a full spoonful of the fish mixture, pulling it up against the side of the bowl to remove the excess.* **2.** *With a second moist spoon, smooth and shape the top of the quenelle.*

3. *Hold the same spoon over the fish mixture.* **4.** *Run it under the quenelle and scoop it out of the first spoon.*

5. *Turn the spoon over and place the quenelle in a buttered pan. Continue until all the quenelles are formed.* **6.** *Cover the quenelles with buttered parchment paper (see page 248 for how to cut the paper). Ladle boiling water onto the side of the paper as the quenelles cook.*

FISH QUENELLES

1 **pound very cold skinless fillet of nonoily fish (fluke, flounder, pike, salmon, striped bass, scallops)**
⅛ **teaspoon freshly ground nutmeg**
Dash of cayenne
Salt and freshly ground pepper to taste
1 **egg**
1½ **cups heavy cream**
1 **teaspoon butter**
1½ **quarts salted boiling water**
White wine sauce (see following recipe)

1. Remove all fish bones (many fillets of flatfish have a bone remaining toward the head of the fillet; it can be removed with a v-shaped incision).
2. Cut fish into 2-inch pieces. Place in bowl of food processor. Add nutmeg, cayenne, salt and pepper.
3. Using the chopping blade, blend for about 15 seconds. As blade turns, add egg and then cream through funnel of processor. Blend for a few seconds more until smooth.
4. Butter a shallow pan such as a gratin or a roasting pan.
5. Form the quenelles, using large soup or serving spoons, which you must keep moist by dipping them continuously into warm water. Take a heaping spoonful of the mixture in one spoon, enough of it to create the desired football shape of the quenelle. Smooth and shape the mixture with another spoon. Then, with the spoon used for shaping, scoop the mixture cleanly into the pan.
6. Cut wax paper or parchment into the shape of the pan; cut a hole in the center about an inch in diameter, butter one side of the paper and cover the quenelles with the buttered side.
7. Ladle all the water over the paper, then bring the water back just to simmer. Reduce heat and simmer gently for 5 minutes.
8. Remove wax paper and turn quenelles once. Cover again and turn off the heat.
9. Serve immediately or leave quenelles in water for up to half an hour before brief reheating. Serve with white wine sauce.
Yield: Six servings.

WHITE WINE SAUCE

1 **tablespoon butter**
3 **shallots, finely chopped**
2 **tablespoons flour**
½ **cup white wine**
1 **cup fish stock (see stock recipe, page 13; clam juice can be substituted)**
¾ **cup cream**
Juice of ½ lemon
1 **tablespoon butter**

1. In a small saucepan, melt butter and add shallots, flour and wine, whisking well. Cook for several seconds. Add fish stock and cook 5 minutes more, or until reduced to 1¼ cups.
2. Add cream and bring to a boil, whisking occasionally. Remove from heat. Add lemon juice. Pour through a fine-mesh strainer and swirl in butter.

LADLES & SKIMMERS

The instruction may seem unappealing and almost incidental, one little chore in the midst of a flurry of others included in a recipe: It tells you to skim off the fat and the scum from the surface of a soup, gravy or sauce. Trivial though it may seem, the skimming procedure does matter considerably. A taste of grease lingering on the lips can ruin the impression of a soup.

There are a number of approaches to skimming the fat. You are usually told to skim a liquid as it simmers. That's because simmering helps release fat instead of homogenizing it into a mixture as boiling would. It is also possible to remove the fat after a soup or sauce has chilled and the fat has hardened on the top. I have done this on occasion but feel it is less thorough.

The tool I like most for skimming is a shallow ladle. I settle the bowl of the ladle into the liquid so that the ladle's rim is just below the surface, and then move it in a gentle, circular fashion near the side of the pot. The fat is forced up against the side and rebounds in ripples that fall into the ladle. It's a good idea to place paper toweling across the surface of the liquid to pick up any remaining spots of fat.

What recipe writers describe as a scum forming on the surface is the sediment released by meat and bones and brought to the top by the turbulence of the simmering liquid. In the preparation of a stock, you will see it as foam. It does no harm to the flavor, but if it is left in the stock it will cause undesirable cloudiness. A slotted spoon will remove it, but it is done more easily with a circular, perforated skimmer.

Incidentally, for removing the fat from a sauce a good new device that is an adaptation of an old design is a plastic cup with a spout that pours liquid from the bottom rather than the top. So you transfer the gravy into this cup, the fat rises, and the gravy is poured out from beneath it. Works every time.

1. *A metal skimmer with small holes is the best tool for removing foam and scum from the surface of stock.*
2. *To remove the fat, hold a shallow ladle just below the surface near the rim of the pot where the fat collects. Move the ladle gently in a circular motion until the fat gathers in the bowl.*

3. *After the stock has been strained and refrigerated, gather the fat that has accumulated by running a slotted spoon over the surface.* **4.** *A slotted spoon is also used to lift and drain sautéed vegetables. In this case, I don't want the quiche shell to become soggy with the fat in which I sautéed the zucchini.*

CHICKEN STOCK

5	**pounds chicken bones**
2	**cups coarsely chopped onions**
½	**pound carrots, coarsely cut, about 2 cups**
1	**cup coarsely cut celery**
1	**clove garlic**
10	**sprigs parsley**
1	**bay leaf**
½	**teaspoon thyme**
10	**peppercorns**
16	**cups water**

1. Blanch bones in a 6-quart stockpot, covering with water, and bringing to a boil. When it boils, discard the water and rinse the bones thoroughly and return to stockpot.
2. Add the rest of the ingredients along with 16 cups of water and bring to a boil.
3. Reduce to a slow simmer. As it rises to the surface, skim fat and scum thoroughly using a ladle for fat and a perforated metal skimmer for scum. Cook for 2 hours, skimming every 15 to 20 minutes.
4. Strain through a fine sieve (a chinois is just right) into a stainless steel bowl, which will allow for rapid cooling. Two people are required to pour it out of the pot; one person working alone would have to ladle it out.
5. Cool somewhat before placing in refrigerator (steam from stock will affect other foods if placed in refrigerator too soon).
   Yield: 10 cups.

TONGS

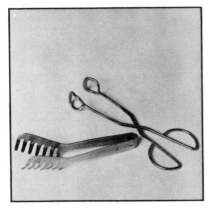

The superheated, supercharged environment of a restaurant's kitchen tends to forge hands that are nearly impervious to high temperature. Nearly, but not entirely. If a chef's hands felt no pain, I guarantee you that in the interest of speed half of his utensils would be discarded and he would work mostly with his bare hands. But even the most experienced chef needs to put some metal or wood between skin and fire or oil.

So when sautéeing a trout he will slide a metal spatula underneath it and then steady the fish with his free hand (see page 52). He generally does not have time for the slower tongs, which are fine for a less practiced hand. Because of my long training as a cook, I don't own fish tongs. But I have nothing against them. I think that fish tongs, which are horizontal in configuration and about 6 inches wide, are a superb, safe extension of the hand. And so are many other tongs. The important thing to remember is to use the utensil designed for the job. I have seen some cooks struggling with those little ice cube tongs that have heads about an inch wide and serrated edges, not realizing that these aren't good for much other than ice and small morsels. The wrong tongs will break and otherwise mar food.

I do own the two tongs pictured here. One operates like a pair of scissors and is marvelous for turning chops without puncturing them. I use it outdoors, over my grill, as well as indoors.

The other is specially designed for spaghetti. These tongs, which look a bit like two long-handled combs joined at the end, allow you to serve pasta with a speed and grace that many cooks have never been able to achieve with other tools. They are also useful for lifting vegetables, such as poached zucchini or corn from the water. A good size is 9¼ inches in length. I prefer stainless steel; nearly all tongs are better if they are made of stainless, rather than the commoner chromed steel, because the chrome tends to wear off.

1. *Because of their comblike construction, spaghetti tongs allow you to pick up large portions of pasta neatly and expeditiously to put on individual serving plates.* **2.** *These tongs, with their scissor-like operation, are useful outside as well as in for turning chops.*

SPAGHETTI PRIMAVERA

4 zucchini (¾ pound)
2 cups small broccoli flowerets
⅓ cup pine nuts
1 pound spaghetti or linguine
4 tablespoons olive oil
1 tablespoon chopped garlic
3 tomatoes (1¼ pounds), skinned and chopped (3 cups)
1 chili pepper
    Salt and freshly ground pepper to taste
4 tablespoons butter
½ cup heavy cream
½ cup Parmesan cheese
10 leaves fresh basil, if available (do not substitute dry basil)

1. Slice zucchini in such a way as to provide varying shapes, some circular, some halved, some on the bias. A mandoline does this especially well (see page 30).
2. Blanch broccoli in boiling water for 3 to 4 minutes and drain; do not overcook. Blanch zucchini for one minute in boiling water and drain. Toast the pine nuts until light brown in a dry steel pan. Watch them carefully to prevent burning.
5. In a gallon of boiling water, cook the spaghetti until al dente. While spaghetti is cooking, heat olive oil in a large skillet. Add the garlic, tomatoes, zucchini, broccoli, chili pepper, salt and pepper to taste. Sauté briefly.
6. Drain spaghetti and add to skillet along with butter, cream, Parmesan cheese, pine nuts and basil. Remove chili pepper from skillet. Grind black pepper to taste. Toss ingredients together in pan and remove to a platter.

Yield: 6 to 8 servings.

MEASURERS, STRAINERS & BOWLS

Everyone knows a cook or two who doesn't appear to measure ingredients carefully and who gets away with it. That's fine, but rarer than it seems. Most people don't get away with it.

Their failures are most often seen in slipshod baking. The spices of a fruitcake might be all wrong, overpowering through an accumulation of little mistakes. Too much vanilla in anything is always conspicuous. Too much flour makes a cake heavier; too little means a loss of body.

I can't emphasize strongly enough the need for precision in some cooking procedures.

If you are making a béchamel sauce, for instance, with the recipe calling for 4 tablespoons of flour, and you hastily scoop up a tablespoon so that each goes into the mixture as a little mound of flour, you may be using 5 tablespoons instead of 4. In that one insouciant moment, the béchamel moves all the way fron silken to leaden.

I know that when I create recipes I fully intend for them to be followed to the letter   at least the first time or two. I want my readers to try it my way with enough exactitude to give them some idea of what a dish tasted like the day I made it in my kitchen. After that, if the dish seems to require some modification to suit personal taste, that's fine.

Of the measuring devices described in this section, the least likely to appear in the home is the scale, and an extra appeal for it seems in order. The absence of a scale makes it difficult to follow some European recipes at all (they rely more on weight designations in the ingredients than do American), and it hampers one's ability to follow some American recipes, too. Beyond that, you'll be astonished at how much more control a scale gives you — when you want to halve the ingredients in a recipe, for instance.

In general, careful measuring is more liberating than it is confining, allowing you to change the flavoring of a dish intelligently because you know just how you made it the last time.

GLASS CUPS

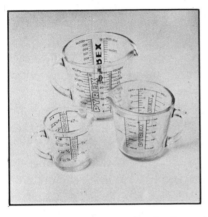

At first, you may think that if you have a whole variety of metal measuring implements you don't need the glass kind. This is not so for a number of reasons.

With solids, you intentionally fill the measuring cup or spoon to the brim and then level it off exactly so that you are in complete control. But the reason glass or clear plastic containers are necessary for liquids is that you can't fill a container to the brim with liquid without having it slosh over.

To fill it to any of a series of levels marked on the container, you have to be able to see the level of the liquid and read the markings clearly. Measuring cups that are nearly opaque and that come with raised letters and numerals rather than brightly colored ones are infuriating to work with. I don't understand how they ever got onto the market.

I have four 1-cup glass containers, two of 2 cups and one of 12. The large one comes into play when I'm making a sherbet or measuring off stock.

The most interesting use of a clear glass measuring cup doesn't have much to do with measuring. When I need to clarify butter — for a sauce such as a béarnaise — I've found that this cup becomes almost central to the endeavor. You place the requisite amount of butter into the cup, place the cup in boiling water and watch as the butter melts, with the solids separating out. Some of the solids sink, others rise. In a glass measuring cup you see that happening as clear as can be. You then take a small ladle and remove the solids from the top, allowing those on the bottom to remain undisturbed. Then gently pour off only the clarified butter (the fact that the measuring cup has a spout is valuable here). The solids on the bottom should stay right there.

1. *Put butter in a glass measuring cup and place it in a large pan of boiling water.* **2.** *When the butter has melted, use a small ladle to remove the foam from the top and discard it. Carefully pour off the clear liquid, which is clarified butter, discarding the solids that have settled on the bottom.*

BÉARNAISE SAUCE (for fish, chops and steaks)

¾ **pound butter**
4 **tablespoons wine vinegar**
2 **tablespoons chopped shallots**
2 **tablespoons chopped fresh tarragon or 1 teaspoon dried**
½ **teaspoon peppercorns, crushed with bottom of heavy saucepan**
3 **tablespoons water**
3 **egg yolks**
 Salt to taste
 Cayenne pepper to taste

1. Put the butter in a 2-cup glass measuring cup (this allows visibility, which will facilitate separating the whey and foam from the clarified liquid). Place the measuring cup in a shallow saucepan with enough boiling water to reach a level about 2 inches up the side of the cup. When the butter is melted, remove the cup from the water but leave the saucepan with its water simmering on the range. Ladle the foam from the surface of the butter. Leave the whey that has settled to the bottom undisturbed. Let butter cool to about 120 degrees.

2. Place vinegar, shallots, tarragon and peppercorn in a small slant-sided fait-tout saucepan and reduce it until dry; let cool.

3. Add the water and yolks to the shallot and tarragon mixture and place the saucepan in pot of simmering water. With a thin wire whisk, stir rapidly in a controlled fashion so that all of the mixture is moved (a figure-8 motion is best, occasionally extending outward to get the edges). Just before it is thoroughly thickened, remove the sauce from the heat for the last seconds of whisking. The mixture is done when it is thickened to a pastelike consistency.

4. Off the heat, pour clarified butter into the egg mixture slowly in a very thin stream, beating continuously with the whisk to form an emulsion, as in mayonnaise.

5. Add salt and cayenne to taste and serve alongside broiled fish, steaks and chops.
   Yield: 1½ cups.

METAL CUPS & SPOONS

Every cook needs a good set of inexpensive measuring spoons. Spoons intended for dining won't do; although called tablespoons and teaspoons, they actually vary considerably in capacity. The same is quite obviously true of cups. Ordinary cups vary greatly in size, and only one intended for measuring should be trusted.

Measuring spoons usually come in a set of four: tablespoon, teaspoon, half teaspoon and quarter teaspoon. They are sold in one metal or another or in plastic. The best, to my mind, is stainless steel. Besides being easy to clean, stainless is rigid and allows you to fill the spoon and then neatly sweep a knife or spatula across the top to make the measurement absolutely accurate.

For larger quantities, you'll need a variety of containers, metal cups for most solids and glass or clear plastic for liquids (more about glass in the following pages). It shows foresight if you have several sets of measuring cups and spoons. Since all the ingredients necessary for a given dish ought to be laid out near you before you start, it is convenient to measure a quarter cup of sugar and simply leave it in the container until it is called for.

The container for that quantity of sugar should be a metal one that has a capacity of precisely ¼ cup so that it performs just as the measuring spoons do; you fill it to the brim and level it off with a spatula. In addition, you'll want containers of ⅓-, ½-, and 1-cup capacity.

With metal cups and spoons, take care that the handle is long enough to be comfortable and that it is sturdy (when you gently bend some of these they stay bent, failing a rather basic test).

1. *To measure flour or sugar, place it in the proper size metal measuring cup over a sheet of wax paper. Run a flexible spatula over the cup to make sure it is level. This is especially important in baking, where quantities must be exact.*

SCALES

The first scales I ever used were of the balance beam type, which work much on the same principle as a doctor's scale. But I gave them up forever the day I acquired a spring-based scale, which operates something like the common bathroom scale. The reason I prefer it is because the spring-based one has the ability to "zero." Zeroing means that no matter how much is in the container on top of the scale at any given time — or how much the container itself weighs — the scale can be reset at zero so each ingredient can be precisely measured as it is added. If you are making a cake that calls for some ingredients in volume and some in weight and some, such as eggs, merely by number, it is possible to put in 2 cups of flour, ½ cup of rum and 2 eggs and then drop that ½ pound of nuts into the mixture simply by pushing the scale's setting back to zero just before adding the nuts.

There are a number of zeroing spring scales on the market (although not all spring scales have this ability, so be wary). Their varying designs, mostly in plastic, suit different needs and tastes. Some of them are too limited in their capacity. You want a scale that can truly weigh several different ingredients at once, or perhaps several potatoes at the same time. The one I've used for many years is by Soehnle. I mention it by name because I much prefer it to all the others. It has a compact circular base, on top of which goes a roomier container than any I've seen elsewhere. The container is actually a mixing bowl of about 8 inches in diameter and 3½ inches in depth, which means that in preparing some small cakes the ingredients can be weighed and actually mixed in the same bowl. Mine is cheerfully red and sits in the center of my work place, where it belongs.

THERMOMETERS

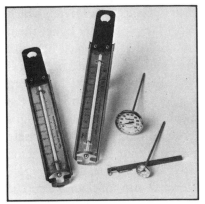

Thermometers come in a great variety, each designed for its own task, so that the attained heat in meat or fat or in candy can be measured. And almost always, it is safer to use a thermometer than not.

The best meat thermometers are the so-called instant kind. They are small and thin, allowing you to pull a roast out of the oven quickly, test it and, if it is not yet done, return it to the heat. Unlike the big, clumsy kinds you see so often, these thermometers make a relatively small hole, so only a little juice will be lost. And since they don't need to be left in the meat, they won't conduct heat as others do, actually cooking the meat around the rod at a different rate than the rest of the roast.

A second and truly important thermometer is made necessary by the fact that most ordinary oven thermostats are untrustworthy. Out of curiosity, I have often tested them to see how accurate they were and have found that ovens vary from the set temperature by as much as 50 degrees. This is no little betrayal. A variation of 20 or 30 degrees from the desired temperature can have noticeable results, a soufflé falling, for instance. If the soufflé is cooked at too low a temperature, its walls will not attain a sufficient stiffness to support it as it rises. Chicken that is roasted at heat that is too low will taste more baked than roasted. It will not attain the crisp skin that one wants while the flesh retains its moisture. To achieve this, chicken should be roasted at 425 degrees.

The first step toward remedy of a problem, or even toward learning that there is a problem, is to obtain a first rate oven thermometer. One that I like a lot is made by the H-B Instrument Company. It comes in its own folding case, which, when opened, is a metal stand that gives it a firm base. In addition to being an extraordinarily accurate instrument, it is, because of this excellent stand, a very mobile one. It is possible to move the thermometer from one spot in the oven to another. This will tell you not only whether the oven thermostat is performing properly but also whether the oven has hot spots. If the oven does turn out to have hot spots, that is no cause for despair. Although hot spots are an annoyance, the awareness that they exist should alert you to the need to turn a roast or pastry from time to time and thus prevent uneven cooking.

If the oven as a whole is off by, say, 20 or 30 degrees, then there are two possible courses of action: take the temperature variance into account when setting the thermostat, or call in a repairman. The important thing is to know you have the problem and must do something.

1. *When making ice cream, it is important that the temperature doesn't go over 175 degrees because you will end up with the cooked flavor of eggs and milk. Test it frequently with an instant thermometer.* **2.** *A deep-fat thermometer rests on the bottom of the pan and tells you when the fat is the desired temperature, never over 375 degrees.*

HAZELNUT BRITTLE

1 cup granulated sugar
½ cup light brown sugar
¼ cup dark corn syrup
¼ cup water
2 ounces sweet butter
½ teaspoon baking soda
1 cup hazelnuts, coarsley chopped

1. In a saucepan, combine the sugar, syrup and water. Bring to a boil and cook until the mixture reaches 300 degrees, according to a candy thermometer.
2. Add the butter and baking soda and with a wooden spoon blend gently. Stir in nuts and immediately pour onto a cool, greased, nonporous surface such as marble. Be careful! The mixture is very hot. Smooth the mixture with a narrow spatula and with the edge of the spatula mark off squares of the desired size. Before candy has cooled and hardened entirely break it into squares or rough pieces.
Yield: One pound.

CHINOIS

Some sauces and cream soups require a smoothness that can best be described as silken. And when that transcendent smoothness is achieved it is done by a traditional tool, the fine-meshed chinois, so named because it once reminded someone of the shape of a coolie's hat. Both the shape and the construction of the screen are crucial to doing certain jobs properly. The screen in a good chinois is so fine that it looks like woven silver cloth rather than a metal strainer.

I turn to my chinois to make such sauces as a bordelaise, which is comprised of shallots and wine and perhaps some demi-glace. The chinois is placed in a pot or bowl that is the appropriate size to hold it firmly, and the sauce is poured in. Then I take a small long-handled whisk — it needs to be able to fit down into the base of the chinois — and rotate it rapidly with the palms of my hands forcing the mixture through the screen. What is happening is that the shallots are, in effect, puréeing and binding with the liquid. An alternate method is to force the mixture through the screen with a small ladle, gently plunging the ladle downward until the job is accomplished. Whether using whisk or ladle, the results are much smoother than can be accomplished by any other method, including using a food processor.

Imagine how well this chinois does with a cream of chicken soup, as it binds the stock and the roux. Or how useful it is in making a crème anglaise (see recipe, page 58), when you want to be sure to eliminate any remaining egg solids.

Another use is in preparing the clearest of broths. There, you don't want to purée the ingredients. What you want is the pure liquid, leaving behind all solids. Rather than use any tool to force the soup through, I tap the chinois on its rim to encourage the liquid to pour through and do nothing more vigorous than that. The size of a chinois comes into play here. Because it is large and funnel shaped, it allows you to pour the stock and its ingredients rapidly into it without fear of sloshing all over your work space. A convenient size chinois is about 8 inches in diameter.

The design I prefer has a heavy wire outer skeleton, which protects the screen if it is dropped. It also gives the chinois the support it needs to stand in a pot while one pours a large volume of soup through.

Most often a chinois is made of tinned steel, which has the advantage of being relatively inexpensive and is adequate for most kitchens. Heavy use over time may wear through the tin, however, and might result in rusting. I have seen a chinois or two in stainless steel, which, of course, will not rust but costs about twice as much as tinned steel.

1. *To make any kind of smooth sauce or soup, pour the mixture through the chinois. For sauces, tap the rim with your hand or a wooden spoon to encourage the liquid to pass through. For a soup force it through with a ladle or whisk.*

CRÈME D'AVOCATS (Cream of avocado soup)

2 tablespoons butter
3 tablespoons finely chopped onion
2 ripe, unblemished avocados
2 teaspoons lemon juice
6 cups rich chicken broth
3 cups heavy cream
2 egg yolks
   Salt and freshly ground pepper to taste
2 tablespoons port wine

1. Heat the butter in a large saucepan and add the onion. Cook, stirring, until wilted.
2. Meanwhile, peel the avocados and remove the pits. Finely dice enough of the flesh to make ½ cup. Add the lemon juice to the diced avocado to prevent discoloration.
3. Blend the remaining avocado flesh in a food processor. There should be about 2 cups.
4. Add the puréed avocado to the saucepan along with the chicken broth and stir with a wire whisk. Add the cream and blend well. Let simmer over low heat about 20 minutes.
5. Beat the egg yolks and add a little of the hot soup. Return this to the saucepan and cook briefly. Add salt and pepper to taste. Force the mixture through a chinois and heat in a saucepan. Add the port wine and the reserved diced avocado. Serve hot.

   Yield: 12 servings.

FOOD MILL

Over the years I have developed some enduring allegiances to various pieces of equipment. One of them is this conical food mill, a kind of rigid chinois. I bought the one I use to this day 30 years ago, and then bought two similar ones in recent years as wedding presents for my daughters.

Mine is made of steel, but most commonly these days they are aluminum, which is a good, sturdy material for the purpose. The one I have comes with a stand that allows it to straddle a pot or bowl, and some of the new aluminum ones do, too. I've seen other mills equipped with only a hook that grasps the rim of a pot; the hook works far less well than the stand because it simply isn't as stable. My mill is 7¼ inches deep and 7 inches in diameter and requires the use of a tapered wooden pestle that is 10 inches long.

It is wonderful for puréeing vegetables such as string beans or lima beans, allowing you to push the soft flesh of the vegetable through the perforations while the skin is left behind. It is good for making sauces or soups that are meant to be smooth but not fine. If, for instance, you want a thick-bodied onion soup with a smooth texture, you can force the soup through the mill, in effect reducing the pieces of cooked onion to a pulp.

And it is far more efficient than anything else I know about for preparing mashed potatoes, an elementary dish that nevertheless can benefit from proper technique. And when it is done right, with the perfect texture imparted to it by this mill, its simplicity is transformed to elegance.

When you force the potatoes or anything else through the mill, hold the pestle in an open palm, so that its rounded handle can rotate as you move the tool rapidly along the wall of the chinois, using your whole arm in a broad circular motion.

1. *Use a wooden pestle that has the same cone shape as the mill to force potatoes, or any vegetable, through.*
2. *Move the pestle in a circular motion all around the sides.*

CARROT PURÉE

2 pounds carrots, roughly
  sliced
  Salt to taste
2 tablespoons butter
½ cup cream (or 2 more
  tablespoons butter)
  Fresh nutmeg

1. Place the carrots in a deep saucepan and cover with salted water. Bring to a boil and simmer for 10 minutes.
2. Purée the carrots in a conical or rotary food mill (this step can be done in the food processor but it will lose the desired coarse texture). Stir in the butter and cream and two gratings of nutmeg.
   Yield: 6 to 8 servings.

MASHED POTATOES

2 pounds Maine or Long
  Island potatoes, peeled
  and cut into ½-inch slices
  Salt to taste
1½ cups milk
3 tablespoons butter
  Freshly ground pepper to
  taste

1. Place the potatoes in a deep saucepan and cover with salted water. Bring to a boil and simmer until tender, about 15 minutes more.
2. Meanwhile, warm the milk but do not let it boil.
3. In a food mill (not a food processor, which will produce an unappealing paste), purée potatoes as fast as possible so they don't cool. Do this over a saucepan. Add butter and pepper and beat with a wooden spoon until thoroughly blended.
4. Over low heat, add the milk, stirring thoroughly with the wooden spoon. After the milk is added, test for texture. Add more milk if a thinner purée is desired. Add salt to taste.
   Yield: 4 to 6 servings.

   Variations: For extra creamy potatoes follow same procedure but use cream instead of milk. For an elaborate embellishment of mashed potatoes — it's known as pommes mont d'or — add 2 egg yolks and a dash of freshly ground nutmeg immediately after the milk and mix well. Place in a gratin dish, smooth the top with a narrow spatula and, with the side of the spatula, create a wavelike design; top with a ¼ cup of grated Gruyère or Parmesan cheese and place under the broiler until nicely browned.

COLANDERS

Among the humblest of my tools are my colanders. And yet, as I used one to strain pasta one day, I was rather proud of it. This particular one is actually part strainer, and sometimes it is called a spaghetti strainer. It is 10 inches in diameter with a handle 6½ inches long, flat-bottomed and perforated all around. It looks like a pot used for buckshot practice.

So there I was, having just made some fresh noodles that I was about to toss with warmed fresh tomatoes and fresh basil. With all that freshness, the last thing I wanted was for the noodles to get soggy. I wanted them out of the water as fast as they were done. I reached for the colander, held it suspended over the sink (because of its design there is no need to find a purchase for it) and poured the noodles and water through it at once. I agitated the colander briefly to remove all the water and then poured the pasta back into its pot to be tossed with the tomatoes. It was fast and just right.

The same type of motion, the quick transfer of food from boiling water, is done often with other foods, such as boiled potatoes. The potlike colander comes into play more than one might imagine.

Colanders of this type are usually equipped with a hook on one side so that they can be firmly suspended on the rim of a large pot (the handle supports one side, the hook the other). This ability is useful for numerous tasks. In the preparation of a clear consommé, for instance, you might line the colander with cheesecloth and strain the liquid through it. Or you could use the colander to separate a fish stock from the bones and other solids (letting the bones continue to drip over the liquid below to drain all the essence from them).

The one caution I have about this colander is that it ought to feel sturdy when you buy it; some do not, and almost certainly the weak ones will not survive for long. I have been somewhat baffled by versions of this colander with holes only on the bottom. For my purposes, that appears to be an inferior, slow-draining design.

I also use the more familiar colanders as well, the bowl-shaped types that sit on legs or a broad pedestal and are 9 or 10 inches in diameter. They are fine for methodical washing and draining jobs. I wash berries or spinach in a large bowl (or just in the sink) and drain them in this colander. Incidentally, I never wash anything directly in the colander because some sand or other sediment will unquestionably collect in it, defeating the purpose.

1. *A pot-shaped colander drains pasta quickly and efficiently. Hold the colander over the sink and pour the spaghetti in. Then shake the colander and pour the spaghetti back into the pot for saucing, all in one movement.* **2.** *The pot-shaped colander is also useful for rinsing other foods before cooking.*

PASTA WITH FRESH TOMATOES AND BASIL

1¼ **pounds fresh tomatoes**
1 **pound fresh noodles (see recipe, page 216) or ½ pound dry**
4 **tablespoons olive oil**
1 **tablespoon chopped garlic**
1 **whole hot pepper**
  Salt and freshly ground pepper to taste
⅓ **cup chopped basil**
6 **tablespoons grated Parmesan cheese**

1. Place the tomatoes in boiling water for 10 to 12 seconds, remove with a slotted spoon and peel with a paring knife. Cut into ½-inch cubes.
2. In a large pot of boiling water (at least 2 quarts; the more water the better), cook the noodles, stirring occasionally with a two-pronged fork.
3. When the noodles are almost finished (fresh noodles will be done in 3 or 4 minutes), begin the sauce. Heat the oil and garlic (be careful not to brown the garlic) in a shallow skillet. Add the tomatoes, along with the hot pepper and salt and pepper to taste, heating them at high flame just enough to warm but not to cook.
4. Drain the noodles in a colander, pour back into pot and toss with tomatoes, basil, Parmesan and freshly grated pepper.
   Yield: 4 servings.

STRAINERS

Oh, I know you already own a strainer, and chances are it is adequate. Strainers, after all, are the simplest of devices: a bowl of wire mesh suspended on a metal frame. They are most commonly used for the separation of liquids from solids, and just about every one I've ever seen, unless it had been punctured in some way, did the job well enough. It is possible, however, to make a variety of relatively challenging demands on a strainer, and you may find you need more than one kind. A strainer with fine mesh is called for in certain chores and one with coarser mesh suits others.

I think of one of my fine-mesh strainers immediately when making crêpes, to take one example. The reason is that the crêpe batter can sabotage you with lumps that go undetected, and straining will eliminate them. I also strain many sauces. A strainer with a coarse screen is called upon to turn hard-cooked egg yolks into mimosa for a salad or a garnish by forcing them through with fingers or a rubber spatula. I also use mine to make very fine bread crumbs for the lightest of breadings.

Of course, for all of this work the strainer has to be well built. The wires should be strong enough and woven together well enough to take the force of a rubber spatula or a wooden spoon. In the coarse mesh, I find that most standard American aluminum strainers are at least good enough.

A marvelous, relatively new Italian stainless steel strainer with fine mesh is on the market these days. It's produced by Efeppi, distributed by Rowoco. Its bowl is shallow, which diminishes the stress put on the mesh. This is the one I've been using to strain sauces. A surprising feature of this tool — surprising because most strainers are so homely — is its sleek good looks.

Incidentally, the cleaning of strainers can be annoying because the mesh clogs and sometimes resists efforts to unclog it. I find that a stiff brush is the best approach, under forcefully running water.

1. *To strain crêpe batter, or a small quantity of sauce, this wide, fine-meshed strainer produces the same results as a chinois. Push the solids through with a rubber spatula.*

COPPER BOWLS

Rarely have function and beauty so perfectly married as they have in the copper mixing bowl. The copper bowl, a gorgeously gleaming bit of symmetry, is virtually essential for beating egg whites. It is true that egg whites can be beaten in a stainless steel bowl, too, but not with any hope of gaining the volume and the lightness that emerges from a copper bowl. It is said that something inherent in copper enables it to interact with egg whites to make them fluffier.

The copper, to do its work well, needs to be so clean that it is unmarred by the slightest film of grease or, for that matter, by a spot of yolk that has slipped into the bowl along with the whites. You avoid contaminating the whites with yolk, of course, by learning to separate eggs flawlessly. (A common method is to crack an egg with a sharp stroke of the noncutting edge of a knife blade, which renders a much neater split than the edge of a countertop, and then move the yolk back and forth from one shell half to the other over a bowl until the white has slipped out.) You keep the copper bowl clean — at least traditional cooks do — by rubbing it with salt and the flesh of a lemon and by using it for egg whites exclusively.

Copper bowls come in a variety of sizes, from 9 to 14 inches in diameter. The 12-inch size is large enough to prevent the whites from splashing over the sides. Just as you can use a stainless steel bowl for the egg whites, you can also use a nontraditional tool to beat them, an electric hand mixer, and I know cooks who do it with good results. Nevertheless, I find that the volume of beaten egg whites is much enhanced by the use of a balloon whisk (see page 53) whose shape fits the bowl precisely.

A final thing to keep in mind in the use of bowl and whisk is that you must beat the egg whites until they reach the proper consistency. The usual test for that is that the whites should provide a peak as you lift the whisk up, but they should still be moist.

1. *Put egg whites into a clean copper bowl and tip the bowl so that the whites will stay around the whisk. Start beating with a balloon whisk, moving only the hand and the wrist.*
2. *When the whites have reached the soft peak stage, add sugar. Beat until stiff peaks form, but don't overbeat because the whites will break down.*

STEEL MIXING BOWLS

In the class system of the kitchen, mixing bowls are the proletariat. With the exception of the copper bowl, which is elegant and aloof, reserved for the single task of beating egg whites, mixing bowls are used every day for countless chores, and they are as indispensable to a cook as spoons or knives. The most versatile are in stainless steel.

Stainless is light in weight and thus less cumbersome than some other materials; it is easy to clean and will not chemically interact with food in any way. It will not chip, shatter or melt. It is relatively inexpensive.

Most important, I think, is its ability to chill and heat more rapidly than will a plastic or ceramic bowl, an ability that pays off, especially when you want to whip cream in a cold bowl. The bowl also can quickly be converted into the top of a double boiler simply by placing it over a pot of steaming water.

Steel mixing bowls can readily be used as molds — to make, for instance, a charlotte bavaroise, in which ladyfingers line the bowl and Bavarian cream fills it.

Don't shrink from buying a number of bowls, from the very small to the very large. They will all find a use. If you don't now own a big bowl, perhaps 12 or 13 quarts in capacity, it may be difficult to imagine what service such an enormous container can perform. But it is marvelous for washing the greens of a salad, or cleaning mussels or straining stock. An 8-quart one is good for proofing bread, 5 quarts for whipping cream, 3 quarts for making mayonnaise and 1½ quarts for beating eggs for scrambling.

There are several qualities, in addition to size, to look for in a stainless steel bowl. One is shape. The best design has rounded rather than straight sides so that it can accommodate the head of a whisk properly. The bowl should be flat-bottomed and sturdy so that it is stable. The way I test the stability of a bowl on display in a store is by taking a whisk off the rack and placing it in the bowl. If the two tip over and clatter to the floor, the bowl is not for me. (This testing method, by the way, is also useful for attracting the attention of sales help.)

Depending on the storage area in your kitchen, you might want to look for bowls with rings on the side so they can hang. An advantage in buying mixing bowls in a set all of precisely the same design is that several will fit inside a single large bowl.

BEURRE MAÎTRE D'HÔTEL

¼ pound soft butter, cut
  into small pieces
  Juice of 1 lemon
4 tablespoons finely
  chopped parsley
  Salt and freshly ground
  pepper to taste

In a small mixing bowl, mix all the ingredients with a rubber spatula until smooth. When steak or chops are done, spread butter sparsely over the meat. It is also a fine embellishment for broiled fish.

Yield: ½ cup.

FRENCH POTATO SALAD

8 new potatoes (2½
  pounds)
  Salt to taste
⅓ cup chopped onion
2 tablespoons finely
  chopped shallots
¼ cup finely chopped
  parsley
½ teaspoon finely chopped
  fresh thyme, when
  available (do not
  substitute dried thyme)
¼ teaspoon chopped garlic
¼ cup dry white wine
⅔ cup vegetable oil
  Freshly ground pepper

1. In a large saucepan, cover the potatoes with water and add salt to taste. Bring to a boil and simmer for 20 minutes.
2. While the potatoes are still warm, peel them and cut them into ¼-inch-thick slices. Place them in a large mixing bowl and using a large rubber spatula combine all the ingredients with the potatoes, being careful to break the potato slices as little as possible. Place in a warm spot until ready to serve. If the salad has been standing for a while, stir from the bottom before serving.

Yield: 6 to 8 servings.

POTS & PANS

I have said with confidence that the home cook's dilemma on what to acquire in the way of knives has been eliminated — given one's ability to spend the requisite amount of money on high carbon stainless steel. In the realm of pots, the confusion over what to buy is much greater today than ever. The reason for that is the proliferating availability of good pots and pans. And it remains true that no single material, from copper to aluminum to iron, stands out as best for all jobs. So one still needs to acquire pots and pans in a variety of materials and designs. It is thus illogical to buy them in sets; rather, one ought to shop for them with particular cooking chores in mind. In the ensuing discussions of pots and pans I will describe the specific merits of each utensil. Here I will make a number of generalizations about materials and maintenance.

Copper

After many years at the top, copper still is the most nearly perfect material for the cooking of food. A good pan requires that heat be distributed well to all its parts so that there are no hot spots to burn ingredients while the rest go undercooked. This is especially true in the making of sauces, where the heat should spread out from the ring of fire and climb the walls of the pot. A bad pot, usually something in thin stainless steel or thin aluminum, will almost always transfer too much of the heat directly from the fire right through the base of the pot. When that happens there will invariably be a ring of burned food at the bottom, a sure sign of poor heat distribution. Heavy gauge copper is among the best materials for distributing heat evenly.

In addition, a pan is often required to be responsive, which means it should get hot when the heat of the fire is raised and cool when the

fire is turned down. A pan's inability to do that takes away a great deal of a cook's flexibility in preparing a delicate dish in precisely the right fashion. Copper is exquisitely responsive.

Copper's drawbacks are primarily on the side of care. Because it is somewhat toxic if too much is eaten (minute amounts are actually required for good health), copper is generally lined with some nontoxic substance such as tin or steel. Scientists assert that copper only poses a problem when the food it contains is acidic and thus eats away at the metal, so that the food combines with a bit of the copper, which is then ingested. So the beating of egg whites, which are not acidic, in an unlined copper bowl is nothing to worry about. But the simmering of a tomato sauce in an unlined pot might indeed result in gastric distress. The tin lining, which is more common than the steel, works beautifully. A thin wash of tin is protective enough and does not inhibit the copper's performance in any way. The problem with it is that the lining will ultimately deteriorate. Scouring can damage it and, if the pot is left empty on heat for too long, the tin might even melt. Deterioration requires relining. Steel lining is more durable, but copper pots with steel linings are usually not as responsive as those with tin.

High costs are associated with good copper pots because the pots are initially the most expensive of all and because, if they are lined with tin, the relining is costly. Moreovr, they require frequent plishing with copper cleaner.

Stainless steel

For years, I wouldn't have dreamed (except in nightmares) of cooking with stainless steel. It distributes heat too poorly. But now manufacturers have taken this durable, easily maintained metal and made it useful, even superb, in the kitchen. The most successful design of all those I've tried is one incorporating a plate of aluminum or copper (not a thin wash of copper, which is useless) under the pot. The copper or aluminum distributes the heat throughout the base. This cladding, however, is unable to aid the pot's sides. So when you are simmering a stew in one of these designs you definitely lose something tangible when the heat fails to climb and surround the ingredients adequately. Nevertheless, the level of ability of these pots is so high for most jobs that I believe few cooks can go very wrong by owning several.

Aluminum

If I were equipping a restaurant on a low budget, I would mostly buy heavy gauge aluminum pots. They distribute heat well and transfer it intensely for good browning (although they are not especially responsive). They are inexpensive and they look fine, as if they mean business. There are problems to be considered, of course. Aluminum, first of all, interacts with some sauces, especially those containing eggs, and thus cannot be used in those instances. Moreover, to be any good, aluminum has to be very thick (sometimes designated as professional grade), and thus this material, with a reputation for its lightness, can become astonishingly heavy. A large aluminum skillet takes a good deal of strength to manipulate.

Iron

Iron pots and pans are in many ways the darlings of my kitchen. They are so inexpensive and available almost anywhere. Their ability to absorb an enormous amount of heat and transfer it to food for high-heat cooking is superb, and they can also be very gentle, the heat glid-

ing uniformly up the sides of a pot, making this material superb for skillets, where one wants high heat, and for casseroles, where one wants a simmer. Iron, unfortunately, is stubbornly unresponsive to heat reduction. You can't expect to turn down the flame and have the pot cool; it will burn to extinction anything in it before responding to the absence of fire. It is also brittle and can crack. And it can rust, which means it requires careful seasoning.

My method for seasoning iron is to wipe it thoroughly with vegetable oil. Then I pour a small amount of additional oil into the pan and bake it in the oven at 450 degrees for 15 minutes. Remove the pan, wipe it out and repeat the procedure two or three times. After that, the pot can be washed occasionally without too much worry of rusting. What will often happen over time, if one cooks at high heat, is that carbon will build up on the exterior of the pot. When the buildup is so extensive as to be unsightly, I place the pot in the electric oven, turn the oven on to self-clean and let the oven clean itself and the pots at the same time. Then the seasoning procedure must be repeated.

Enameled iron

The way to avoid a lot of the annoyance of cast iron is to acquire an enameled pot or two. But the enamel I've seen is never chip-proof, and once it does chip, a brightly colored pot quickly becomes ugly. Moreover, if the interior is scratched, baring the iron, food will stick and burn. You'll find, too, that enamel decreases the pot's cooking ability in some degree. Enameled skillets will never sear meat the way naked iron will. Yet enameled casseroles are excellent because they, like iron, hold and distribute the heat so well. An enameled iron saucepan is fine for sauces — it won't impart any undesired flavor to some delicacy as naked iron might — but it takes far too long to heat these pots, if all you want to do is boil water.

Black steel

For many cooking chores, raw steel is magnificent. It will transfer and distribute heat with blinding speed. For cooking fast and hot, as one does with chicken livers, say, or an omelet, there is nothing like it. It browns food beautifully and is very durable. It is also quite inexpensive. It needs to be seasoned as iron does. Otherwise it quickly rusts.

Nonstick surfaces

Throughout this book I say very little about Teflon and its succeeding generations of nonstick surfaces. The fact is that I use it rarely. But I nevertheless believe that every kitchen should have one of these pans. The latest types do not peel, as the early ones did, although they still scratch rather easily, which means they have to be treated with extraordinary gentleness. A nonstick pan proves to be almost a required utensil for some nouvelle cuisine dishes that call for very little oil. And it does make the production of omelets or crêpes easier (although the texture that results is less to my liking than what one obtains using black steel).

Glass

There are few uses for glass pots and pans in the kitchen. They're not bad as gratin pans (see page 120), and they can boil water. But glass copes with heat terribly; no kitchen needs a glass pot.

SAUTOIR

This is one of those pans that really ought to be in copper. In French it is known as a sautoir (because it sautés); in recipes I frequently refer to it simply as a heavy, straight-sided skillet. In so many preparations it acts first as a sautéeing pan and then as a kind of enormous saucepan (I have in mind a pan that is at least 12 inches in diameter, although there are useful smaller sizes, too). So it must be extraordinarily responsive to heat, as any good sautéeing pan would be, and then it must be able to hold and distribute the heat evenly, as any good saucepan would.

These pans are heart-stoppingly beautiful, of course, and once you have one you'll feel compelled to use it (not wanting it to serve merely for decoration). A big sautoir is superb in sautéeing chicken pieces at very high flame for, say, a curried chicken or a chicken basquaise. It can easily handle pork chops to be covered in a rich tomato sauce. It's the right pan, too, in which to simmer meatballs immersed in tomato sauce.

The pan needs to be built magnificently. In sautéeing large pieces of food, such as chicken or chops, the cook has to agitate this big pan frequently. So it should be sturdy and should have a handle that allows for a firm and relatively cool grip. Workmanlike yet handsome copper pots frequently have iron handles that are effective because the heat does not travel well from one metal to another. Although lids for copper pots are notoriously difficult to find, one is especially useful here when the sautéeing stage is left behind for a simmering stage.

While there is nothing like copper for the kind of work I've been describing, there is one, perhaps overwhelming, drawback to these pans. Large copper sautoirs are heavy. Before buying one, grasp the handle toward its base, with your hand on top of the handle and the remainder of the handle wedged under your forearm so that your whole arm and not just wrist and hand are holding the pot. See whether it is too heavy for you. If it is, either try a smaller one or settle for a similar design in a lighter material. There are similar pans in aluminum and in stainless steel with aluminum cladding on the base. Akin to the sautoir are the so-called chicken fryers that show up in enameled iron, but those pans usually have short handles that limit their use somewhat. They are also very heavy.

Because these copper sautoirs are generally lined with tin they come with the usual maintenance problems, which I discuss in the introduction to this chapter.

1. Place the chicken pieces in one layer in a large, straight-sided skillet, known as a sautoir. Brown the pieces evenly on all sides. 2. Add onions and seasonings and cook, turning with a spatula.

CHICKEN BASQUAISE

2 tomatoes (¾ pound)
8 skinless, boneless halves chicken breast (2¼ pounds)
Salt and freshly ground pepper to taste
4 tablespoons olive oil
¼ pound onions sliced (1⅓ cups)
1 tablespoon finely chopped garlic
½ pound green pepper cut into julienne strips (2 cups)
½ pound red sweet pepper cut into julienne strips (2 cups)
1 bay leaf
½ cup white wine
¼ cup chicken stock
¼ cup coarsely chopped parsley

1. Peel tomatoes by dropping them in boiling water for 10 to 12 seconds, allowing to cool and then removing skin with paring knife and fingertips. Remove seeds by cutting tomatoes in half, grasping dome of tomato and squeezing gently, shaking seeds out over a pan. Chop into pieces roughly ¾ inch in size.
2. With a utility knife, remove all excess fat and fiber from chicken breasts. Sprinkle them with salt and pepper. Heat oil in a heavy, deep skillet (a sautoir) and place breasts in pan, flat side down. Brown lightly and, using narrow metal spatula, turn breasts to brown the other side, about 4 minutes on each side. Remove chicken to platter; cover with foil.
3. Place onions in pan and brown lightly at high flame, stirring with wooden spatula. Add garlic, stirring to be sure not to burn it. Add all the peppers and sauté for 3 or 4 minutes. Add tomatoes and bay leaf, wine and stock.
4. Place chicken and pan juices back in pan; cover and simmer for 5 minutes. (If desired, this step and next can be done 45 minutes or an hour after earlier steps.)
5. Remove chicken, return to serving platter and cover; cook vegetables for five minutes at high heat uncovered to reduce liquid. Remove bay leaf.
6. Pour the vegetables over the chicken and sprinkle with parsley.
Yield: 6 to 8 servings.

MEATBALLS WITH TOMATO SAUCE

1 teaspoon vegetable oil
½ pound onions, finely chopped (1⅓ cups)
3 pounds lean chuck ground in food processor
1 teaspoon finely chopped garlic
½ cup chopped parsley
⅛ teaspoon chili powder
Salt and freshly ground pepper to taste
1½ cups fresh bread crumbs
2 eggs
1 tablespoon olive oil
2 tablespoons chopped parsley for garnish

1. Prepare the tomato sauce (see following recipe).
2. Heat the vegetable oil in a small skillet and sauté the onions for 2 or 3 minutes; do not brown. Allow to cool. Combine onions and remaining ingredients except 2 tablespoons parsley in a medium size mixing bowl and knead with moistened hands sufficiently to bind but not so much as to make it mushy.
3. For each meatball, roll about 3 tablespoons of the mixture in moistened hands. The balls should be 1 ½ inches in diameter. When done, there should be 35 or so.
4. Using a black iron skillet, brown the meatballs thoroughly, turning them frequently with a spatula. As soon as each meatball is brown, remove it to the simmering pot of sauce, making sure that each ball is mostly submerged in the sauce. Shake the pot occasionally to allow the meat to settle .
5. Simmer for ½ hour and skim off fat. Serve with pasta. Garnish with parsley.
Yield: About 6 servings.

TOMATO SAUCE

4 tablespoons olive oil
1 cup chopped onion
1 tablespoon chopped garlic
1 28-ounce can Italian tomatoes in thick purée
2 cups tomato purée
¾ cup water
2 teaspoons dried basil
1 teaspoon chopped rosemary
½ teaspoon oregano
Salt and freshly ground pepper to taste
1 whole chili pepper

1. Heat the oil in a large straight-sided skillet (a sautoir) and sauté onion and garlic.
2. With chopping blade in place, put tomatoes and their purée into the container of a food processor and purée for about 5 seconds. Pour tomatoes into the skillet, along with additional purée and water.
3. Add all the seasonings, and simmer. Before serving, remove chili pepper.
Yield: About 6 servings.

CURRIED CHICKEN

3½ pounds chicken, cut into
    serving pieces
    Salt and freshly ground
    pepper to taste
2 tablespoons butter
1 medium onion, chopped,
    about ½ cup
⅓ cup chopped celery
1 tablespoon chopped
    garlic
3 tablespoons curry powder
1 bay leaf
2 medium tomatoes, peeled
    and cored (1 cup)
1 large apple, diced (1 cup)
1 banana, diced (¾ cup)
1½ cups chicken stock

1. Sprinkle the chicken with salt and pepper to taste.
2. In a heavy, wide saucepan (a sautoir), melt butter, add the chicken and sauté briefly without browning.
3. Add onion, celery, garlic, curry powder and bay leaf, stirring with a wooden spatula and agitating the pan. Cook slowly for 3 or 4 minutes.
4. Add the remaining ingredients, stirring. Bring to a boil, cover and simmer for 20 minutes.
5. Uncover and reduce at medium flame for 5 minutes.
6. Remove the chicken pieces to a platter. With a stiff wire whisk, stir sauce in pan to bind ingredients and thicken sauce, but be careful not to lose the coarse texture. Pour sauce over chicken.
7. Serve with chutney on the side.
   Yield: 4 to 6 servings.

PORK CHOPS IN MUSHROOM AND TOMATO SAUCE

4 center cut pork chops,
    about 1½ pounds
    Salt and freshly ground
    pepper to taste
1 teaspoon peanut or
    vegetable oil
½ cup chopped onion
1 teaspoon chopped garlic
¼ pound sliced mushrooms
1 tablespoon red wine
    vinegar
1 cup Italian tomatoes in
    thick purée
¼ cup water
½ teaspoon rosemary
1 tablespoon freshly
    chopped basil, if available

1. Sprinkle chops with salt and pepper.
2. Heat the oil in a heavy skillet (a sautoir) large enough to hold the chops in one layer. When it is very hot and smoking slightly, add the chops. Turn the chops when well browned, in about 3 minutes, and brown on other side. Pour off fat. Place the onion and garlic in the pan and stir well, cooking for several seconds.
3. Add the mushrooms and cook for a minute. Add red wine vinegar. Add tomatoes in purée, water and rosemary. Cover and cook at low flame for 20 minutes.
4. Uncover and reduce the liquid, if necessary, to produce a thick sauce. Just before serving, sprinkle with freshly chopped basil.
   Yield: 4 servings.

FAIT-TOUT SAUCEPAN

By far my favorite pot is a slant-sided saucepan known in French as the sauteuse evasée (evasée refers to the slanted sides). I have also seen it called a fait tout because it's supposed to be able to do everything. And that's almost literally true.

The sloped sides of the sauteuse make it superb for anything that needs to be stirred. If you can lay your hands on one in a store, try the stirring motion for a second and you'll see how much freer the motion feels when the sides of the pot are slanted.

The slopes also mean that there are no sharp corners at the bottom. So a whisk will find the bottom of the pot more accessible than it is in other saucepans. This matters especially in the preparation of sauces such as a hollandaise or béarnaise, both of which need to be stirred constantly and thoroughly so the egg-heavy mixtures remain smooth as they slowly warm.

The wide top and the relatively narrow bottom of this pot are intended to allow considerable evaporation, a characteristic that makes the pot serve well in reducing a sauce. (The converse ought to be kept in mind, too: Pots that are deep with proportionately narrow tops should be used when you want to avoid the loss of liquid.)

The pots come in a range of sizes. The larger ones, starting at about 9 inches in bottom diameter, are excellent for sautéeing chunky foods that need to be cooked rapidly and thus moved about vigorously, such as lamb or veal kidneys.

I have seen slant-sided sauteuses in aluminum, but they are commonest in tin-lined copper because aluminum will discolor sauces containing eggs. In any case, this is one pot that really ought to be copper. Sauces need that gentle, even heat more desperately than almost any other creation in the kitchen.

1. *Put water and egg yolks in a fait-tout pan and place in a larger pan with simmering, not boiling, water. Stir constantly in a figure-8 motion with a wire whisk.* **2.** *When sauce is thickened, remove the pan from heat and whisk in clarified butter in a thin stream. Season and strain through cheesecloth.*

HOLLANDAISE SAUCE

1 **pound butter**
4 **tablespoons water**
4 **egg yolks**
   Salt to taste
   Cayenne pepper to taste
½ **tablespoon lemon juice**

1. Place the butter in a 1-quart glass measuring cup (this allows visibility, which will facilitate separating the whey and foam from clarified liquid) and put cup in saucepan with enough boiling water to rise about 2 inches up the side of the cup. When butter is melted, remove cup from water and ladle foam from surface. Leave the whey that has settled to the bottom undisturbed. Let butter cool to about 120 degrees.

2. In a saucepan, preferably a slant-sided fait tout, place the water and yolks. Place saucepan in a pot of simmering water. With a thin wire whisk, stir rapidly in a controlled fashion so that all of the mixture is moved (a figure-8 motion is best, occasionally extending outward to get the edges). Just before mixture is thoroughly thickened remove from heat for another few seconds of whisking. The mixture is done when it is thickened to a pastelike consistency.

3. Pour the clarified butter into the egg mixture slowly in a very thin stream, beating continuously with the whisk to form an emulsion as in mayonnaise. Be careful not to pour in the sediment at the bottom of the cup. Guard against allowing the mixture to adhere to wall of pot.

4. Add salt, cayenne and lemon juice.

5. Strain through cheesecloth to remove any coagulated egg or pits. Serve with poached or steamed vegetables such as asparagus or artichokes.
Yield: 2 cups.

OTHER SAUCEPANS

The common straight-sided saucepan is a workhorse of the kitchen. I don't think it's excessive to have five saucepans in sizes ranging from ¾-quart capacity to 4½ quarts. The smallest one might be used to melt butter or hard-cook a single egg. Those in between should be near at hand to prepare vegetables or a small quantity of fish stock. The largest can be called into play for soup or pasta.

The most frequent error, I think, is to take these pans too lightly, to imagine that since they have so little character just about any pan will do. That's true enough if all you want to do is boil water. But what if you want to use one of these pans to boil milk for a custard sauce, or perhaps to prepare a thick tomato sauce? In other words, some subtler cooking may need to take place in the plain old saucepan — and then you want to be sure it can distribute heat as well as one of your better pots.

In shopping for saucepans in any size, look for those that are gently curved at the base. Some pans have sides that are perpendicular to the base, and if you ever want to make a sauce in a saucepan, a sauce that requires constant whisking, you'll find that the whisk can't get to the base of the pan's wall at all, and some sticking and burning will certainly result. Another point to keep in mind is that every saucepan should have a lid that fits well (even though, as I know all too well, the storage of lids is a problem). A lid fits well when snug but with a little give so that it can be removed even as it expands through heating.

The reason for being sure that all these pans have lids is that each saucepan — at one time or another — will be asked to simmer food such as rice or a soup with little loss of moisture, and each one will need to bring water rapidly to a boil. This is a procedure that is accomplished much more quickly when the pot is covered.

Almost all of my saucepans these days are made of stainless steel with some kind of cladding, aluminum or copper, on the bottom. There are many enameled iron saucepans on the market, but they are a poor choice because they heat so slowly you simply waste too much energy trying to do something as elementary as boiling water for an egg or reheating soup.

HEAT DIFFUSER

The heat-diffusing gadgets that are sold under a variety of brands — the best known and perhaps the most effective is the Flame Tamer — are among those devices that don't seem to be really necessary in the kitchen, until you acquire one. Then it's astonishing how often it is used. What these little devices do is soften and distribute heat so that almost anything can be kept warm, and nothing can burn.

The Flame Tamer is an 8-inch round of steel, rather like a wheel with a layer of air between two surfaces. It is the air that acts to diffuse and soften the heat, just as air does when it is trapped between a storm window and a home's ordinary window.

Once a heat diffuser is within easy reach, it can be used to keep coffee warm (in fact, I advocate doing that with the plunger-type coffee makers; see page 162). It can serve as a kind of double boiler for melting chocolate and the like. In a double boiler, the cook is using the fact that the water cannot rise above 212 degrees to ensure that the temperature is kept low and even. Setting a saucepan containing chocolate over a Flame Tamer will do very much the same thing, virtually guaranteeing that the chocolate will not become too hot.

The heat diffusers are especially good under a casserole that will simmer for a long time at the lowest possible heat, a heat so low that the range may be incapable of providing it. These gadgets are inexpensive, durable and, when you think about it, terribly clever.

1. *A heat-diffusing device such as a Flame Tamer is almost essential when making sauces and custards that need to cook over very low heat. Otherwise the eggs would curdle. And when cooking the custard base for ice cream, it must be stirred constantly and removed from the flame when the custard registers 180 degrees.*

STOCKPOT & SOUP KETTLES

The making of good stock requires no special skill, just diligence and a big pot. Moreover, it takes about as much effort to make ½ gallon of stock as it takes to make 3 gallons, and stock stores well in the freezer. So you might as well be ambitious.

As for the size of the pot, at a minimum you will need one that can hold about 5 pounds of meat and bone, along with vegetables such as celery, carrots and onions and a bouquet garni of herbs and spices, all of that to be covered by water. A 6-quart pot should suffice. A 16-quart pot, which is the size I prefer for the home kitchen, can handle 8 pounds of meat and bone or more and will produce great quantities of stock.

Stockpots are tall and relatively narrow to diminish the evaporation of liquid and to allow the bubbling liquid to travel vertically through layer after layer of ingredients, extracting what it can from all of them.

The material the pot is made of can be nearly anything without loss of cooking quality. Most commonly, however, it is aluminum or stainless steel. Copper in a stockpot adds nothing in function. The metal of a stockpot can be extremely thin, but I like stockpots that have some heft to them so that I can use them for other purposes (a stew, for instance, cooked in a pot that is too thin will burn where the bottom of the pot develops hot spots).

Once you're committed to making a stock on some grand scale do it right and especially cautiously the first time. When the stock is supposed to simmer, be sure that's all it does. Boiling will incorporate the fat and sediment into the stock, making it cloudy and greasy. Be sure to skim the scum and fat from the top periodically. And cook it long enough, 4 or 5 hours of uncovered simmering for a beef or chicken stock, to get everything the ingredients have to give. Strain it when you're done (the most adequate tool — the one that will result in the least splash — is a chinois, see page 74).

If you're having trouble maintaining a simmer, some kind of heat-diffusion device, such as a Flame Tamer, will help.

Professional stockpots have spigots at the bottom so that the clear stock can be drained until there is nothing left in the pot but the fat and sediment that had been on top. Most of us can get along well enough without one of those, however, as long as the skimming is done conscientiously.

The difference between a stockpot and a soup kettle is that the soup pot is shallower and wider. This allows you to reach into the pot to stir onions or leeks before the liquid is poured into it. It makes the stirring of a soup much easier, too. That's especially necessary for a clam chowder, which has many solids that may burn if not stirred every now and then. And any creamed soup needs to be stirred to avoid burning. The pot isn't limited to soup, of course; it's fine for boiling beef or ham, as well. The one I use has an 8-quart capacity.

VEAL STOCK

5 pounds veal bones
½ pound carrots, coarsely cut (2 cups)
½ pound onions, cut into chunks (2 cups)
2 cloves garlic, cut in half
1 cup coarsely cut celery
20 cups water
1 bay leaf
½ teaspoon thyme
10 parsley sprigs
10 peppercorns
1 cup Italian tomatoes in thick purée

1. Preheat the oven to 425 degrees.
2. Place veal bones in a heavy, shallow roasting pan (about 2 inches deep) and roast for 30 minutes to brown them. If bones are large, crack them open with a cleaver first.
3. Add the carrots, onions, garlic and celery to the roasting pan. Continue to roast for about 15 minutes.
4. Transfer the bones and vegetables to a 6-quart stockpot. Place the roasting pan on the range over high heat. Pour in 1 cup water and scrape the solids to dissolve; add this liquid to the stockpot.
5. Add the remaining water, bay leaf, thyme, parsley, peppercorns and tomatoes in purée. Bring to a boil and reduce to a slow simmer. Skim immediately and thoroughly with a shallow perforated metal skimmer by pressing it down gently over the ingredients so scum and fat rise through holes. Then remove scum and fat to a waiting pot. Skim every 15 or 20 minutes for the first hour, and continue to simmer uncovered for 5 more hours, skimming occasionally. Strain and cool.
Yield: About 3 quarts.

MANHATTAN CLAM CHOWDER

24 chowder clams
4 cups water
4 strips bacon
2 cups finely diced carrots
1½ cups celery cut into small cubes
2 cups chopped onion
1 cup chopped green pepper
2 cloves chopped garlic
1 teaspoon thyme
1 bay leaf
2 cups tomatoes
4 cups potatoes cut into ½-inch cubes
Salt and pepper to taste

1. Wash the clams well. Drain.
2. Place the clams in a large saucepan and add the water. Simmer until shells open.
3. Meanwhile, chop the bacon and put it in a soup kettle. Cook until bacon is rendered of its fat. Add the carrots, celery, onion and green pepper. Cook about 5 minutes, stirring often.
4. Add the garlic, thyme and bay leaf.
5. When the clams open, drain them but reserve both the clams and their liquid. Add 10 cups of clam liquid to the bacon mixture. (If there are not 10 cups, add enough water to make 10 cups.) Add the tomatoes. Cook 15 minutes.
6. Remove the clams from the shells and discard the shells. Chop the clams finely on a flat surface or put them through a meat grinder, using the small blade. Add them to the kettle and add the potatoes. Add salt and pepper to taste and cook about 1 hour.
Yield: 8 to 10 servings.

OVAL FISH PAN

To sauté fillets of fish in a classic, simple fashion, you dredge them in milk, then flour, cook them in very hot oil and serve them with lightly browned butter and lemon juice.

Any frying pan can accomplish that, more or less. But a black steel oval fish pan has several advantages. Its shape, for one thing, is the shape of fish fillets. So the fillets will fit the pan neatly. None of them will be forced up the sides, where the fish will cook at a different rate than the rest. And there will not be great bare spots in the pan, areas that are empty because the fish's shape and the pan's just don't mesh. A large bare spot is to be avoided because it is precisely where a pan will burn if you are cooking at high heat, as I do much of the time.

In addition, the black steel browns food better than anything but cast iron — and cast iron responds to heat too slowly to suit me in the sautéeing of fish fillets.

When you cook the fillets in one of these oval fish pans, what you want is a deep, handsome browning without drying the interior of the fillet. If you try this dish in, say, stainless steel or in an aluminum pan and then in one of these black steel ones, the difference will take your breath away, so pale might those done in the first two seem.

Incidentally, once you've managed to get the surface of the fish so marvelously crisp be sure to follow the instructions in the recipe accompanying this discussion. The lemon juice should be poured over the fillets before the butter. Done in that order, the juice will cause the butter to bubble attractively and the result will be a crackling exterior. If you make the mistake of mixing lemon and butter together first (as many restaurants do), the crisp surface will turn soggy, and the virtue of using the best pan for the job will have been lost.

Because a black steel pan rusts fast, some precautions are necessary. For one thing, it needs to be seasoned properly with oil. And then wash the pan rarely. (If it is reserved only for fish, this will cause no problem.) Instead, wipe it with a paper towel while still warm and scour it with coarse salt if there is any food adhering to the surface.

A good size for this pan — it will hold 4 modest bluefish fillets — is 14 inches from head to base.

1. *To turn fish, slip a wide spatula under the fillet and hold the top with your free hand. Quickly turn the fish back into the pan.*

FILLETS OF FISH MEUNIÈRE

2 pounds fish fillets
(flounder, fluke, striped
bass, blue fish)
Salt and freshly ground
pepper to taste
¼ cup milk
½ cup flour
4 to 5 tablespoons
vegetable oil
6 tablespoons butter
Juice of ½ lemon
Half lemon, sliced for
garnish
3 tablespoons chopped
parsley

1. Sprinkle the fillets with salt and pepper to taste.
2. Dip each fillet in milk and then dredge in flour, patting flour to be sure it adheres.
3. Heat the oil in an oval black steel fish pan (it should be very hot to prevent sticking) and place in pan as many fillets as will fit in one layer.
4. Brown thoroughly, then turn with slotted metal spatula and brown on the other side. Depending on the size of the fish, the process will take about 2 minutes on each side. While the fish is browning on the second side, baste the top with hot oil from the pan to prevent drying. Transfer fillets to a warm platter.
5. While the pan is still warm, wipe it clean with a paper towel and return it to medium heat to melt the butter, agitating the pan as butter melts to prevent burning.
6. Squeeze lemon juice over the fillets. Pour the butter over them and garnish with lemon slices and parsley.
   Yield: 4 servings.

FISH POACHER

Of all the fine ways of cooking fish, not one is so nearly perfect as poaching. Take a whole fish, simmer it in a liquid that can be as primordial as sea water or as refined as a stock of wine and vegetables, and the result is a dish that is moist, delicate and pure in flavor.

The procedure is quicker and less complicated than it looks, but there is a serious hazard. If the fish is clumsily handled, it will break, losing its juices and its looks.

I remember the time I poached a striped bass in a friend's kitchen. The fish was so large and difficult to remove from the pot that I had to be as much acrobat as cook, maneuvering the fish into a towel so that I could safely transport it, as if it were some invalid on a makeshift stretcher, onto a platter.

The way to avoid such harrowing manipulations is to buy or borrow a fish poacher. A fish poacher is an elongated pot with a rack that sits on the bottom. The shape, of course, is useful because it means you will use only as much stock as necessary; a large round pan often forces the cook to fill the unoccupied area by diluting the stock too much. And it is the rack of the poacher, with handles at either end, that allows you to lift out the fish absolutely intact.

The pots come in lengths ranging from 16 inches or so for people who spend most of their waking hours thinking about trout, to 40 inches for people who go down to the sea in search of more frightening fish. The most useful size, I think, is 24 or 28 inches, which is big enough to easily accommodate a four-pound striped bass that will serve six or eight people. It can also be used for smaller fish laid end to end.

Fish poachers are made of aluminum, tin-plated steel, stainless steel or tin-lined copper. To my mind, all those materials are at least adequate. A good middle-priced choice is the tin-plated steel. It is sturdier than aluminum and it is every bit as efficient as expensive copper, although not as handsome.

1. *Use scissors to cut the fins from the fish and, if the head is left on, cut out the gills on either side of the head.* **2.** *Lay the fish on a large piece of cheesecloth and roll it over and over until the fish is securely enclosed.*

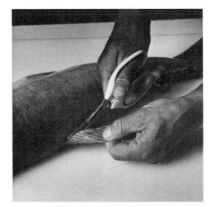

3. *Tie the fish loosely at 4-inch intervals. Don't pull the kitchen twine too tight or it will mark the fish.*
4. *Lay the wrapped fish on the rack of the poacher. If the liquid doesn't cover the fish, add water to the court bouillon. Bring to a boil and cook.*

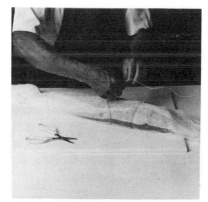 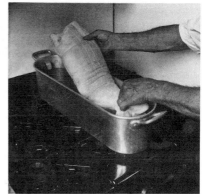

5. *When the fish is done, lift out the rack and discard the vegetables.*
6. *Gently roll the fish onto a cutting board and remove the strings.*

7. *Unwrap the fish by carefully rolling it to open the cheesecloth. Leave the fish on the cloth.*
8. *Using a paring knife, gently remove the skin on the exposed side of the fish and scrape off any black part. Lift the fish with the cloth and invert it onto a serving platter. Remove the skin on the other side.*

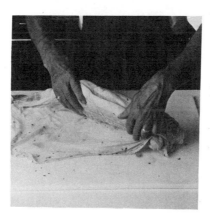 

POACHED SALMON WITH SAUCE GRIBICHE

Court Bouillon

2 medium onions, cut into
  chunks (1¾ cups)
3 carrots, cleaned and
  sliced on the bias (1 cup)
2 stalks celery, sliced on
  the bias (1¾ cups)
2 cloves garlic
1 bay leaf
10 peppercorns
4 sprigs parsley
8½ quarts water
4 sprigs fresh thyme
  Salt to taste
⅛ teaspoon chili pepper

The Salmon

1 6-pound salmon, cleaned
  (striped bass or red
  snapper can also be used)
  Sauce gribiche (see
  following recipe)

The Garnish

2 medium tomatoes
2 hard-cooked eggs
1 tablespoon peanut or
  olive oil
2 cups fresh steamed
  broccoli flowerets

1. Prepare the court bouillon, combining all ingredients in a 24-inch fish steamer; cover and bring to a boil with steamer resting on two burners. Simmer for 20 minutes and allow to cool.
2. Meanwhile, use scissors to remove the fins from the salmon, but leave the tail on. If the head is on, leave it but remove the gills.
3. Cut cheesecloth to a length about 2 inches longer than the salmon. Place the fish down on it and roll it in the cloth. Tie the cloth closed in four places with twine. Leave the ends untied, but fold them under the fish.
4. When court bouillon is ready, place fish gently into the tray in the pot. Bring to a boil and simmer about 15 minutes on a single burner.
5. Let the fish rest in steamer for 15 or 20 minutes. Lift fish out of steamer on its tray; place it on a cutting board and open up the cheesecloth wrapping, but don't remove it entirely since the cloth underneath the fish will be a useful aid in moving it. Remove the skin on the exposed side of the fish with a paring knife. Gently scrape away brownish fat to reveal the pink meat. Cradling the fish in cheesecloth, lift it to a serving platter, rolling gently onto the platter so that side with remaining skin is up. Remove cloth entirely. Clean skin and brownish fat from fish. Make the fish glisten with a light brushing of oil.
6. To prepare the garnish, cut the tomatoes in quarters. Quarter the eggs. Slice an incision most of the way lengthwise through the skin side of each tomato section and place the wedge of egg in it. Brush lightly with oil.
7. Ladle sauce gribiche over the fish. Place tomato and egg garnish around it. Place broccoli flowerets between the egg and tomato segments. The salmon can rest for an hour or two, if desired, and then be served lukewarm with sauce added at last minute.
Yield: 6 to 8 servings.

SAUCE GRIBICHE

1 tablespoon Dijon
  mustard
2 tablespoons finely
  chopped shallots
3 tablespoons finely
  chopped onion
1 hard-cooked egg, sieved
1 egg yolk
  Salt and freshly ground
  pepper to taste
¼ cup red or white wine
  vinegar
1 cup vegetable oil
½ cup olive oil
1 tablespoon chopped
  parsley
1 tablespoon chopped fresh
  tarragon
2 tablespoons chopped
  chives

Place mustard, shallots, onion, egg and yolk, salt, pepper and vinegar in a mixing bowl. Blend briefly with a whisk. Slowly pour the combined oils into the bowl, whisking to create a light emulsion. Add parsley, tarragon and chives. Blend well with a whisk.
Yield: 6 to 8 servings.

VEGETABLE STEAMER

In a restaurant the vegetables often arrive at the table possessing a magnificently rich color that is not easy to duplicate at home. One of the reasons, of course, is that professional cooks have their secrets, not all of them especially appealing when the truth is out. A bit of ammonia, for instance, will keep colors bright. Less offensive sounding and also effective is baking soda. But both additives change the texture of the food for the worse, and in any case there are better approaches.

The one I like best is the steaming of vegetables, which has many benefits: It won't sap the nutrients of food the way boiling will; it leaves food firmer, too. But the color is what takes your breath away. Asparagus are a marvelous way to prove this point.

Steamers come in a variety of shapes. Some cooks prefer deep ones that allow them to stack a great volume of vegetables into the steamer at the same time. These steamers are round with baskets that descend into them. They are superb for steaming potatoes, a procedure that leaves the potatoes firmer, less soggy and more flavorful than the boiled variety. I most often use a rectangular aluminum pot (12 inches long and 8 inches wide) made by Tournus. In it goes a perforated tray on a stand that suspends the tray above the water. The process requires about an inch or an inch and a half of boiling water.

It is designed for the longer vegetables but it is adaptable to other uses. I find it perfect for steaming two small lobster. Steamed lobster, like steamed vegetables, retain a flavor that can be lost in other cooking procedures. The rectangular shape of this steamer is also useful for fish fillets that can be steamed and then sauced.

And when clams are prepared in any steamer there is an interesting byproduct. Once the clams have popped open to demonstrate that they are done, you will notice that a broth has formed below the tray as the juices of the clams and the water mix. It is a clean, flavorful broth, undamaged by contact with the clams' shells.

In buying any steamer, be sure the lid fits securely, or the pot will not adequately contain the steam. It is not terribly important that the aluminum or steel be thick because the steam and not the metal will transport the heat. The only drawback to thin-gauge steamers is that you must be careful not to drop them. Once the pot is dented the tray or steaming basket may never fit in properly again.

1. *Bring about an inch of water to a boil in the bottom of a steamer. Put the food on the rack and lower it into the pan. Cover tightly and cook until just tender.* **2.** *Lift out the rack (I use whatever is handy; in this case a long fork and a kitchen towel) and drain the vegetables.*

STEAMED FISH IN MUSTARD SAUCE

3	**egg yolks**
2	**tablespoons cold water**
12	**tablespoons clarified butter (see note)**
	Salt to taste
2	**teaspoons lemon juice**
2	**tablespoons Dijon mustard**
⅛	**teaspoon cayenne pepper**
1½	**pounds fillet of sea bass or striped bass**

1. Bring ½ inch of water to a boil in a straight-sided skillet.
2. In a slant-sided saucepan, place egg yolks and cold water and whisk briefly. Place saucepan into skillet with boiling water. Whisk mixture constantly, using a figure-8, making sure all of the mixture is moved so it will not stick. When egg yolks become custardlike, remove the pan from the water and add clarified butter in a steady stream while whisking. Continue beating and stirring constantly until all of the butter is added.
3. Add lemon juice, mustard and cayenne and mix well. Salt to taste. Let sauce stand in a warm spot until fish is ready.
4. Put about 1 inch of water into a steamer and bring to a boil. Place fish on steamer tray and cover pot. Salt as desired. Cook at high heat for 3 to 4 minutes. Do not overcook.
5. Remove the fish to a warm platter and pour sauce over it or serve separately.

   Yield: 4 servings.

   Note: To clarify butter, let butter melt in a glass measuring cup in a pan of boiling water. Skim the foam from the top. Pour off the clear liquid without disturbing the solids on the bottom.

STEAMED POTATOES

1½ pounds small red potatoes
4 tablespoons melted
 butter
 Juice of 1 lemon
2 tablespoons chopped
 parsley

1. Scrub the potatoes and, with a swivel-bladed vegetable peeler, remove only a narrow band around the center of each potato, forming a decorative belt.
2. Bring 1 inch of water to a boil in a steamer. Place potatoes on tray and steam for 10 to 15 minutes. The potatoes are done when they offer little resistance if pierced with a paring knife or fork.
3. Remove potatoes from the steamer and place on a platter. Pour butter over them. Sprinkle with lemon juice and parsley and serve.

Yield: 6 to 8 servings.

ASPARAGUS VINAIGRETTE

1½ pounds asparagus
2 teaspoons Dijon mustard
2 teaspoons red wine
 vinegar
⅓ cup vegetable oil
 Salt and freshly ground
 pepper to taste
⅓ cup finely chopped red
 onion
2 tablespoons chopped
 parsley

1. Cover the bottom of steamer with 1 inch of water and bring to a boil.
2. Cut off the white portions of asparagus stem and peel asparagus, holding the tip and moving the peeler toward the base. Place in steamer and cook at high heat, covered, for 3 to 4 minutes, or until tender but not soft. Do not overcook; they should still be al dente.
3. To prepare the sauce, put mustard in a small mixing bowl, add vinegar and start beating with a wire whisk while steadily adding the oil in a thin stream. Add salt, pepper, onion and parsley and blend.
4. Pour the sauce over the asparagus or serve separately. Asparagus can be hot or cold.

Yield: 4 to 6 servings.

DUTCH OVEN

When prepared correctly, there is nothing so satisfying as a rich daube of beef, the familiar French stew. And I prepare daubes frequently for my own satisfaction as well as for guests. My mother used to labor diligently over her big black iron Dutch oven cooking those daubes, and the Dutch oven was the first pot I bought when I came to this country.

But I am restrained from waxing nostalgic about these pots by a sense of irritation when I realize the most significant reason for having one in this country today. The reason comes blaring forth when I use mine to brown the beef for a daube, an absolutely critical step in any such dish because it is what ultimately gives the stew its color. The meat should be richly browned on all sides, seared really.

These days, the meat often resists browning. Liquid bubbles up from it, preventing the requisite drying of the surface. That is because American beef is far too frequently aged poorly. It reaches the home kitchen too moist. It will bubble and foam infuriatingly for many minutes, turning a pallid gray.

But if it is going to brown at all, it will do so in a big black Dutch oven. The reasons for the special competence of that pot are several. First is black cast iron's ability to transfer an even, intense heat extraordinarily well (better than cast iron that has been enamelized). Also, the shape of these classic Dutch ovens is such that they allow for a lot of browning surface on the bottom, just as a frying pan would.

In addition, the width of the pan (taken together with the fact that it is relatively shallow, compared with, say, a stockpot) allows the steam to escape as completely as possible.

Once the browning is done, a good pot needs to have a tight lid, as these almost invariably do, and it needs to be able to distribute the heat all around the stew. Stainless steel pots, for that reason, are poor for stewing, because they cannot draw heat up their walls the way iron can.

These iron pots, which are today virtually the same as they were generations ago, come in a number of sizes and are generally very inexpensive. One of 4½ or 5 quarts is ample in capacity if you cook for four people. If you plan to make a stew to serve eight or ten, then something closer to an 8-quart pot is required, and even these larger ones are still not expensive. If you intend to buy only one, buy the bigger pot; it will provide more surface for browning.

1. *To brown meat, cook it in small batches so that all the pieces come in contact with the bottom of the pan. Be sure the fat is hot and use a wooden spatula to turn the meat so all sides brown evenly.* **2.** *After adding the vegetables and flour, add the wine or other liquid and stir the pieces so that everything is evenly coated.*

BEEF STEW WITH RED WINE

2 tablespoons vegetable oil
5 pounds brisket of beef, trimmed of excess fat and cut into 1½-inch cubes
  Salt and freshly ground pepper to taste
½ pound onions, coarsely chopped (2 cups)
1 tablespoon finely chopped garlic
1 pound whole small mushrooms
½ pound carrots, halved or quartered, depending on size, and cut into 1½-inch lengths
¼ cup flour
4 cups red Burgundy wine
1 cup water
4 sprigs fresh thyme, or ½ teaspoon dried
6 sprigs parsley
2 whole cloves
1 bay leaf

1. Heat the oil in a large black iron Dutch oven. Thoroughly brown a third of the meat at a time, sprinkling it with salt and pepper on all sides. As the meat is browned, remove it to a platter and do the next batch. (If you try to brown all of this quantity at once there will not be enough bottom surface to do the job; to speed things up, you can use a black iron frying pan in conjunction with the pot for the browning stage.) Discard fat in the pot and return all the meat to it.
2. Add onions, garlic, mushrooms and carrots. Add flour and stir to coat the meat and vegetables. Add the wine and water and stir.
3. Prepare a bouquet garni, wrapping thyme, parsley, cloves and bay leaf in cheesecloth. Tie the top with string, trimming the bouquet garni so there is no excess cloth in the pot to absorb gravy. Place it in pot. Cover and simmer slowly for 2 hours, or until meat is tender. If the stew persists in bubbling vigorously even at low flame, use a Flame Tamer to diffuse heat. Cook for 10 more minutes uncovered to reduce the liquid somewhat. Discard the bouquet garni.
4. Serve with noodles, rice or parsley potatoes.
   Yield: 8 to 10 servings.

BOEUF EN DAUBE PROVENÇALE

3½ pounds stew meat (round or chuck), excess fat trimmed away
Salt and freshly ground pepper to taste
3 tablespoons olive oil
¾ pound small white onions (about 12)
1 pound mushrooms
2 tablespoons chopped garlic
¼ cup flour
½ cup Italian tomatoes in thick purée
1½ cups beef stock
1 cup red wine
½ teaspoon saffron
1 bay leaf
½ teaspoon thyme
1 whole chili pepper
½ pound carrots, cut into 2-inch pieces (split thick pieces down the middle)
20 green, pitted olives
¼ cup chopped parsley

1. Cut the meat into 1½-inch cubes and sprinkle with salt and pepper.
2. Heat the oil until very hot and brown meat thoroughly on all sides. This is best done in a large black iron Dutch oven.
3. Add whole onions, mushrooms and garlic. Add flour, stirring to coat the meat and vegetables, and brown.
4. Add tomatoes in purée, stock, wine, saffron, bay leaf, thyme, chili pepper, salt and pepper to taste and bring to a boil. Scrape the bottom so that nothing sticks to burn; cover and simmer for 1 hour, occasionally scraping the bottom.
5. Add carrots and cook for about ½ hour longer.
6. Blanch the olives briefly in boiling water and drain to wash the salt away. At the very end, place olives in the daube. Serve with chopped parsley as garnish.

Yield: 6 to 8 servings.

OVAL ROASTING PAN

Nearly everyone is under the impression that he can roast a chicken properly. But the evidence — the finished chicken — is often an indication that a cook esteems himself too highly. The errors that can be made are many.

Once a cook is committed to roasting at high temperature, as I am, a good roasting pan becomes invaluable. It needs to be one that can be easily manipulated for rapid basting.

My preference for many years now is for pans that are not specifically meant for roasting at all. They are the oval gratin pans in enameled iron (gratin pans used for their intended purpose are described on page 120). The biggest advantage they offer is in their shape. You can pull one toward you, tilt it slightly, and the juices will all gather in the curved end where they can be readily scooped up by a basting ladle and spread over the chicken. Pulling the shelf part way out of the oven and then tilting the pan forward and grasping the far end with a towel is much safer than trying to reach into the depths of the oven with your arm.

Also in the pan's favor is the fact that it has no corners that are vulnerable to burning. Juices in corners burn because they are uncovered by the chicken as it roasts. The enameled oval pan also distributes heat evenly, as all cast iron does, which is another bit of insurance against burning.

One needs to avoid burning the juices in the pan because burning will be disastrous in the production of a sauce afterward. To produce a sauce I frequently deglaze the pan, removing it to the range top where I pour off the fat and pour in some white wine and stock or water, which is then reduced at high flame. Since deglazing produces a sauce by dissolving all the solids on the bottom of the pan, it is obvious that burnt solids will make the sauce bitter.

Oval gratin pans come in many sizes. One with a base that is 12 inches long is right for a chicken of 3 or 4 pounds. One that is 15 inches at its base can handle two small chickens or, perhaps, a single capon.

1. Truss and season the chicken. Rub it all over with butter and butter the roasting pan. Lay the chicken on its side with the onion, neck and gizzard. 2. As the chicken cooks, baste it frequently with pan juices. I like an oval-shaped basting spoon that you move sideways rather than push away from you.

ROAST CHICKEN

1   3½-pound chicken, allowed to sit at room temperature for at least 15 minutes, and its giblets
    Salt and freshly ground pepper to taste
2   tablespoons butter
1   medium onion (⅛ pound)
½   cup water or chicken stock

1. Preheat oven to 425 degrees.
2. Remove the fat from the cavity and wash and truss the chicken (see pages 39-40). Sprinkle the cavity with salt and pepper to taste. Rub chicken and an oval roasting pan with butter. Sprinkle salt and pepper on the skin, if desired.
3. Place chicken on one side in roasting pan surrounded by neck, gizzard and onion. Reserve the liver. Roast for 20 minutes. Turn chicken on other side and, using a basting spoon or other large spoon, baste the roast. (The roast should be basted each 10 minutes thereafter throughout the cooking period.) Roast for another 20 minutes. Reduce heat to 375 degrees. Place the chicken on its back for final roasting stage. After 10 minutes, remove all fat from the pan and add ½ cup of water or stock and the liver to the pan. Place back in the oven for final 10 minutes, where simmering liquid will deglaze the pan as chicken roasts, creating a gravy. Remove from the oven (the bird should now be at about 160 degrees internal temperature).
4. Pour the cavity juice into the roasting pan. Remove trussing string. Let the chicken rest in the pan 10 minutes before removing to a board for carving (see pages 7-9). Place carved pieces back in the roasting pan and spoon gravy over them just before serving.
   Yield : 4 servings.

RECTANGULAR ROASTING PAN

An oval roasting pan is perfect for a single chicken, but food that is bigger or more blocky in shape, such as a leg of lamb (or two good-sized chickens), requires a rectangular metal pan.

In acquiring one or several, keep in mind that each pan needs to be the right size for the chore at hand. To baste a roast, which really ought to be done every 10 minutes or so, the cook has to be able to dip into the pan to ladle out the juices. A pan that is too small will make that job impossible. Thus, a roasting pan should be at least large enough to allow the easy intrusion of a basting spoon. But not too large. A pan that leaves much more room than a spoon's width presents a problem of its own: It will offer too much empty surface and thus cause the juice to evaporate rapidly and perhaps burn.

A similar problem crops up with flimsy pans, which warp, causing some juice to collect in a puddle while elsewhere it is burning. That kind of mishap is the undoing of a proper sauce, which owes much of its flavor to deglazing. Deglazing is done by loosening and diluting the pan sediments with liquid such as stock or wine. Burned sediments thus lead to a harsh tasting gravy.

Should the sides of the pan be high or low? I tend to stay away from high-sided pans because they hold the moisture around a roast, resulting in a steamed effect.

Since a roasting pan will often be called upon to carry a heavy burden, it ought to have handles that allow a firm grip. And for cooks who are not especially strong, the pan ought to be light — stainless steel or aluminum, rather than iron — so that it does not greatly add to the problem of removing a large roast from the oven.

The only reason to buy an expensive copper roasting pan happens to be a rather persuasive one; these pans look marvelous when they are brought directly from oven to the sideboard or buffet.

1. *For large roasts, or two chickens, a rectangular pan is the most efficient. There is enough space to allow you to baste the roast, but not enough to create hot spots where the flavorful drippings will burn. The pan should not be too crowded because air will not be able to circulate around the meat.*

ROAST PORK WITH SAGE

1 3½- to 4-pound center
  cut pork loin roast
4 cloves garlic
  Salt and freshly ground
  pepper to taste
1 tablespoon sage
2 small white onions,
  peeled
½ cup chicken broth

1. The roast will be easier to carve if the continuous flat bone at the top of the ribs is cut away. If this is done, save the bone.
2. Preheat the oven to 400 degrees.
3. Cut the garlic into slivers. Using a paring knife, make gashes at various points in the fat of the roast as well as between the meat and the rib bones. Stud the holes with garlic slivers. Sprinkle the roast with salt and pepper. Rub the sage all over the roast.
4. Arrange the roast meaty side down in a shallow roasting pan. Chop the bone into pieces and scatter them around the roast. Add the onions. It is not necessary to add any liquid at this time.
5. Place the roast in the oven and bake. Baste the roast at frequent intervals as the fat accumulates. When the roast has baked 30 minutes, turn it bone side down. Continue basting and roasting 30 minutes.
6. When the roast has cooked a total of 1 hour, reduce heat to 350 degrees. Pour off all the fat from the pan. Add the chicken broth and cover the roast lightly with foil. Bake 30 minutes longer. Serve hot or cold with pan juices.
   Yield: 6 to 10 servings.

FILET DE BOEUF ROTI AU JUS (Roasted fillet of beef)

1 well-trimmed, tied, 11-
  inch length of fillet of
  beef, about 2¼ pounds
  Salt and freshly ground
  pepper to taste
1 tablespoon peanut,
  vegetable or corn oil
1 tablespoon butter

1. Preheat the oven to 425 degrees.
2. Sprinkle the meat on all sides with salt and pepper. Rub with oil.
3. Place the beef in small, shallow roasting pan and bake for 20 minutes, turning once or twice as it roasts.
4. Pour off the fat from the pan and add butter to the pan. Continue baking 3 to 5 minutes.
5. Remove the roast from the oven and remove the strings. Cover with a light layer of foil and let stand in a warm place about 10 minutes. Serve sliced with the pan liquid.
   Yield: 6 to 8 servings.

ENAMELED IRON CASSEROLES

Although it can look rather gimmicky in its avocado green or so-cheerful yellow, there is no question but that enameled iron is an important addition to cookware. It distributes heat beautifully, is only moderately expensive and is often very good looking. But it also heats slowly, tends to chip and is heavy to work with.

The two brands of pot I prefer are Le Creuset of France and Copco from Denmark. The casseroles made by both companies all function extremely well. They have heavy, tight-fitting lids that will contain moisture and heat so that a stew can cook for hours on a very low flame bathed both in simmering liquid and in steam. It is the nature of thick cast iron that allows for this heat retention and distribution, of course. The enamel merely eliminates the rust problem of iron. However you do get rusting if the pot chips, baring the metal. Be sure to use wooden spatulas so you don't scratch the surface, and clean the pot with a sponge or soft brush, not a rough scraper. A hint of rust is also possible on the base of the pot, which is not enamelized as the rest of the pot is, but that is an insignificant problem. It can be avoided by careful drying.

More important as a problem is that enameled pots are not especially good at browning and thus are limited in their use for stews. For those stews that require browning you either have to do your best with the enamel or else brown in a cast iron, steel or aluminum pan and transfer the meat to the casserole. The poor browning ability, however, is a plus when you want to avoid darkening a sauce, as is the case in a blanquette of veal.

Several times while cooking in a casserole you may need to lift the lid to stir the ingredients, or add new ones. So my preference is for a casserole with a center-of-the-lid handle.

1. *An enameled iron casserole is excellent for what we call white stews, such as blanquettes and fricasees, where the meat is not browned. For a blanquette, the veal is blanched and drained before adding it to the casserole.* **2.** *Add flour and stir to coat all the meat and vegetables, but do not let the flour brown.*

3. *Add stock and stir well again with a wooden spatula to combine. Bring the liquid to a boil, cover and lower heat so that the stew just simmers.*

IRISH STEW

3 pounds lamb shoulder with bone, or mutton, cut into stewing pieces

2 large onions (¾ pound), sliced

½ pound cored cabbage, sliced (2 cups)

1½ pounds Long Island or Maine potatoes cut into ⅛-inch slices (4 cups)

5 cups lamb or chicken stock

1 teaspoon chopped garlic

1 bay leaf

2 sprigs fresh thyme (optional)
   Salt and freshly ground pepper to taste

2 tablespoons chopped parsley for garnish

1. Place lamb, vegetables and potatoes in enameled iron casserole and cover with water; bring to a boil and drain.
2. Cover with stock; add garlic, bay leaf, thyme, salt and pepper. Bring to a boil and simmer uncovered for 1 hour. Skim foam as necessary. Serve with sprinkling of parsley.

Yield: 6 to 8 servings.

VEAL BLANQUETTE

4 pounds lean veal neck
and shoulder, cut into
1½-inch cubes
4 sprigs parsley
4 sprigs fresh thyme, or ½
teaspoon dried
1 bay leaf
2 cloves
2 tablespoons butter
24 small whole white onions
(¾ pound)
1 tablespoon chopped
garlic
½ pound whole small
mushrooms (2 cups)
¼ cup flour
1 cup white wine
3 cups veal or chicken
stock
Salt and freshly ground
pepper to taste
⅛ teaspoon freshly ground
nutmeg
Dash cayenne pepper
½ pound carrots cut into
1½-inch chunks
1 cup cream
Juice of 1 lemon, strained
2 egg yolks

1. To ensure whiteness of the veal, begin by soaking it in cold water for 1 hour. Drain in a colander and place meat in a large heavy pot, such as an enameled iron casserole. Cover with water and bring to a boil for 2 minutes, stirring. Remove from water, rinse and drain.
2. Prepare a bouquet garni by wrapping parsley, thyme, bay leaf and cloves in cheesecloth; tie the cloth closed and trim off excess material.
3. Melt the butter in the pot. Add meat and then, stirring as each ingredient goes in, add onions, the garlic and mushrooms. Sauté for about 5 minutes, being careful not to brown the meat. Add the flour, stirring to coat thoroughly. Add the wine, stock and bouquet garni. Add salt, pepper, nutmeg and dash of cayenne. Bring to a boil and reduce to a simmer.
4. After ½ hour, add the carrots. Simmer for another ½ hour, or until meat is tender. Cook at high heat, uncovered, for an additional 10 minutes to reduce the liquid somewhat. Discard the bouquet garni.
5. In a mixing bowl or small saucepan, whisk the cream, lemon juice and egg yolks. Add a cup of the liquid from the pot and whisk. Turn the heat off under the casserole. Stir in the egg and cream mixture. Serve with buttered rice.

Yield: 4 to 6 servings.

POACHED CHICKEN WITH CREAM SAUCE

1 3-pound chicken, washed,
   trussed (see pages 39-40),
   fat removed
1 onion (about ¼ pound),
   peeled
2 whole cloves
4 carrots, cut into 2-inch
   pieces
4 stalks celery, peeled and
   cut into 2-inch pieces
1 clove garlic
1 bay leaf
½ teaspoon dried thyme
3 sprigs parsley
10 peppercorns
   Salt to taste
   Cream sauce (see
   following recipe)

1. Place the chicken, neck and gizzard in an enameled iron casserole or heavy, deep saucepan. Cover with water (about 10 cups).
2. Stick 1 clove in each end of the onion and drop into pot.
3. Place the remaining ingredients except cream sauce into the pot and bring to a boil, uncovered. Simmer for about 35 minutes. Remove chicken to a cutting board.
4. Remove skin if desired, carve and place on serving platter surrounded by vegetables. Spoon sauce over the chicken or serve on the side.

Yield: 4 servings.

CREAM SAUCE

2 tablespoons butter
3 tablespoons flour
1½ cups chicken stock from
   chicken pot, passed
   through a fine sieve
½ cup cream
   Juice of ½ lemon
   Dash cayenne pepper
2 tablespoons chopped
   fresh parsley or tarragon
   (optional)

1. Melt the butter in a slant-sided fait-tout saucepan and add flour, stirring with a wire whisk to keep it smooth. Add stock, whisking rapidly. Simmer for 5 minutes.
2. Add the cream and cook for another 5 minutes, whisking.
3. Season with lemon juice and dash of cayenne. Sprinkle with parsley or tarragon.

DEEP FRYER

Deep-fat frying has gotten itself a bad name, unwarrantedly. Home cooks think of it as greasy and fattening — which is palpably untrue since deep-fried food, cooked correctly, absorbs little oil and results not in some soggy mess but in food that is crisp. They also think of it as wasteful, to use a quart or two of oil at once, but in fact the oil is easily preserved for later use.

A good start in introducing yourself to this cooking method is the purchase of a decent fryer and basket. Commonly, deep-fat fryers are electric, but I have never seen an electric one that did the job to my satisfaction. In these modern gadgets, which have proliferated in the past few years, the oil too often fails to return to the proper temperature fast enough after food is placed in it. What I prefer is the sort of design that has been around for a long time — a simple black steel pot and basket, with a rod on the lip of the pot to support the basket after it emerges from the oil. That basket hanger allows for easy draining of chicken or shrimp or potatoes.

Almost any oil with a neutral flavor works well. The problems arise when the oil gets too hot. If the oil burns — burning is signaled by brown smoke — flavor is destroyed and the oil is ruined.

An important accessory is a deep-fat thermometer, which will tell you when the heat level of the oil verges on the 400-degree mark, a dangerous area. How far below it one stays depends on the food in the pot. Chicken, for instance, should cook more slowly than shrimp — 325 degrees for the former, 360 for the latter. The accompanying recipe is for scallops. One for french fries appears on page 72.

Some hints: To be on the safe side, don't fill the pot much more than about halfway with oil. When the food is first dropped into the oil at, say, 380 degrees, the oil will expand rapidly, filling the pot. It will then cool somewhat and settle back down, bubbling productively as it does its job. If the basket is too full — or the pot too small for the amount of food placed in it, the oil will cool rapidly, falling out of the deep fry zone on the thermometer. In that event, the basket can be raised briefly while the oil regains a useful heat. A good size pot is 5 inches deep and 10½ inches in diameter.

Be sure the ingredients are dry before they are placed in the pot. If they are not, there will be a period of ferocious splattering just after the food is lowered into the fat. Also, don't use salt during the cooking process, because it causes oil to break down more quickly than the oil otherwise would.

To reuse the oil, strain it carefully through a piece of cloth and refrigerate it. Generally, two to four uses are possible before the oil must be discarded. Deterioration can be detected by dipping white bread into the oil. Dark specks on the bread mean the oil has expired.

The steel of the pot becomes well seasoned through use. Each time the pot is washed, wipe it carefully and then heat it on the stove for 30 seconds or so to remove any last drop of moisture.

1. Dredge the well dried scallops first in flour then in the egg mixture. They must be thoroughly and evenly coated to make the bread crumbs adhere. 2. Use your fingers to toss the scallops in bread crumbs so they are coated on all sides. Don't be stingy with the crumbs — they are the secret to a crisp exterior.

DEEP-FRIED SCALLOPS

1 egg
4 tablespoons water
1 tablespoon vegetable oil
Salt and freshly ground pepper to taste
2 cups fine fresh bread crumbs
½ cup flour
1 pint bay scallops
Enough vegetable oil to fill the fryer halfway
4 wedges of lemon

1. With a wire whisk, combine the egg, water, oil, salt and pepper in platter. Place bread crumbs on another platter. Place flour on a third platter.
2. Dredge the scallops in flour, then in egg mixture and bread crumbs, tossing them well in the crumbs so they are thoroughly coated. Hold the scallops and jostle them gently with the fingers, shaking off excess coating.
3. Heat oil in fryer to 350 degrees, as determined by a deep fat thermometer.
4. Pour the scallops into the basket over the sink or some toweling rather than over oil so that any remaining loose breading will not fall into the pot. Immerse scallops in the oil. Fry for 1 minute, agitating the basket constantly, and remove to a platter layered with toweling. Serve hot with lemon wedges as a garnish.
Yield: 4 servings.

GRATIN PAN

Designating a dish as au gratin means that it is supposed to have a crusty top, usually comprised of a sauce of cheese and eggs and sometimes bread crumbs. In these dishes, such as potatoes or broccoli au gratin, the crust is the prize. It needs to be perfectly intact — that is, one doesn't want any watery separation to take place — and there needs to be enough of it to go around. There should not be a mound of potatoes, in other words, accompanied by just a little bit of crust.

The vessel best suited for the production of most of these dishes is a piece of equipment bearing the same name as the food; it is a gratin pan. It can be round, oval or rectangular, and most commonly it is about 1½ inches deep. The material can be copper, stainless steel, enameled iron, aluminum, glass or anything else imaginable. It really doesn't matter much because the food, in many cases, is cooked elsewhere and then transferred to the gratin pan for a brief period under the heat of a broiler. So you aren't relying on this vessel's material, in those instances, to do any special job of heat conduction.

You are relying on it to be beautiful, however. Usually the gratin pan will be a presentation pan, in which the dish is carried directly to the table, where its crusty top can be displayed before it is shattered in the process of serving.

I have a couple of suggestions on how to ensure that the gratinée turns out well. To protect against separation of the sauce's ingredients, never place the pan so high that the sauce is nearly touching the flame; the appropriate distance is about 2 inches. A crust-saving trick I use is to introduce a little water into the oven just as the sauce begins to brown. I hurl 2 tablespoons of water right onto the wall of the broiler to produce a burst of steam. I envision it acting as suntan lotion does on the human skin, protecting the crust of the gratinée so it doesn't crack.

There are times when a slightly deeper gratin pan is useful. If what you want is a fillet of sole au gratin, for instance, then that is one of the dishes that might be cooked entirely in the oven — baked not broiled. It will need to be in the oven longer, therefore, and you want to avoid drying out the fish before the crust is done. A deeper pan, holding somewhat more of the ingredients, will be able to retain more moisture. A cassoulet au gratin (cassoulets are bean dishes with a variety of other ingredients, such as goose and sausage, mixed in) would also require a deeper pan for the baking procedure. And then there are the sumptuous pommes dauphinoise, which differ significantly from pommes au gratin. In the latter, the potatoes are precooked before they are sliced and sauced and placed under the broiler. But the dauphinoise is baked entirely in the gratin pan and thus benefits from a bit more depth.

1. *The primary use for a gratin pan is for a dish that will have a crisp crust, such as the potatoes in the accompanying recipe. Pour the sauce over the potatoes and sprinkle the cheese evenly over the top.* **2.** *I also use the gratin pan as a bain marie for such things as timbale molds.*

POMMES DAUPHINOISE

2½ pounds potatoes
1 tablespoon butter
2 cups sliced onions
   Salt and freshly ground pepper to taste
2 cups milk
½ cup cream
1 bay leaf
   Freshly grated nutmeg
¼ pound Swiss or Gruyère cheese, coarsely grated

1. Preheat the oven to 375 degrees.
2. Peel the potatoes and cut them into ⅛-inch slices (with a mandoline, if available). Put them in a mixing bowl containing cold water to remove starch. Drain.
3. Butter a gratin pan and pour the potatoes and onions into it. Add salt and pepper and toss.
4. Pour in the milk and cream. Place bay leaf in center of potatoes. Sprinkle with several gratings of nutmeg. Bring to a boil. Turn off the heat. Add the cheese, spreading it evenly over the top. Place in the oven for 40 minutes.
   Yield: 8 to 10 servings.

NOODLES AU GRATIN

¾ pound medium or fine egg noodles
2 tablespoons butter
   Salt and pepper to taste
⅛ teaspoon grated nutmeg
1 cup heavy cream
¼ pound grated Gruyère or Swiss cheese, about 1¼ cups loosely packed

1. Preheat the broiler.
2. Cook the noodles in boiling salted water until tender. Drain. Return the noodles to the kettle and add half the butter, salt, pepper and nutmeg. Toss to blend.
3. Spoon the noodles into a gratin dish. Heat the cream and pour it over the noodles.
4. Sprinkle the cheese over the noodles and dot with the remaining butter. Run under the broiler until cheese melts and browns.
   Yield: 4 servings.

CAST IRON SKILLET

The cast iron skillet is an extraordinarily important piece of equipment. The fact that it still matters in cooking will not, I'm sure, surprise anyone. And yet in these days of fancy pots and pans one might wonder why the cast iron seems so special. The material, after all, has been around for 4,000 years, and it has been used for cooking during much of that time.

The reasons are several. Cast iron does many of the things a pot is supposed to do: It distributes heat magnificently, with wonderful evenness and great intensity. And, unlike the copper sautoir (see page 88), the cast iron pan is very inexpensive.

Mine is 11½ inches in diameter and I use it frequently, especially when I want to sear meat to seal it while leaving the inside moist, perhaps rare. It can sear so quickly because of its intense heat. And quick searing is the trick in, say, a beef paillarde, which is thin but needs to remain rare at its interior.

I think of my cast iron pan first for a delightful dish called hamburger au poivre. I crush whole peppercorns by rocking a saucepan over them, press the coarse pepper into hamburger patties and then place them in the preheated iron pan. The iron will take a while heating up, and I generally let it warm for several minutes.

When the meat is done, I remove it, pour off the fat, add butter and some shallots to the hot pan and sauté briefly. I deglaze the pan by dissolving the remaining meat solids with red wine. When the wine has reduced somewhat, I swirl sweet butter into it and pour it over the hamburgers.

Another reason I enjoy having this pan around has to do with a dish called pommes macaire, in which baked potatoes are mashed, seasoned (salt, pepper and nutmeg), moistened with butter and pressed into the cast iron pan, which serves as a mold. The potatoes are baked again until they brown and then they are unmolded and cut into wedges like a pie.

You'll find, too, that if you need to brown meat for a stew and the stewpot has an inadequate surface for doing the browning, you can brown the meat in the skillet and then transfer it.

The responsiveness of cast iron — or rather the lack of it — is the reason it is far from an all-purpose pan. You can't just turn down the heat and expect the pan to start cooling at once. So foods of some delicacy cannot be cooked in it. And, of course, the pan needs thorough seasoning to prevent rusting.

1. *For hamburger au poivre, put peppercorns on a flat surface and use a heavy saucepan to crack them (I'm using a fait-tout pan). Hold the front of the pan on the surface and rock the back down and away from you.* **2.** *Dredge the hamburgers in the crushed peppercorns until they are evenly coated on both sides.*

3. *Cook the hamburgers in the cast iron frying pan over high heat, turning them only once. Remove and pour off all the fat.* **4.** *Deglaze the pan by adding wine and scraping the pan with a wooden spatula as the wine reduces.*

5 *When the wine is reduced, swirl in butter to thicken the sauce.* **6.** *Pour the sauce over the hamburgers.*

HAMBURGER AU POIVRE

2¼ pounds chuck
2 tablespoons black peppercorns crushed with bottom of heavy saucepan
  Salt to taste
3 tablespoons butter
2 tablespoons finely chopped shallots
¾ cup dry red wine
1 tablespoon chopped parsley

1. In a food processor, chop the chuck, taking care not to make it mushy by overchopping.
2. Prepare the peppercorns by crushing them with the bottom of a heavy saucepan (I always use my slant-sided fait tout).
3. Form unseasoned chopped meat into 8 patties of equal size. Sprinkle with salt and dredge all over with crushed peppercorns, pressing them in gently so that they adhere.
4. Heat a heavy iron skillet briefly and add 1 tablespoon of the butter.
5. Place patties in the pan and sear on both sides. When red juices bubble out of them, they are very rare. Shortly afterward they will be medium rare. Be sure not to dry out the meat through overcooking.
6. Remove patties to a warm platter. Pour off all fat from the skillet. Add 1 tablespoon of the butter to the skillet and add the shallots, sautéing briefly. Pour in wine. With a wooden spatula, scrape the pan's bottom to dissolve solids. Reduce to one-quarter original volume. Swirl in remaining butter as thickener. Spoon over each patty.
7. Sprinkle parsley over patties and serve.
   Yield: 8 servings.

STEAK BORDELAISE

4 10-ounce New York cut steaks (or boneless rib steaks or boneless strip loin steak)
  Salt and freshly ground pepper to taste
3 tablespoons butter
2 tablespoons chopped shallots
½ cup red wine
2 tablespoons chopped parsley

1. Sprinkle the steaks with salt and pepper.
2. Place a well-seasoned iron skillet over heat and make it very hot (it will smoke when hot enough). Sear steaks at high flame.
3. When steak is brown on both sides, cut down the flame to allow slower cooking. Cooking time is 6 to 8 minutes on a side.
4. Remove steaks to a serving platter and keep warm. Discard the fat in the pan and add 1 tablespoon butter and the 2 tablespoons of shallots. Cook for several seconds. Do not burn them.
5. Add red wine and deglaze the pan at high flame by scraping the bottom of the pan with a wooden spatula to dissolve the solids. Cook until reduced to one quarter of original volume.
6. Swirl 2 tablespoons of butter into sauce, pour over steak and garnish with parsley.
   Yield: 4 servings.

CRÊPE PAN

A crêpe pan is not an omelet pan, but it's close. At least the one I use is. The preparation of a good crêpe requires speed — the rapid transfer of heat — and dexterity on the part of the cook. So the pan needs to be light and the material it is made of needs to be very capable indeed. As with the omelet pan, black steel is the choice here. The crêpe pan is shaped somewhat differently from the omelet pan, with sides that are gently curved to allow for the easy intrusion of a small narrow spatula to turn the crêpe. Some accomplished cooks are able to flip the crêpe, and here, too, the sides are well suited to this. The size I prefer in a crêpe pan is 5½ inches in bottom diameter.

The most important maneuver in preparing a crêpe is in the action of the wrist. Hold the pan in one hand tilted downward slightly and, using a 1-ounce ladle, pour the batter into the pan toward the top. Then, with a quick figure-8 movement — this is where that wrist action is crucial — distribute the batter evenly and thinly over the surface of the pan. The crêpe is turned when the edges begin to brown. The perfect crêpe has a lacelike appearance to it. Oddly, this look is imparted to it by black steel and not by Teflon or other nonstick surfaces. But anyone who makes crêpes only rarely and therefore has been unable to accumulate the required amount of experience, will find the nonstick surface is a good enough substitute, preventing the failure that often comes with inexperience.

A nonstick pan also avoids the need for seasoning that the black steel requires lest it rust. But you can be certain of this: The texture does make a difference, and learning to make crêpes well in black steel is more than worth the effort.

1. *The strained crêpe batter should fall from a ladle in an even stream without any lumps.* **2.** *Ladle about an ounce of batter into one side of a very hot crêpe pan.*

3. *Quickly tip the pan forward, up and around in a figure-8 motion. The bottom of the pan should be covered with a thin layer of batter.*
4. *When lacelike holes form and edges are slightly brown, turn the crêpe with a narrow, flexible spatula and cook briefly on the other side.*

5. *The finished crêpe.*

CRÊPES MARTINIQUE WITH RUM

4 tablespoons butter
2 cups sliced banana
2 tablespoons sugar
8 crêpes (see following recipe)
¼ cup cream
¼ cup rum

1. Melt the butter in a shallow pan. Add the banana and 1 table-spoon of the sugar. Sauté briefly until just hot, turning bananas frequently.
2. Butter a large shallow pan such as a gratin pan or presentation pan, perhaps 12 inches in diameter. With serving spoon, place some of the banana mixture in each crêpe and roll closed. Arrange crêpes in greased pan. Place over low flame, pour in cream and sprinkle with remaining sugar. Pour in rum. Cook for about 1 minute and serve, usually 2 crêpes per person.
Yield: 4 servings.

BASIC CRÊPE

2 eggs
1 cup flour
2 teaspoons sugar
  Pinch of salt
½ teaspoon vanilla
1¼ cups milk
4 tablespoons butter

1. In a mixing bowl blend the eggs, flour, sugar, salt, vanilla and milk.
2. Melt 2 tablespoons of the butter in a small saucepan and add it to the batter, whisking briefly. Pour mixture through a fine-mesh strainer, pushing solids through with a rubber spatula. The finest mesh is required to ensure a thin, smooth batter. Let batter rest about 20 minutes before use.
3. Melt the remaining butter to brush the crêpe pan as necessary. If a black steel crêpe pan is well seasoned it will need little or no butter before receiving batter. If it is not well seasoned, brush it thoroughly before each use.
4. Using a ladle, pour about 1 ounce of batter into very hot pan, rapidly tipping and moving the pan in a figure-8 motion so that the batter quickly spreads evenly and thinly over the surface, covering the surface completely and slightly up the wall of the pan, if necessary, to keep it evenly thin throughout. This will take practice.
5. Brown the crêpe on one side, about 40 seconds. The signal that it is time to turn the crêpe is slight browning at the edge. Then turn it with a narrow spatula to brown the other side. The consistency is correct if the crêpe is lacelike when it is done.
6. Crêpes can be stacked and covered with plastic wrap and refrigerated until needed.

Yield: About 24 crêpes.

Note: The crêpes can be made quite satisfactorily in a nonstick pan rather than one of black steel. But it is my experience that such pans do not yield the desired lacey look.

BLACK STEEL FRYING PANS

The black steel frying pan has no current popularity. But in any professional kitchen this pot is never idle, used constantly for sautéeing and for omelets. In my kitchen there are three used all the time: 8, 11 and 13 inches in diameter. The main virtue of these frying pans is that they transfer heat from fire to food rapidly and thoroughly so that browning is done with extraordinary efficiency.

Cast iron browns food well, too, of course, but there are many instances in which you want the pan to cool rapidly, and cast iron just won't do that. The extreme responsiveness of a steel pan is invaluable in cooking calf's liver, for instance. It is the perfect heating property for scaloppine. And it means that a chop can be browned thoroughly without its center being overcooked, since the pan will respond at once to a lowered flame.

Another property that makes this pan the primary one for sautéeing potatoes and other vegetables is its lightness. To sauté vegetables you hold the pan's long handle almost at the end, tilt the pan down and away from you and then, with a quick wrist motion, slip the ingredients back over themselves. Needless to say, in cast iron or enameled iron that flipping motion would be exhausting, if possible at all. The 11-inch pan is the one I use most for sautéeing.

In preparing an omelette fines herbes, I turn to that same 11-inch pan. I pour the mixture into it, stir it vigorously, let it set for a few seconds and begin to fold the side nearest me toward the opposite side of the pan. The next step is the one where this utensil is without parallel: To make the opposite side of the omelet fold back toward me, I lift the pan off the range with my left hand, tilting it away from me, and strike the base of its handle two or three times with the fist of my right hand. The resiliency of the steel causes it to rebound as it is struck, hurling the omelet back onto itself.

Since this steel is at the other extreme from stainless — meaning it rusts very quickly — it has to be treated properly, like cast iron. It should be seasoned well with oil. And it should be used, generally speaking, for the same foods time and again to prevent imparting unwanted flavors to the food. Thus, an omelet pan should be saved for eggs and potatoes and the like and never used for fish. If you are disciplined about that, the pan will almost never need to be washed; just wipe it clean while it is still warm and perhaps scour it with coarse salt to remove any adhering particles. Once the pan has been well and constantly used, an occasional washing with soap and water will do it no harm.

For omelets and some other jobs I also have used the nonstick Teflon-coated pans and their successive generations, such as T-Fal. With each new generation of this material the pans get better. They no longer peel the way they once did. They do still scratch, however. And they impart to omelets a texture that reminds me a bit of pancakes. I don't like the omelet as much as when it emerges from a raw steel pan. But the difference is only a nuance, and I would recommend these pans to anyone who finds omelet making to be too elusive a skill in the steel pans. I also recommend these pans as a way of cutting down on oil and other fats. In fact, in some nouvelle cuisine cooking there is so little fat required that a nonstick pan is almost a necessity.

For an omelette paysanne:

1. *Add eggs to the potatoes and onions and stir all over the bottom with the back of a fork to let the eggs flow.* **2.** *When the bottom of the omelet is set, hold a plate over the pan and invert the omelet onto it.*

3. *Slide the omelet back into the pan and cook for about 30 seconds. Spoon vinegar around the periphery of the omelet.* **4.** *Slide the omelet out onto a plate and cut into wedges to serve.*

OMELETTE PAYSANNE

3 tablespoons oil
½ pound potatoes, boiled
with skin, cut into ⅛-inch
slices
Salt and freshly ground
pepper to taste
6 eggs
1 tablespoon coarsely
chopped parsley
½ cup diced Swiss cheese or
Gruyère
1 medium onion, sliced
(about ½ cup)
2 tablespoons butter
1 teaspoon vinegar

1. In 11-inch black steel frying pan, heat oil until it smokes slightly.
2. Place the potatoes in the pan, spreading them along the bottom as evenly as possible to facilitate complete browning. Cook, turning occasionally with a steel spatula. Add salt and pepper to taste.
3. Meanwhile, beat eggs in a mixing bowl and add parsley. Stir in the cheese.
4. As potatoes turn lightly brown, add the onion to the pan, turning occasionally. When potatoes are thoroughly brown, drain most of the oil and add butter to the pan.
5. Add the egg mixture to the potatoes and onions, stirring gently with the rounded base of an ordinary fork to allow the egg to flow to the bottom. Let set, at high flame.
6. When the mixture has solidified, shake the pan to be sure the omelet is loose. Turn the omelet by inverting a plate over the pan and quickly inverting the pan. Then slide the omelet back into the pan. The final stage of cooking is brief, only about 30 seconds.
7. Spoon vinegar around periphery of eggs and transfer back to plate.
8. Cut into wedges and serve, either hot or at room temperature.
Yield: 2 or 3 servings.

SAUTÉED CALF'S LIVER WITH PARSLEY

1¼ pounds calf's liver
(4 slices)
Salt and freshly ground
pepper to taste
2 tablespoons oil
5 tablespoons butter
3 tablespoons flour
2 tablespoons vinegar
3 tablespoons chopped
parsley

1. Sprinkle the liver with salt and pepper to taste.
2. In a black steel skillet, heat the oil and then melt 1 tablespoon of the butter.
3. Dredge the liver in flour and place in pan. Cook about 3 minutes on each side.
4. Rinse and brush the pan out in clear water. While pan is still warm, add remaining butter, browning the butter slightly while agitating the pan to prevent burning. Add vinegar, swirling it through the butter, and pour over the liver.
5. Garnish with a sprinkling of chopped parsley.
Yield: 4 servings.

SAUTÉED POTATOES

1½ pounds Idaho or
California potatoes
(about six) with skin
Salt to taste
2 tablespoons peanut,
vegetable or corn oil
Pepper to taste
2 tablespoons butter
2 tablespoons chopped
parsley

1. Scrub the potatoes and place in a straight-sided saucepan. Cover with water, add salt, and bring to a boil, continuing to cook until tender, about 20 minutes.
2. Drain in a colander and, when cool enough to handle, cut into ⅛-inch-thick slices with paring knife.
3. Heat oil in a black steel pan until it starts to smoke slightly. Place potatoes in pan and add salt and pepper, shaking the pan a bit to keep the slices separate. Flip occasionally or turn the potatoes with a flexible slotted spatula.
4. When crusty brown, remove potatoes from the pan and pour off all the oil. Melt butter in the still-hot pan and return the potatoes to brown for about 30 seconds. Remove and serve with a sprinkling of parsley.
Yield: 4 to 6 servings.

For a folded omelet:

1. *Melt butter in the pan until it foams but is not brown. Pour in the beaten eggs.* **2.** *Hold the fork parallel to the pan and move it all over the bottom while shaking the pan to let the egg flow.*

3. *When the eggs are set, tip the pan away from you and roll one third of the omelet over with the fork.* **4.** *With the pan still tipped, bang the handle with your fist, which will make the far third of the omelet fold back on itself.*

5. *Shape the omelet neatly with a fork.* **6.** *Hold the pan vertically and turn the omelet out onto a warm plate, seam side down.*

OMELETTE FINES HERBES

6 eggs
1 tablespoon chopped
   tarragon
2 tablespoons chopped
   parsley
2 tablespoons chopped basil
2 tablespoons chopped
   chives
   Salt and freshly ground
   pepper to taste
2 tablespoons butter

1. Place all ingredients except the butter and 1 tablespoon of herb, to be reserved as garnish, into a mixing bowl and beat well with a fork.
2. In a pre-warmed 11-inch black steel frying pan, melt the butter and pour in omelet mixture.
3. Stir mixture over high heat with the rounded base of a fork and at the same time push the edges of the mixture toward the center. When the mixture has nearly solidified, stop stirring and let set for a few seconds.
4. Holding the pan so that it is tilted away from you, use the fork to fold the near side of the omelet halfway to the other side.
5. Firmly grasping the handle with one hand, lift the pan off the range, still tilted away from you, and strike the base of the handle two or three times with the side of the fist of your other hand. This will cause the far edge of the omelet to fold back on itself, completing the envelope. Use the fork to press the omelet closed at the seam. Roll out onto a platter, seam side down. Sprinkle remaining herbs on the top of each omelet.
Yield: 2 servings.

SAUTÉED MUSHROOMS AND GARLIC

¼ cup vegetable oil
1 pound small whole
   mushrooms (4 cups)
1 tablespoon olive oil
1 tablespoon butter
   Salt and freshly ground
   pepper to taste
1 tablespoon chopped
   garlic
2 tablespoons chopped
   parsley

1. Heat vegetable oil until it smokes slightly in a large black steel frying pan. Place the mushrooms in pan and sauté at high heat, repeatedly tossing them until the moisture evaporates. Pour mushrooms into a colander to drain them. Remove oil from pan.
2. Heat olive oil and butter in the pan. When butter is melted and pan is very hot, return mushrooms to it and brown them, tossing repeatedly. Add salt and pepper to taste. Add the garlic and parsley. Sauté for a few seconds, being careful not to brown the garlic. Remove from the pan. Serve as an appetizer or side dish.
Yield: 4 servings.

STEAK & CHOP GRILL

I am not especially partial to broiled meat, at least as it is generally done in the oven. Broiling in the oven tends to impart a baked flavor. I much prefer a grilling technique widely favored in France and not unknown here. It is a technique that uses an iron pan designed with parallel ridges along its bottom.

The pan I have used in recent years is rectangular in shape (14 by 8 inches), making it especially suitable for a large steak, and it has a spout for pouring off excess fat.

The reason a porterhouse or châteaubriand seems to benefit so much from the ridged pan is that not only do the ridges keep the meat away from the fat, which might make it soggy, but also the pan is able to sizzle the meat much as an outdoor grill would do. It creates a seared, flavorful exterior while retaining a moist interior.

The method for grilling meat in one of these pans is to get the pan as hot as possible before placing the meat in it. Leave it empty on top of a full flame for four or five minutes, and you can be sure it will be hot enough. If the meat is lean, it helps to brush it with oil before placing it in the pan. Then sear it rapidly on both sides to seal it. After the searing, you will want to keep an eye on the meat to be sure that it's not burning. As the meat cooks, pour off any excess fat.

One of the many pleasing results of this kind of cooking is the pattern the ridges of the grill make on the meat. It's a good idea to rotate the steak or chop so that you get a crisscross effect (in addition to being a more elaborate pattern than the simple horizontal lines, the crisscrossing sears more of the meat).

The one kind of flat meat I would not prepare in this manner is a thick pork chop, which must, of course, be cooked thoroughly. It would be burned on the outside before the inside could be done.

1. *Heat the empty grill for 4 or 5 minutes, then place the seasoned and oiled chops on the grill. Sear them on both sides over high heat, turning with tongs. Lower the heat and continue to turn the chops and move them around.* **2.** *Drain the fat frequently by holding the chops with a rigid spatula.*

PAN-BROILED LAMB CHOPS WITH ROSEMARY

1 teaspoon chopped garlic
1 teaspoon dried rosemary,
  chopped
6 1½-inch thick lamb chops
  (2½ pounds), trimmed of
  excess fat
  Salt and freshly ground
  pepper to taste
1 tablespoon olive oil

1. Combine the garlic and rosemary, chopping with a chef's knife to create a paste. Place the chops in a tray or pan and rub the garlic and rosemary mixture into them. Sprinkle with salt and pepper. Pour oil over the chops and rub again with hands.

2. Preheat a chop grill on top of the stove. Sear the chops for a few seconds at high heat and then cut down the flame to allow the meat to cook through. Turn frequently and pour off fat as necessary. Stand each chop on edge to burn the fat away. Also brown the bone on the sides. The result should be a browned appearance all over the chop. Cook for a total of about 10 minutes.

3. If desired, serve surrounded by pan-broiled zucchini (see following recipe), pouring any of the remaining seasoned olive oil from the zucchini pan over the dish.
   Yield: 6 servings.
   Note: This dish can be prepared similarly in the broiler section of the oven.

PAN BROILED ZUCCHINI WITH ROSEMARY

3 medium zucchini (1
  pound), cut lengthwise
  into thirds
  Salt and freshly ground
  pepper to taste
½ teaspoon chopped garlic
½ teaspoon dried rosemary,
  chopped
2 tablespoons olive oil

1. Place the zucchini in a shallow pan. Sprinkle with salt and pepper, garlic and rosemary. Spoon oil over the zucchini and toss thoroughly with the hands. Let sit for 15 minutes or more.

2. Place the zucchini on a hot chop grill (or under oven broiler). If it is to be served with chops do this step just as the chops are done. Cook about 2 minutes on each side.
   Yield: 4 to 6 servings.

DOUFEU

The doufeu oven has a knack for survival. Originally this heavy, capacious pot with a broad depression in its lid was used to surround braised meat with heat. The pot sat on the fire, and coals were placed in the lid's shallow well. Its name derives from that use. Doux feu means soft fire. In fact, braising refers in French to hot coals. The coals are mostly gone in these days when modern ovens can surround food with heat, but the doufeu oven remains because of a tenacious ability to adapt.

That depression in the lid is no longer called upon to hold coals; it is filled with cool water or even ice cubes instead. The principle that is thus brought into play is simple: If the lid of a pot can be kept cool, it will intensify the condensation of steam within the pot so that as the steam strikes the inside of the lid it returns to its more substantial, watery state and drips down onto the food below, basting it continuously.

Using a doufeu in my own kitchen, I applied this method to veal chops en cocotte. Because I knew the condensation in the pot would keep the veal moist, I needed to add very little liquid to the pot beyond what the food would yield ordinarily. There was a little butter, mushrooms, vinegar and seasonings. The butter was necessary for browning the chops first. Ordinarily in such a dish, one would have to use stock or wine or some other liquid to prevent the meat from drying. But here the mushrooms and the meat, along with the butter left in the pot and the little vinegar, would prove to be more than ample. At the end, there was a considerable amount of the natural liquid as a sauce for the meat. The chops had a deep, pure flavor.

Many another dish is cooked well in this pot. In particular, I like it for chicken, loin of pork and roast veal. It can be used to produce a stew, too. But for a stew, I would add a bit of liquid, although not as much as with other pots. Actually, the doufeu can be used simply as a handsome casserole, forgetting about the depression in the lid.

But, however it is used, the pot ought to possess certain important characteristics: It should be made of heavy gauge metal — cast iron, enameled cast iron or aluminum — that will distribute the heat evenly and hold it well. Most commonly, these days, it is made of enameled iron, which is less capable in browning the meat but is otherwise excellent. (If you choose, meat can be browned in a cast iron or a steel pan first and then placed in a pot such as this.)

The lid, and this is extraordinarily important, ought to fit tightly, since the loss of moisture is obviously antithetical to the whole purpose of the pot. As for size, a 5-quart doufeu is generally adequate.

LOIN OF PORK EN COCOTTE

2½ pounds loin of pork
    (center cut)
    Salt and freshly ground
    pepper to taste
1 clove garlic, cut into 4
    slivers
1 tablespoon vegetable oil
1 large onion (¼ pound)
1 bay leaf
½ teaspoon thyme
1¼ pounds medium potatoes,
    peeled
¼ cup water
¼ cup coarsely chopped
    parsley

1. Sprinkle salt and pepper over the entire roast, working it into the meat with the hands. Pierce the back of the roast with a paring knife in four equidistant spots between ribs and push slivers of garlic into holes.
2. Heat the oil in a doufeu pan. Place the roast, fat side down, into pan and cook at medium heat for 5 minutes, or until brown. Brown all remaining surfaces and onion, too, so that gravy will have good color.
3. Remove all fat from the pan. Turn roast fat side up. Place bay leaf on roast and sprinkle with thyme. Position potatoes around the meat and sprinkle them with a little salt. Cook uncovered for another 5 minutes, shaking the pan occasionally to brown the potatoes (turn with a fork if necessary to expose all sides of potatoes to heat).
4. Pour ¼ cup water into the pot and cover tightly. Pour ½ cup of cool water into the depression in the cover. Continue to cook at low flame for about 2 hours, occasionally replenishing water in the lid.
5. Remove roast to a warm serving plate; surround with potatoes and onion and pour pan juices over all. Sprinkle with parsley and serve.
    Yield: 4 to 6 servings.

VEAL CHOPS EN COCOTTE

4 veal chops, ¾-inch thick
    (about ½ pound each)
    Salt and freshly ground
    pepper to taste
3 tablespoons butter
2 tablespoons finely
    chopped shallots
½ pound whole mushrooms
1 bay leaf
¼ teaspoon thyme
3 tablespoons vinegar
4 tablespoons chopped
    parsley

1. Cut the tail of each chop part of the way through at the base so it will fold. Sprinkle with salt and pepper to taste.
2. Heat the butter in a doufeu pan until it bubbles. Place the chops in the pan and brown on both sides at high heat, about 5 minutes each side. Distribute shallots around the chops.
3. Put mushrooms and bay leaf in the pot. Sprinkle thyme over the chops. Shake the pan a bit to distribute the ingredients. Cook for 5 minutes, still uncovered. Add the vinegar.
4. Cover and pour water into the lid of the doufeu pan. Cook at low flame for 30 minutes. Uncover and reduce liquid to two-thirds its original volume.
5. Serve the chops in their sauce, garnished with parsley.
    Yield: 4 servings.

CLAY POT

A clever prehistoric approach to cooking was to wrap game in wet clay and place it on hot coals. The method must have worked reasonably well, retaining the meat's moisture and flavor as the clay hardened around it. The cooking vessels had to be shattered at each use, of course, to get at the meat.

Wet-clay cooking has been back with us now for several years. Luckily, this time around, the pots are reusable, and they offer an attractive and effective mode of cooking.

They generally take the form of a covered casserole made of porous clay. Before each use, a pot's top and bottom are soaked for ten minutes or so in a sink filled with water. This causes the pot to absorb the water like a rigid sponge. In the oven, the pot will slowly release its moisture. The steam thus created prevents food from drying out, with the use of little if any fat or oil, and allows the seasonings to permeate the food.

The method is especially effective with tough cuts of meat. An inexpensive 3-pound roast beef will cook quickly (perhaps in less than an hour) in one of these pots and will emerge tender. The flavor is rich and pleasant, if unusual, a combination of potting and roasting. The color, however, is likely to be a bit on the gray side. I have been especially satisfied with the ability of these pots to cook lamb shanks.

Clay pots are an obvious boon to anyone trying to avoid as much aggravation as possible, because roasts done in them generally don't need to be turned or basted. With chickens — which roast superbly in these pots — browning can be enhanced by a single basting about 10 minutes before the cooking is done. Then the roast should be left uncovered for the remaining time.

The claim has been made by advocates of these pots that they save time because they allow you to cook at a higher-than-usual temperature and therefore for a shorter period. The claim is debatable, however. In some instances, the cooking time is in fact relatively brief. In others it is so long it verges on the ridiculous. In one audacious recipe I've seen that was meant to show the versatility of the pot, trout were cooked for 45 minutes at 425 degrees!

When cooking with these pots, keep in mind many cautions. An important one — and one that's easy to forget — is not to put the hot pot on a cool surface. If you do, it may shatter (leaving you to feel roughly as clever as prehistoric man). Instructions that come with the pots tell you not to use a preheated oven because it, too, would create an extreme temperature change that might do some damage. In fact, I have placed mine in a preheated oven with no disaster.

The pot should be washed only with a stiff brush and hot water, not soap, which will clog the pores. Some clay pots come partly glazed to facilitate cleaning but the glaze, of course, diminishes the porosity of the pot. The pots come in sizes ranging from one that will accommodate 2½ pounds of food to one that will handle 14 pounds. The most useful is the standard size, which takes up to 6 pounds.

CHICKEN COOKED IN A CLAY POT

1 3½-pound chicken
1 tablespoon fresh, finely
   ground black pepper
   Salt to taste
1 small onion, peeled
½ cup tightly packed
   parsley
1 bay leaf
½ teaspoon thyme
2 tablespoons butter
4 to 8 small carrots,
   trimmed, peeled and cut
   in half crosswise
8 small to medium fresh
   mushrooms
¼ teaspoon crushed hot red
   pepper flakes
½ cup canned tomatoes

1. Preheat the oven to 450 degrees.
2. Place a clay pot in a basin of cold water and let it soak for at least 10 minutes. Drain well.
3. Sprinkle the inside of the chicken with half the ground pepper and salt. Stuff the cavity with the onion, parsley, bay leaf and thyme.
4. Sprinkle the outside of the chicken with the remaining ground pepper. Rub the breast and legs of the chicken with butter.
5. Arrange the chicken breast side up in the bottom of the clay pot. Arrange the carrot pieces and mushrooms all around the chicken. Sprinkle with hot red pepper. Place pieces of tomato on top of the vegetables.
6. Cover the pot with the lid. Place in the oven and bake at 450 degrees for 1 hour and 30 minutes.
7. Carve the chicken and serve it with its natural juices.
   Yield: 4 servings.

LAMB SHANKS BOULANGÈRE

1 tablespoon chopped
   garlic
1 teaspoon fresh thyme, or
   ½ teaspoon dried
2½ pounds potatoes, peeled
   and cut into ⅛-inch slices
   (about 6 cups)
2 cups onions
¼ cup chopped parsley
2 bay leaves
   Salt and freshly ground
   pepper to taste
4 lamb shanks, about 1
   pound each, trimmed of
   excess fat
4 tablespoons butter

1. Preheat the oven to 450 degrees.
2. Soak a clay pot, top and bottom, for at least 10 minutes.
3. Combine the garlic and thyme by chopping them together finely.
4. In a mixing bowl, place the potatoes, onions, thyme and garlic mixture, parsley, one of the bay leaves and salt to taste. Toss together well.
5. Sprinkle the shanks with salt and pepper. Place two in the pot, cover with a layer of half the potatoes. Place remaining two in pot and cover with remaining potatoes and one bay leaf. Distribute the butter over potatoes. Sprinkle with pepper.
6. Cover and bake for 1½ hours, or until so tender that the meat easily comes off the bone.
   Yield: 4 servings.

WOK

Everyone by now has heard all about the wonders of stir-frying vegetables in a wok — just a drop of oil, rapid cooking, all the nutrients preserved. But chances are, if you're like many people of my acquaintance, you still haven't acquired a wok and have survived without one.

The truth is that you can stir-fry reasonably well in a big skillet. So there is no mandate, even during the current popularity of Chinese cooking, to have one of these bowl-like pots in the kitchen.

Nevertheless, there is no doubt that a wok makes life easier for Chinese dishes such as the stir-fry of vegetables and beef accompanying this discussion. The shape of a wok allows you neatly to contain a great volume of vegetables and other foods while rapidly agitating them over a large cooking surface. The agitation of the vegetables and meat — the Chinese approach to sautéeing, actually — is accomplished with a shovel-shaped spatula.

The distribution of heat throughout a wok is terribly important, and for that reason I prefer rolled steel or iron to thin stainless steel or aluminum. The steel, of course, requires seasoning (see pages 86-87) or it will rust. Some people say a wok should never again be washed after the initial seasoning, which I think is a bit extreme as advice. Just dry it carefully after each washing, and keep it well-oiled.

A good-sized wok is at least 14 inches in diameter. They are frequently sold with some useful ancillary equipment. In addition to the shovel-like spatula and shallow ladle, you generally see a long-handled strainer that is used to remove delicate foods, such as tempura, from the oil. The ring that fits under the wok is intended to stabilize it over the heat source, but I never use it because it holds the wok too far from the heat. You'll find it useful to have a colander or other large metal straining device to place the food in as it is removed from the wok. The one pictured here is the traditional design.

1. *The secret to successful stir-fried dishes is to have all the ingredients near at hand, chopped and measured, so that you can add them quickly as called for in a recipe.*
2. *Heat a wok over a high flame and pour in the oil. Using a Chinese spatula, distribute the oil over the sides of the pan.*

3. *Stir-fry the food by quickly scooping and tossing it with the spatula, distributing it all over the surface of the wok. The cooking is done in seconds.* **4.** *Drain the food as called for in a recipe by scooping it into a wide metal strainer placed over a pot to catch the oil. Or use a metal colander.*

SHREDDED CHICKEN WITH BEAN SPROUTS

4 chicken breast halves, skinned and boned
3 teaspoons cornstarch
1 egg white (beaten lightly)
3 tablespoons dry sherry or shao hsing wine
Salt to taste
1 cup peanut, vegetable or corn oil
4 cups bean sprouts
⅓ cup thinly shredded, fresh red or green, long hot peppers
3 teaspoons sugar

1. Place the chicken on a flat surface and slice it thin on the bias. Shred the slices as fine as possible. (This is easier if the meat is partially frozen before slicing and the slices stacked before shredding.)
2. Using the fingers, blend the shredded chicken with the cornstarch, egg white, 2 tablespoons of the wine and salt to taste. Refrigerate for 30 minutes.
3. Heat the oil in a wok and, when it is warm but not piping hot, add the chicken mixture. Cook, stirring, just until the shreds separate and the chicken loses its raw look. Drain in a sieve-lined bowl to catch the drippings and set aside. Pour off all but 4 tablespoons of the oil.
4. Heat the 4 tablespoons of oil, then add the bean sprouts and salt to taste. Cook, stirring constantly, about 45 seconds in all. Drain.
5. Rinse out and wipe the pan. Add 2 tablespoons of oil and, when it is hot, add the hot pepper shreds. Cook briefly and add the bean sprouts, the chicken, salt to taste, the sugar and the remaining tablespoon of wine. Stir just to heat thoroughly. Serve hot.
Yield: 4 to 8 servings.

STIR-FRY BEEF AND VEGETABLES

3 tablespoons sherry
1 teaspoon sugar
2 tablespoons chicken
  stock (or broth)
1 pound chilled lean flank
  steak
2 tablespoons cornstarch
3 tablespoons dark soy
  sauce
1 cup peanut oil
4 green peppers (¾ pound)
2 medium onions
1 clove garlic, chopped

1. In a small mixing bowl combine the sherry, sugar and stock.
2. Using a cleaver, cut steak crosswise in strips 2 inches wide. Pound the meat once or twice with the side of the cleaver to make it more compact. Then, with cleaver parallel to the cutting surface, slice the steak horizontally along the length of each strip. Do this twice so each strip yields three thin slices. Stack the three strips on top of each other and slice crosswise into strips ⅛ inch wide.
3. Toss the meat with the cornstarch to coat thoroughly. Add the soy sauce and 2 tablespoons of the oil. Marinate at least 10 minutes.
4. Cut each pepper in half with the cleaver. Pull out the seeds and the core. Cut into ¼-inch strips (4 cups). Cut the onions in half and place flat side down. Cut into ⅛-inch slices (1½ cups).
5. Pour the remaining oil into the wok. Using a spatula, distribute it all over the surface. When oil begins to smoke, place half of the meat in the wok, stirring and tossing rapidly with the spatula. When meat browns, in about 30 seconds, remove it to strainer alongside the wok. Cook second half.
6. Discard all but 2 tablespoons of oil, which should be left in the wok. Place the peppers and onions in the wok and cook rapidly, tossing and stirring, for about 30 seconds. Add the garlic and toss for a few seconds. Return meat to the wok. Add stock, sherry and sugar mixture. Toss for another 30 seconds and remove to a platter.

Yield: 4 to 6 servings.

PAELLA PAN

For the cook who likes to spend free time feeding as many friends as possible, paella is a blessing, a lavish and generous dish of many flavors and textures that can be ruined only through practiced negligence.

A magnificent paella intended for six or eight people contains such a variety of meat and seafood as well as rice and vegetables that its preparation requires an enormous pan. The pan used for ages, the traditional paella pan, is certainly big, with shallow, sloping sides. It does facilitate the manipulation of all those ingredients as they are cooked separately and together. A true Spanish paella is cooked over an open fire, and when the cooking is done the pan is used as a serving platter, presented as a mountain of colorful morsels.

The accompanying recipe does not require any outdoor cooking, but it is still flamboyantly effective. It uses the same Spanish pan, first on top of the range and then in the oven to finish off the job.

My steel pan (pictured here) is 18 inches in diameter, less than 2 inches deep and does not have a cover. The preparation of the paella using this pan involves browning many of the ingredients in it individually, removing each as it is browned, then joining them with the required liquid, spices and rice for a period of baking.

There is also a modified paella pan and a modified approach, which I have found satisfactory on occasion. The pan is unconventionally deep (3 inches deep and perhaps 15 inches wide) and made of aluminum. Although deeper than the traditional pan, its design still allows the server or the guests to forage around for a little of this and a little of that, a search that would be awkward in pans any narrower or deeper.

The aluminum pan, with its excellent heat-distribution ability will do a better job of browning the chicken, ham and sausage that so often go into the paella than the thin steel of the traditional pan, but because it is not as wide it will accommodate less.

In these relatively deep aluminum pans, all of the cooking can be done on top of the stove. But then the pan needs to be covered while the rice is cooking toward the end of the preparation. If the pan has no lid, aluminum foil may be used as a cover.

At least as important as having an adequate pan for the paella is remembering not to stint on the ingredients. The fun is in the profusion. And, especially, don't neglect the seasoning. The saffron for instance is expensive, but without it a paella suffers greatly.

1. *Brown the chicken pieces in hot oil in the paella pan, turning them frequently, and remove.* **2.** *Sauté the lobster pieces in the same oil and remove them with a skimmer or a slotted spoon so the oil remains in the pan. Cook the shrimp and the sausage in the same way and then pour off the oil.*

3. *Add more oil and cook the pork, then add the vegetables. Cook, stirring with a wooden spatula, until the moisture has evaporated. Add the rice, chili pepper and water.* **4.** *Add the previously cooked ingredients, then top with mussels and clams. Place in the oven to bake.*

PAELLA

¾ pound chorizo (if unavailable, substitute hot Italian sausage)

2 large tomatoes (¾ pounds)

1 1½-pound lobster

½ cup olive oil

1 3½-pound chicken, cut into 10 pieces
Salt and freshly ground pepper to taste

12 medium shrimp (½ pound before shelling)

½ pound of loin of pork, most of the fat trimmed away, cut into ½-inch pieces

3 onions, coarsely chopped (1½ cups)

1 teaspoon finely minced garlic

2 large red peppers (¾ pound), cut into ½-inch strips

½ teaspoon saffron

2 cups converted rice

1 chili pepper

2 cups water

12 large mussels

8 littleneck clams

1 cup frozen green peas

¼ teaspoon olive oil

1 lemon, cut into 8 wedges

1. Preheat the oven to 375 degrees.
2. Pierce the sausage with a fork in several places and blanch in boiling water for 5 minutes. Cool and slice into ½-inch pieces.
3. Place the tomatoes in boiling water for 12 seconds. Remove skin with a paring knife. Cut in half and chop into ½-inch chunks, about 2 cups.
4. Cut the claws and legs off the lobster in a single piece, remove the tail and slice the body into 1-inch pieces. Remove and discard the small sac inside the lobster near the eyes.
5. Heat ¼ cup of the olive oil in a paella pan. Sprinkle chicken with salt and pepper and sauté, moving pieces around the pan, until thoroughly browned. Remove to a large platter.
6. Sprinkle lobster pieces with salt and pepper and place in same hot oil. Sauté 2 or 3 minutes until shell is deep red. Remove to platter.
7. Sprinkle shrimp with salt and pepper and sauté very quickly, about 1 minute, being careful not to overcook.
8. Sauté sausage pieces 2 or 3 minutes. Remove to the platter. Discard oil in paella pan.
9. Heat remaining ¼ cup oil in pan. Sprinkle pork with salt and pepper and sauté 2 or 3 minutes until lightly browned on both sides.
10. Add onion, garlic, peppers, salt and pepper to taste, tomatoes and saffron. Cook, stirring, about 5 minutes, until moisture from vegetables has evaporated.
11. Add the rice and mix in thoroughly. Add the chili pepper. Pour in the water. Bring to a boil and place previously sautéed ingredients on top, the shrimp last. Add mussels and clams. Place in oven for 25 minutes. Remove from oven and toss lightly to distribute all ingredients throughout the dish.
12. Put the peas in a colander and rinse under warm water. Drain and put in a bowl. Pour ¼ teaspoon olive oil over peas and sprinkle them over the paella. Garnish with lemon wedges. Serve directly from paella pan.

Yield: 6 to 8 servings.

COUSCOUSSIÈRE

Couscous, grains of semolina made from wheat, is as commonplace in North Africa as pasta or potatoes are elsewhere. In this country, couscous is rare, the object of an almost cultish affection. To those who adore it, couscous, a nearly tasteless cereal, serves as a kind of tabula rasa for the flavors of any number of meats, vegetables and sauces that are poured over it, the grain lending its name to the entire dish. Couscous traditionally prepared is not boiled; it is steamed so that each grain can swell slowly without binding to any other grain. It is frequently steamed over an aromatic simmering stew. More simply these days, there is very good instant couscous available. Boiling water is merely added to it; it swells up in a few minutes and the job is done. For both methods it is extremely attractive — providing a suitable Moroccan air to the whole enterprise — and somewhat more effective to bring the traditional vessel, the couscoussière, into play. For steaming couscous, it is possible to improvise, by placing a colander in a deep pot or by using a double boiler with a steamer insert. But since a couscoussière is specifically designed for steaming the semolina over stew, it tends to facilitate the job. With the instant variety, if you take the couscous just after it has swollen for a short while and place it in the steamer section it, too, will have the opportunity to absorb some of the delightful aroma produced by the stew below.

The couscoussière is actually two separate units. A rounded, deep-bottom pot holds the stew. The top unit is a strainer, perforated only on its bottom. The strainer intrudes into the lower unit only slightly, perhaps less than half an inch, so the semolina will not become soggy.

Couscoussières have been made in earthenware and copper. Their most recent incarnation is in aluminum, which is a thoroughly adequate material for the purpose. A 6-quart pot easily contains a pound of uncooked couscous in its steamer and enough stew to serve eight.

1. *The stew that flavors and accompanies couscous cooks in the deep, rounded bottom part of the couscoussière.* **2.** *The couscous steams in the shallow, perforated top. Stir it with a two-pronged fork so it is loose and no grains stick together.*

LAMB COUSCOUS

2 tablespoons olive oil
2 pounds lean lamb
  shoulder meat without
  bone
2 pounds lean lamb necks,
  with bone
1½ pounds onions, peeled
  and quartered (5 cups)
4 quarts cool water
¼ cup honey
½ teaspoon saffron
2 teaspoons powdered
  ginger
1 teaspoon black pepper
1 stick cinammon
1 teaspoon ground cumin
½ teaspoon turmeric
⅓ cup raisins
5 or 6 medium carrots, cut
  into 2-inch lengths (2
  cups)
3 medium yellow squash,
  quartered and cut into
  2-inch lengths (4 cups),
  or use same quantity of
  pumpkin
4 medium zucchini, halved
  and cut into 2-inch
  lengths (3 cups)
1 16-ounce can chick-peas,
  drained and washed
2 pounds medium-grain
  precooked couscous
¼ pound butter
  Tabasco sauce

1. Place oil and then meat in the bottom section of a couscoussière. Begin cooking at medium heat on top of the range. Add 1 cup of the onions and stir. Stirring and shaking the pot occasionally, sauté about 5 minutes without browning. Add water, honey and spices and cover. Bring to a boil. Let simmer for 1 hour.
2. Add raisins, carrots, squash, zucchini and chick-peas; return to the boil and simmer for ½ hour more, skimming fat and scum as needed.
3. Pour couscous into a mixing bowl and pour in 3 cups boiling water, add salt to taste. Stir and let sit 2 to 3 minutes. Place couscous in top section of couscoussière and put it on top of base to steam for 5 minutes and absorb flavors from below. Be sure the couscous does not touch the liquid. Stir occasionally with a fork.
4. Add butter and fluff the couscous with a fork. On a large platter, arrange couscous in a ring around the periphery with room for stew in the middle. Serve with Tabasco sauce on the side.
Yield: 8 to 10 servings.

SABAYON POT

In my "60-Minute Gourmet" columns in *The New York Times* and in the books that grew out of them, my focus has been on graceful dishes that can be prepared rapidly and well. A dessert that fits nicely among those dishes is sabayon, a mixture of eggs and wine that takes barely minutes to cook. (In Italian, it is zabaglione.) Sabayon, frothy and rich, has the best chance of success when the appropriate equipment is used in its preparation.

The main complication is the possibility that you will achieve something like scrambled eggs instead of the delicate custard you want.

Sabayon is often prepared in a double boiler to keep the heat low and under control, never rising above 212 degrees. Another aid in preventing overcooking is vigorous whisking during the whole procedure, remembering to remove the sabayon from the heat promptly, pouring it into serving glasses as soon as it has reached soft peaks.

Better than a double boiler for all this is a sabayon pot, a beautiful vessel, usually in copper, with a rounded bottom. You can hold the pot over the boiling water with one hand, thus steadying it perfectly for the vigorous whisking to be done with the other. This specially designed pot has an important advantage over a double boiler, too. It has a rounded bottom that allows the whisk complete access — so that none of the egg yolk will escape to congeal and turn lumpy.

The pot, because it is so pretty and so simple to maneuver, can be brought to the table for preparation there. Then the trick is to hold it steadily over the flame of an alcohol burner until done. A 4-cup pot would serve four; a 6-cup version would serve six.

Over time, the copper will tend to show the greenish effects of oxidation and will need to be cleaned carefully. I often use a combination of salt and lemon juice to polish it. The gleam has its own virtue. This pot, which is more nearly a frill than an essential piece of equipment, helps earn its keep by looking so fine hanging in any kitchen.

1. *Put the sabayon pot in a bowl just large enough to hold it steady. Whisk the sugar and egg yolks until lemon-colored.* **2.** *Add the Marsala and whisk it in well.*

3. *Put the pot in a slightly larger pan with simmering, not boiling, water coming 2 inches up the side. Whisk constantly until the mixture has a custardlike consistency.* **4.** *Pour the sabayon into wine glasses and serve immediately.*

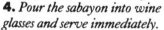

SABAYON

6 **egg yolks**
¼ **cup sugar**
½ **cup Marsala**

1. Place the yolks and sugar in a sabayon pot (resting the pot in a tight-fitting mixing bowl will steady it) and whisk until lemon colored.
2. Add the Marsala and whisk well.
3. Hold the sabayon pot in a pan of simmering water that rises a couple of inches up the pot. Whisk constantly for 2 or 3 minutes until it thickens into a cream. Remove from the heat immediately. Be careful not to overcook, an error that will cause the eggs to solidify.
4. Pour into broad-mouthed wine glasses. Serve immediately.
   Yield: 4 servings.

TERRINES

Ambitious home cooks always get around, sooner or later, to trying one of the most time-consuming and demanding of dishes, the elaborate pâté. They have usually attempted a relatively easy dish first, the pâté campagne, or country pâté, which is essentially blended chopped meat, accomplished rapidly with a food processor.

Then they move on. Pâtés — the complicated and the less complicated as well — are most frequently constructed in a terrine, which is generally a heavy ceramic lidded vessel. When it is oval in shape, it produces a pâté that is especially graceful. But long and rectangular terrines have the advantage of producing uniform slices.

The most elegant of pâtés are assembled, layer by layer, to create a pattern. There might be a layer of forcemeat first and then fillets of duck breast, some more forcemeat and perhaps a layer of chopped truffle. One layer might be a combination of truffle, thinly sliced beef tongue and whole pistachio nuts in a design.

When a pâté is cooking, however, something regrettable often happens to all that work: The pattern starts to break up as the pâté expands and bubbles begin to form. And the compactness of the pâté is lost, which is regrettable in simple ones as well as in the complex. There are at least two ways of restoring that pattern and the compactness. The one that I have always used is a simple device of my own making.

After the pâté is cooked and is ready to cool, I take the cover off the terrine and replace it with a ¾-inch-thick piece of plywood cut to the size of the terrine. On top of that goes a weight of one pound. The weight I have is lead, but it could as well be a one-pound can of peas for all the pâté knows. Be careful here. More weight than that can do its own damage, squeezing out valuable juices and drying the interior of the pâté.

This weight arrangement is left on top of the pâté for at least twelve hours as the pâté is chilled in two stages, the first at room temperature to allow a gradual cooling and settling. When the steam is gone, I put the pâté with its weight in the refrigerator. The result is always the same. When the utility knife cuts through the pâté (it is cut in the terrine) the pattern has been restored and the artistry of the cook is intact. Another way of accomplishing the same goal is to buy a terrine whose lid serves as the weight (such designs are rare, but a 2-quart rectangular earthenware terrine with this feature can be ordered through Bridge Kitchenware; see appendix).

If you like game, as I do, handsome terrines to keep in mind are those with the heads of animals on their lids. Pâté is very frequently made of game, and the terrines come adorned with the heads of rabbit, pheasant, duck, quail or woodcock. The idea, of course, is to fill them with forcemeat of the animal represented on the lid. The wavelike pattern on the side is meant to simulate a crust, as would be used in the preparation of the very elaborate pâté en croute. I should note here that although the French have employed terrines like these for many years they appear to offend the sensibilities of some Americans.

1. *Put a slab of fatback in the freezer for about ½ hour to facilitate slicing it. Using a serrated slicing knife, make short quick sawing strokes to cut slices as thin as possible.* **2.** *Line the bottom and sides of the terrine without overlapping the slices. Leave an overhang of fatback to fold over the top of the pâté.*

3. *Put a layer of meat in the terrine and pack it down with your fist so it is compact all over the bottom.* **4.** *As you add more of the mixture, pack it down so there are no air bubbles. Put a bay leaf on top of the pâté.*

5. *Fold over the fatback and place another slice over the center of the pâté.* **6.** *Place the cooked pâté on a rack to cool and remove the cover. Put a piece of wood on the top and weight the pâté (I'm using a 1-pound piece of lead). If you are adding aspic, do so before weighting the pâté.*

COUNTRY PÂTÉ

12 or more very thin slices unsalted fatback (Caul fat, available in some butcher shops, is also suitable)

3 pounds pork shoulder, 2 parts lean, 1 part fatty

1 pound boneless, skinless breast of chicken, cubed

½ pound chicken livers

¼ cup coarsely chopped shallots

¾ pound boiled ham cut into ½-inch cubes

2 eggs

½ teaspoon freshly ground pepper

⅛ teaspoon allspice

⅛ teaspoon coriander
Dash ground clove
Dash of cinammon

⅛ teaspoon nutmeg
Dash cayenne pepper
Salt to taste

2 teaspoons sugar

1 bay leaf

1. Preheat the oven to 350 degrees.
2. Line the bottom of a 10-cup terrine and then the sides with fat, draping some of each slice over the edge to fold over the pâté.
3. Combine the pork, chicken, chicken livers and shallots in food processor and chop coarsely. Chop only about a third at a time so as not to overload the processor.
4. Place chopped meat, cubed ham and eggs in a mixing bowl. Add all seasonings, except bay leaf. Blend well with hands.
5. Place mixture into terrine in stages, packing it down as you go. Take the folds of fat from the rim of the terrine and fold them toward the center. Place the bay leaf flat on the remaining bare spot of the mixture in the center of the terrine and place a slice of fat over it.
6. Cover and put terrine in a roasting pan containing enough boiling water to rise about an inch around the terrine. Cook for 2 hours, or until an internal temperature of 160 degrees is reached.
7. Remove from oven, uncover and place some kind of weight over the top. I use a slab of wood topped by a piece of lead weighing 1 pound. The result is a more compact pâté, and one in which the fat rises evenly toward the top. Allow to cool, preferably over a rack in a space with good air circulation. Refrigerate with the weight on until chilled and fat is solidified.
8. Scrape off fat, slice and serve with cornichons.
   Yield: At least 10 servings.

TERRINE DE VOLAILLE

1 3¼-pound chicken
1 pound boneless pork butt, both lean and fat, cubed
¾ pound pork fat, cubed
¾ pound lean veal, cubed
½ pound chicken livers
⅓ cup finely chopped shallots
½ teaspoon chopped thyme
½ cup dry white wine
¼ teaspoon ground nutmeg
⅛ teaspoon saltpeter, optional
2 tablespoons chopped black truffles
½ cup pistachios
12 or more very thin slices fatback

1. Skin and bone the chicken. Keep the chicken meat in as large portions as possible but trim away cartilage and all other silvery nerve tissues.
2. Cut the fleshier pieces of chicken, such as the breasts and thighs, into 1½ inch cubes. Set aside in a bowl. Add the scraps of meat to another bowl.
3. Fit a meat grinder with the coarse blade and grind the boneless pork butt, pork fat, veal, chicken livers and any reserved scraps of chicken. Set aside.
4. Combine the shallots, thyme and ¼ cup wine in a saucepan. Cook over moderately high heat until the wine is almost completely reduced. Spoon out the solids and let cool. Add to the ground meat.
5. Sprinkle with nutmeg, saltpeter, truffles, pistachios and remaining ¼ cup wine and blend with the hands. Add the cubed chunks of chicken and stir to blend evenly. Cover with wax paper and a lid and let stand overnight in the refrigerator.
6. Preheat the oven to 375 degrees.
7. Line the bottom and sides of a 10-cup terrine or mold with fatback slices, letting the slices hang generously over the sides. Spoon the chicken mixture into the mold and smooth it over. Fold the overhanging fatback over the filling to enclose it completely. Set the mold in a large basin and pour boiling water around it. Bake for 2½ to 3 hours. The terrine is done when the internal temperature registers 160 degrees on a meat thermometer.
8. Cover the terrine with heavy-duty aluminum foil and place a weight on top of the baked mixture. Let cool on a rack and refrigerate overnight.
9. Scrape off and discard the fat that has accumulated around the meat. Serve sliced.
   Yield: 18 or more servings.

SOUFFLÉ DISHES

The symbol of culinary failure is the fallen soufflé. And it is true that there is nothing sadder than the sight of a soufflé slowly sinking into a dense mass before any of it has ever been touched to the lips. But I think too much is made of the rise and fall of soufflés.

The errors people make at least as often are subtler ones. They dry out the crust or produce a soufflé that is inedibly runny in the center. Frequently, these problems arise from something as basic as the improper selection of a soufflé dish.

The size of the dish can matter. Those with 2- or 3-cup capacities give good results, but the best size for, say, a cheese soufflé to serve four people is a dish with a capacity of 4 or 5 cups that is 2½ inches high. At customary cooking temperatures, this dish will most often deliver a soufflé that is firm on the exterior and moist but heated through at the center.

A dish any larger tends to do just what I want to avoid — produce a dry exterior before it can cook the center adequately. So when I cook for eight, I make two soufflés in 5-cup dishes, rather than one in a 10-cup dish.

For individual dessert soufflés, such as my favorite, the strawberry soufflé in the accompanying recipe, dishes of 1½ cups are called for and work to perfection.

In addition to a dish's capacity, its height is important. When you're shopping for soufflé dishes, you'll undoubtedly see quart-size dishes in the standard 2½-inch height as well as those that are 3½ inches high. I've been disappointed in soufflés produced in the deeper dishes because they are prone to the same kind of failure I've found in those whose capacity is too great.

I do have a big soufflé dish, by the way, one that has a 10-cup capacity, and I do use it. It's attractive for a flan, or for eggplant and lamb. But the only time I would use it for a soufflé is when there is a heavy mixture on the bottom, such as the curried shrimp in the accompanying recipe.

As for the material you should choose, I offer my preference: porcelain. It just looks so lovely. Two of the best brand names are Hall and Pillivuyt. Some people use a charlotte mold (see page 194) for a soufflé, but this mold, marvelous for its intended use, makes an unattractive serving dish and it is tapered toward the bottom, which strikes me as all wrong, because the bottom of the soufflé would cook faster than the rest.

Once you've chosen the appropriate dish, be sure to butter the interior well, especially the sides — the soufflé has to slide right up the walls to rise.

The only thing that comes close to being as sad as a fallen soufflé is a puny one. For the best-looking soufflé, fill the dish completely so that the soufflé will ultimately rise 2 to 3 inches above the rim.

1. *After chilling the soufflé dish, use a pastry brush to cover the inside with softened butter. Be sure the dish is thoroughly coated, including the sides and the rim.* **2.** *Add one third of the egg whites to the mixture and incorporate with a whisk, then gently fold in the rest with a rubber spatula.*

3. *Fill the soufflé dish and smooth the top with a spatula, then run your thumb around inside the rim. This will keep the soufflé from sticking as it rises.* **4.** *When cooked, sprinkle with confectioners' sugar and spoon 2 tablespoons of sauce into each soufflé, or let guests do it at the table.*

CHEESE SOUFFLÉ

1 tablespoon butter
¼ cup grated Parmesan
7 egg yolks
  Salt and freshly ground
  pepper to taste
⅛ teaspoon freshly grated
  nutmeg
  Dash cayenne pepper
6 ounces cream cheese
¼ pound Gruyère, diced in
  ⅛-inch cubes (1 cup)
7 egg whites

1. Preheat oven to 400 degrees. Place cookie sheet in oven to preheat it at the same time. Chill a 5-cup soufflé mold.

2. Using a pastry brush, butter the chilled mold well — especially the wall of the dish — and return to the refrigerator.

3. Combine all ingredients, except egg whites and Gruyère, in a mixing bowl and mix well with a whisk so cream cheese is blended in. Gently mix in the Gruyère.

4. Put egg whites and a pinch of salt in copper bowl. With balloon whisk, beat the whites, tilting the bowl so whites stay around the whisk. It's best to start slowly and build up speed. Beat until stiff. But be careful not to overbeat, which will result in whites breaking down.

5. Place one third of egg whites in bowl with cheese (transfer the whites with the balloon whisk) and stir thoroughly with a stiff wire whisk. Add remaining whites and fold in gently and fast with large rubber spatula, turning the bowl with left hand. Be careful not to overblend since the whites will begin to collapse.

6. Pour and scrape mixture into soufflé dish. The mixture should rise about ¼ inch above the rim. Level the top with a narrow spatula. Run thumb around the periphery to create a channel for expansion. Place on cookie sheet in oven and bake for 10 minutes. Lower temperature to 375 and bake 10 minutes more.
   Yield: 4 servings.

STRAWBERRY SOUFFLÉ

1 **pint strawberries**
8 **eggs, separated**
½ **cup plus ⅓ cup sugar**
  Juice of half a lemon
  Confectioners' sugar
  Strawberry sauce (see
  following recipe)

1. Preheat oven to 450 degrees. Place six 1½-cup soufflé dishes in refrigerator to chill.
2. Remove the stems from the strawberries, wash and drain, then place in food processor, processing until a fine purée.
3. Pour purée into a bowl and add the egg yolks, ½ cup sugar and lemon juice. Beat with a stiff whisk thoroughly to blend.
4. Butter the bottom and sides of the soufflé dishes, paying especial attention to the walls of the dishes, and then return them to the refrigerator.
5. Place egg whites in a copper bowl and, with balloon whisk, beat until stiff. Beat in the remaining ⅓ cup sugar. With large rubber spatula fold the whites into the strawberry mixture.
6. Spoon equal amounts of the mixture into the prepared dishes. The mixture should fill the dishes to about ¼ inch over the rim. With thumb, create a channel around the periphery of the dish to allow for expansion. Place the dishes on a baking sheet and bake 7 minutes. Reduce the oven heat to 425 degrees and bake 7 minutes longer. Serve sprinkled with confectioners' sugar.
7. The sauce is added when each guest, using a spoon, creates a hole in the center of his soufflé and spoons in a generous amount.
   Yield: 6 servings.

STRAWBERRY SAUCE

1 **cup fresh strawberries**
⅓ **cup sugar**
1 **tablespoon kirsch**

1. Clean and slice strawberries. Place berries in a saucepan with sugar and bring to a boil, stirring occasionally. Cook about 1 minute. Add kirsch and remove from flame. Serve hot.

CHEESE SOUFFLÉ WITH CURRIED SHRIMP

4 tablespoons butter
4 tablespoons flour
2 cups milk
Salt and freshly ground pepper to taste
Freshly grated nutmeg to taste (about ⅛ teaspoon)
6 drops Tabasco sauce
¼ teaspoon Worcestershire sauce
1 tablespoon cornstarch
2 tablespoons water
8 eggs, separated
½ cup grated Parmesan cheese
⅔ cup finely diced Swiss cheese
1 pound curried shrimp (see following recipe)

1. Preheat the oven to 400 degrees.
2. Generously butter the inside of an 8- or 9-cup soufflé dish (this preparation requires an unusually large mold) and place it in the refrigerator.
3. Melt the butter in a saucepan and add the flour, stirring with a wire whisk. When blended, add the milk, stirring vigorously. Cook, stirring until thickened and smooth. Season with salt and pepper to taste, nutmeg, Tabasco and Worcestershire sauce. Blend cornstarch with water and stir into the sauce.
4. Remove the sauce from the stove for a minute or so. Beat the yolks briefly and add them to the sauce, stirring vigorously with the whisk. Return the sauce to the heat and cook, stirring constantly all around the bottom of the saucepan, until the sauce starts to bubble. Do not cook more than 5 or 10 seconds, or the sauce may curdle. Spoon and scrape the sauce into a large mixing bowl. Stir in the Parmesan cheese and let the sauce cool briefly. Stir in the Swiss cheese.
5. In a copper bowl, beat the whites until stiff. Add about one third of them to the sauce and beat the whites into the sauce. Fold in the remaining whites.
6. Spoon the curried shrimp into the prepared soufflé dish. Top it with the soufflé mixture. Smooth the top of the mixture and with the thumb create a channel around the edge of the soufflé to allow for proper rising.
7. Place the soufflé in the oven. Bake five minutes and reduce oven heat to 375 degrees. Continue to bake 15 minutes longer. If you want a less moist center, continue baking the soufflé 5 to 10 minutes longer.
8. Serve portions of the soufflé along with portions of the curried shrimp.
Yield: 6 to 8 servings.

CURRIED SHRIMP FOR SOUFFLÉ BASE

1 pound medium-size
  shrimp, 24 to 30
3 tablespoons butter
¼ cup finely chopped onion
6 tablespoons finely
  chopped peeled apple
¼ teaspoon finely minced
  garlic
2 to 3 tablespoons curry
  powder, or to taste
⅓ cup finely chopped
  banana
½ cup fresh or canned
  chicken broth
¼ cup fresh or canned
  tomato sauce
⅔ cup heavy cream
  Salt to taste
1 tablespoon flour

1. To prepare the curried shrimp, peel and devein them. Run under cold water and pat dry with paper toweling. There should be about 2 cups.
2. Heat 1 tablespoon of butter in a saucepan and add the onion, apple and garlic. Cook about 5 minutes, stirring, and sprinkle with the curry powder. Stir about 30 seconds and add the banana. Add the chicken broth, stirring, and stir in the tomato sauce. Simmer about 2 minutes, stirring. Add the cream and salt and simmer about 2 minutes longer.
3. Meanwhile, blend another tablespoon of butter with flour and add it, stirring. Remove the sauce from the heat.
4. Heat the third tablespoon of butter in a skillet and add the shrimp. Cook over high heat, stirring with a spoon and shaking the skillet. Cook about 3 minutes, no longer. Add the sauce, stir until shrimp are coated. Bring to a boil. Remove from heat and use as base for soufflé.

SOUP CROCKS

Little earthenware soup crocks are so common now they seem almost cliché, but don't let that put you off. They are common because they work so well. The crocks excel in baking the classic onion soup au gratin that is the antidote to painful winter days, and they keep the soup hot after it leaves the oven.

The most useful crocks are those with covers, although the covers are employed at no time in the baking of onion soup au gratin. In that instance you want the floating rounds of French bread and the cheese on top of the bread to seal the soup like a lid (and, for the looks of it, the cheese should bubble just enough to drip gracefully over the edge). If you cover the soup while it bakes, the cheese will not brown; if you cover it later, the lid will be redundant since the cheese and bread are serving the same purpose. The lid might also break the cheese crust, ruining its appearance completely.

But the cover is useful if what you want to do is serve plain onion soup with cheese and bread on the side. In fact, using a covered crock is a fine way to be sure any soup will be hot when you serve it. A creamed soup, for instance, can be ladled into the crocks, covered and placed in the oven. The cover, while helping it stay hot, will also prevent a skin from forming on the top.

The crocks are good for other dishes as well. Stew, for example, ought to be served as hot as possible. A pleasant approach is to ladle it into covered crocks before your guests arrive, keep it hot in the oven, and then place a crock of stew alongside each guest's plate to be spooned out at will and then re-covered.

Although crocks like these come in more than one size, the most useful has a capacity of 1½ cups and a rim that is 4 inches in diameter. The reason for the value of this size has to do with onion soup au gratin. A danger is that too much bread will be needed to close off the top and that the bread will start to soak up more liquid than you want it to. The 3½-inch opening has proven to be functionally perfect.

1. Place individual soup crocks on a baking sheet to facilitate removing them from the oven. Ladle the onion soup in and place a slice of toasted French bread on top. Sprinkle liberally with grated cheese.
2. The finished soup will be brown and bubbling on top.

ONION SOUP AU GRATIN

3 tablespoons butter
6½ cups sliced onions
1 tablespoon chopped garlic
3 tablespoons flour
4 cups chicken stock
½ cup dry white wine
2 cups water
1 bay leaf
Salt and freshly ground pepper to taste
6 thin slices French bread, toasted
¼ cup grated Swiss or Gruyère cheese

1. Heat the butter in a deep saucepan and, at high flame, brown the onions and garlic, stirring often. Add flour and cook several minutes longer until flour begins to brown.
2. Add the stock, wine, water, bay leaf, salt and pepper. Bring to a boil and then simmer for 20 minutes, skimming off foam occasionally.
3. Ladle the soup into 6 individual crocks placed on a baking sheet. Float a slice of toasted bread on top and sprinkle liberally with cheese.
4. Bake in a 425-degree oven for 15 minutes.
Yield: 6 servings.

COFFEE MAKER

Mostly I drink tea. The only time I find coffee truly appealing is after a meal heavy with sauces and wines, and then I want some kind of powerful punctuation, an exclamation point to terminate the dining. A strong brew does that for me much the way, I imagine, cigars must do it for others.

I have noticed, of course, that there are an incredible number of coffee makers on the market. Some are good looking, some are ugly. They drip, they percolate or they steam; some are electric, some sit on the stove. Fortunately, I feel no need to choose from among all those contraptions because for some time now I have been satisfied with a wonderful little coffee maker that makes a strong, flavorful drink with very little fuss and very little error.

It is a French-made Melior pot, generically described as a European plunger. It is a beautiful machine: a cylinder of heat-resistant glass in a delicate frame of chromed steel that is evocative of art deco (an acquaintance of mine says it is evocative of the Chrysler Building, but he is irresponsibly expansive about coffee and all things that make it). It has a black plastic, but nevertheless handsome, handle and a domed lid through which fits a rod with a knob on top of it. That rod is attached to a plunger, which is actually an array of four disks that together serve as a filter and which disassemble readily for cleaning. Other plunger-type pots that I've seen provide screens that work less effectively than does this setup.

To make the brew, you place into the glass cylinder a single rounded tablespoon of ground coffee for each desired cup, pour boiling water over the coffee, cover it and let it steep for three to five minutes. (It will help to add that extra tablespoon "for the pot," if you want truly strong coffee.) Then force the screened plunger down through the liquid, separating the drink from the coffee grounds. And that does it. The coffee that pours from the spout can be very strong indeed and some will think of it as bitter and crude; others will think of it as familiarly European because it tastes very much like the coffee regularly served in French restaurants. (The plunger system is commonly used in such places.) The coffee will be especially rich if you use a freshly ground, double-roasted blend that is intended to yield black, powerful coffee. The Melior comes in a range of sizes — from 3 to 12 cups. If you use it for entertaining, anything smaller than the 6-cup will probably be inadequate. In any case, it is possible to make only as little as half a pot of coffee or less in one of these designs.

As much as I admire this pot, it does have one failing which I find tolerable, although others might not. Since it has no heating element and is not intended to sit on the fire, a long period of steeping intended to make it especially flavorful will also allow it to cool noticeably. It will be hot enough for most people still, but not as hot as some like it. An effective remedy is to place a heat-diffusion device such as a Flame Tamer (see page 95) over a very low fire and place the pot on it. That level of heat is low enough not to damage the pot and high enough to keep the coffee from cooling too rapidly.

BAKING

It is my impression that baking has fared less well than other forms of home cooking in recent years. Cooks who entertain with considerable competence will take hours, even days, preparing elaborate dishes, and then go out and buy the pastry that tops it off.

But not always. Every now and then the baking urge strikes and the attempt is made. The problem is that an occasional attempt is likely to be tried without appropriate equipment and the results may well be disappointing.

In this section, I have not included every piece of equipment that would add something to the baking repertoire of the home kitchen. But I describe some of the very basic tools no cook can do without. In addition, since baking is in a surprising degree defined by the shape of the mold employed, I have provided an introduction to some of the molds I hold most dear. The savarin mold, for instance, to anyone who hasn't used one, can be a revelation in the delicacy and the elegance it makes possible.

In this chapter, too, are comments on some relatively recent developments for the home kitchen. The so-called pizza stone is a marvelous addition that I use mostly for baking bread to give it a spectacular crust. The metal French bread loaf pans are also relatively new. And I am grateful they finally came along.

ROLLING PINS

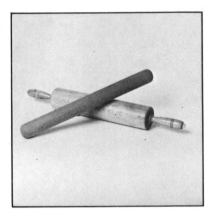

One of the most formidable tasks in French cooking is the preparation of pastry. There is a great deal of precision, speed and delicacy required in the making of croissants or tarts or the patty shells called vol-au-vents. And a good rolling pin is essential.

Remember, a good rolling pin often doesn't cost any more than an inadequate one. So the knack is in knowing what to look for. There are essentially two kinds of pins. The traditional French one is a cylinder of hard boxwood that might be 18 inches long and 2 inches in diameter. It is rolled with the palms of the hands.

The other major design is widely called the American pin, even though it is found in Europe as well. It is a barrel of wood with handles at either end. Sensible barrel sizes for the home kitchen range from 12 to 16 inches in length and are 3 or 4 inches in diameter.

With either kind of pin, you must be sure that the barrel is smooth and perfectly round to ensure uniformity of rolling. And check for dents, gouges or splintering, all of which will cause the surface of the dough to be imperfect. If the pin has handles, be sure that they are sturdy and that they allow the barrel to roll with complete ease.

I use both kinds of pins, but for different purposes. The French pin is exactly suited for the delicate rolling of a pie crust. As you gently roll from the center of a mound of dough outward, rotating the dough as you go along, and work toward a level thickness of about an eighth of an inch, you do need the fine sense of the dough beneath your hands that the slender French pin provides. A more massive pin can roll out the dough too thinly. A heavier pin is precisely what you want for puff paste, which incorporates a large amount of butter into a flour dough that must be smoothed and folded many times. For this work, I prefer a pin with handles and ball bearings.

There are all kinds of variations on the rolling pin that you might want to consider, but they are far from necessities even in the kitchens of very accomplished home chefs. The French-made Tutové pin, which has horizontal ridges around its barrel, is excellent for distributing butter in puff paste. And then there are beautiful marble rolling pins that can be chilled before you begin the work (just as the dough board and the flour can be) to diminish the possibility of the butter melting in the dough, a surefire way of turning the pastry rubbery.

A word about the care and use of wooden rolling pins. Do not soak them; if they retain water the dough will stick to them. Simply wipe them with a damp cloth and, before each use, flour them well to remove any hint of moisture and to diminish friction.

After you've rolled out a pie crust, don't try to lift it with your hands. Wrap the dough around the pin, then unwrap it into the pie plate. Tuck the dough in, and use the roller to cut away the excess. If the plate has an edge to it, run the pin along the top and the job will be done fast and neatly.

1. *For a tart crust, place the ball of dough on a floured surface, preferably marble, and flatten it slightly with a lightly floured rolling pin.*
2. *Put the palms of your hands at each end of the rolling pin and roll from the center of the dough away from you, turning the dough frequently.*

3. *Lift up the dough and lightly flour the board as you go along to prevent sticking.* **4.** *When the dough is a rough circle about 2 inches larger than your tart pan, roll the dough onto the rolling pin.*

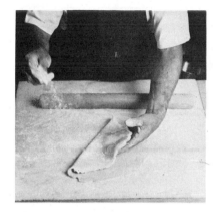

5. *Lift the rolling pin over the tart pan and unroll the dough over it.*
6. *Using your knuckles, press the dough into the sides of the pan without stretching it.*

7. *Run the rolling pin over the top of the pan to remove excess dough.*
8. *The finished tart shell will have a fluted rim.*

BLUEBERRY TART

1½ **cups flour**
  8 **tablespoons butter, cut into pieces**
     Pinch of salt
  ½ **teaspoon sugar**
  4 **tablespoons ice water**
     Pastry cream (see following recipe)
  1 **pint fresh blueberries (strawberries will also do)**
     Currant jelly glaze (see following recipe)

1. Preheat the oven to 375 degrees.
2. Combine the flour, butter, salt, sugar and water in a food processor and blend until the mixture forms a ball, perhaps 30 seconds.
3. Using a rolling pin, roll the dough into a ¼-inch-thick circle about 13 inches in diameter. Pick up the dough by rolling it onto the pin and then unrolling it over a black tart pan with a removable bottom. Press gently into the pan, gathering the dough toward the wall of the pan to thicken the shell's sides. Place it in the refrigerator for 10 or 15 minutes to allow the dough to relax.
4. Cut a round of wax paper a couple of inches larger than the pan. Press it into the mold and weight it down with aluminum weights or beans to hold the dough in place during the initial "blind" baking stage. Bake for 15 minutes. Remove from the oven and take wax paper and weights out of the shell. Bake for another 7 to 10 minutes until light brown. Allow to cool.
5. Spoon cool pastry cream into the tart shell; top with the blueberries.
6. Generously brush currant jelly glaze over the berries so it fills all the spaces. Chill and serve.
   Yield: 6 to 8 servings.

PASTRY CREAM

2 cups milk
½ teaspoon vanilla
3 egg yolks
⅓ cup sugar
1 tablespoon cornstarch
1 tablespoon flour

1. In a medium slant-sided saucepan, bring milk and vanilla to the boil. Remove from heat but cover to keep warm.
2. In a small mixing bowl, combine the yolks, sugar, cornstarch and flour with a wire whisk. Ladle out ½ cup of the warm milk mixture and whisk it into the egg mixture. Add it to remaining milk in pot.
3. Bring to a boil whisking constantly and thoroughly, scraping mixture from side of pot. Transfer to a metal mixing bowl and allow to cool.

CURRANT JELLY GLAZE

½ cup currant jelly
4 tablespoons water

Heat jelly and water in a small saucepan until completely liquefied and reduced slightly (about 5 minutes at medium heat). Pour into a small bowl; allow to cool to lukewarm (if it solidifies before use, warm it again briefly).

SIFTERS

In one of my restaurant jobs, it was necessary to sift great quantities of flour, thousands of pounds of it, in the ordinary course of the work. Time and again as I would look down onto the sifting screen I would notice impurities in the flour, insects that had crept in, and worse. To this day, although screening out contaminants is not the main job of a good sifter, every time I use one of these gadgets I have a certain sense of the hygienic sagacity of it.

The other reasons for sifting flour are a lot more significant. For one thing, the measuring of flour is very important in most recipes and there is no way of telling precisely how much flour you have unless you sift it. The reason is that the environment of the flour, the amount of moisture in the air particularly, will vary the volume. Only by routinely sifting all flour — even presifted — will one batch be the same in volume as another.

A second major reason is that sifting absolutely ensures lightness of the flour, a critical matter in the preparation of sponge cake and other pastries in which a lump is a sin. Sifting is, of course, less than mandatory in the baking of bread, but I do it anyway.

Peripheral uses for sifters are several. For instance, the sifter is a fine way to mix spices and other ingredients that need to be well incorporated into a cake. If you are making a fruit cake with its many spices and sugar to be mixed together with the flour, putting the whole batch into the sifter at once will blend it perfectly.

For sugar alone, sifting can be a good idea to separate the granules and aerate them. The only time it is essential to sift sugar, however, is when making something that must be extraordinarily light, such as a soufflé or the meringuelike dessert known as a floating island.

As a piece of machinery, the sifter is simple, a container of stainless steel, aluminum or tinned steel, at the base of which is an agitator — a metal wheel of some sort, usually propelled by a trigger in the sifter's handle — that forces the flour through a screen. It is far better than a mere strainer would be in several ways, an important one being that it is directional; you can drop the flour where you want it without making much of a mess.

The best capacity for a sifter used in the home kitchen is 5 cups. The commonest sifters have a single screen and an agitator. More complicated ones come with three screens. I prefer the triple screen, because it does the job most completely, but it does have its drawbacks. The spring action operating the two agitators tends to be a bit slower than the single agitator models and to require more strength. The three screens also present more of a clean-up problem. It is best not to wash any sifter (the water would turn some of the flour into glue, clogging the holes). Shake it out instead and then store it in a dry place.

1. *A cookie sheet or jelly roll pan is often floured to prevent sticking. Hold the sifter over the buttered pan and quickly flour the entire surface, shaking off excess.* **2.** *A sifter is also used for sugar, in this case adding the sugar to beaten egg whites for meringues.*

ALMOND CREAM CAKE

The cake
1 **cup heavy cream**
2 **eggs**
¼ **teaspoon almond extract**
1½ **cups sifted flour**
1 **cup sugar**
2 **teaspoons baking power**
  Few grains salt
  Almond topping
2 **tablespoons butter**
⅓ **cup sugar**
¼ **cup blanched, slivered almonds**
1 **tablespoon heavy cream**
1 **tablespoon flour**

1. Preheat the oven to 350 degrees.
2. Whip the cream until it holds soft peaks. Add the eggs, one at a time, beating well after each addition. Stir in the almond extract.
3. Sift together the flour, sugar, baking powder and salt. Add the dry ingredients to the cream mixture; stir until well blended. Pour into an 8-inch greased and floured springform pan. Bake 45 minutes, or until lightly browned on top and a toothpick inserted in the center comes away clean.
4. During the last few minutes the cake is baking, make the almond topping. In a small saucepan, combine the butter, sugar, almonds, heavy cream and flour. Stir over low heat until all the ingredients are blended. Pour the mixture over the cake and bake for 10 minutes longer. Cool on a rack.

Yield: 6 to 8 servings.

BAKING SHEETS

Among the most pedestrian pieces of equipment in the kitchen is the baking sheet. Boring as it may be, however, it should not be neglected. Baking sheets are used very frequently. I place my soufflé dishes on one, for instance, to make their removal from the oven easier. I use these trays as the bottoms for flan rings (see page 183). And, of course, I employ them in the making of cookies, croissants, cream puffs and so on.

As with so many other baking tools, I prefer black steel here because it ensures a deeper, more even crust than would, say, white aluminum. I also always look for a tray that is relatively rigid. I have no compunctions about entering a store, grasping the various trays and twisting them to see how well they're made. Some will offer very little resistance, yielding a kind of popping sound as they twist. That kind of limpness may mean that the sheet will give out just as you remove it from the oven — and the dish will crash to the floor, or the cookies will cascade into the oven. Flimsy trays will also warp over time resulting in uneven baking.

In the preparations for baking, you'll generally want to grease the sheet, and for that a good wide brush (see page 174) is the best tool. It's astonishing how much time can be saved over the use of a small brush. Many cooks will simply reach for a paper towel and grease the sheet that way, but there you run the risk of doing an uneven job, and some of the pastry will undoubtedly stick.

In recipes that require the sheet to be floured after it is greased, the best way to get rid of any excess flour is just to tap the sheet on its side.

The most efficient size to buy is the largest one that will fit comfortably into the oven.

1. *A rigid baking sheet is the perfect base for a flan ring.* **2.** *I also use it to hold individual soup crocks or a soufflé dish to facilitate taking them out of the oven.*

COOLING RACK

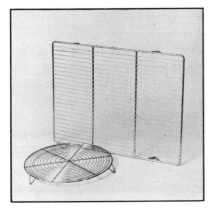

Baking a cake does not end when the oven is turned off. The cooling procedure, while not nearly so involved as the steps that have gone before, needs to be done properly, too.

After a few minutes in which the cake has had a chance to settle slightly, it should be unmolded and — as many recipes insistently specify despite the fact that countless cooks disregard the instruction — placed on a cooling rack, not on a plate.

The reason for taking the cake out of the pan and putting it on a rack is that if the cake is left molded much of the moisture still confined in it will settle to the bottom and stay there, bringing the day's baking to a soggy conclusion. A cooling rack, which is either a grid of interlocking wires or an array of parallel wires attached to a frame, stands on short legs and thus allows the air to circulate about the entire cake, carrying away the moisture. I use these racks for bread as well as cakes, rapidly unmolding a loaf so as not to lose any of its crispness. Pies are normally not unmolded, but I place them on a rack anyway. At least that way the air can pass beneath the pie pan and help cool the pie evenly and quickly.

Beyond its employment in cooling pastry and bread, a rack has a number of other uses. For instance, it is an excellent aid in the glazing of pastry, such as éclairs or cakes.

For glazing you need a baking tray in which the rack can sit. With this arrangement you can glaze the top of the pastry with, say, a mixture of melted chocolate and rum, vigorously and expeditiously pouring the chocolate over the top, smoothing it with a spatula then recovering the drippings from the tray.

The same holds true for the preparation of an aspic glaze. Chicken that is about to become encased in aspic and some colorful garnish can be placed on the rack and coated there with a minimum of mess.

In buying a rack and tray, it is sensible to get the largest your countertop can comfortably accommodate. An adequate size is 12 inches wide and 18 inches long, which is big enough to hold bread as well as cake. If you have a limited amount of space, a relatively small round rack intended for cake will be of some use. When buying a rack, see that it stands level and is sturdy. The spokes should be firmly attached to the frame.

While I am on the subject, I'd like to reiterate a warning I often give about cooling anything that has been cooked. Do not become so impatient that you shove the cake or whatever into the refrigerator while it is still steaming. What will happen is that the refrigerator will fill with steam, perhaps forming unwanted crystals, and certainly destroying the evenness of the temperature within it. When the temperature of a refrigerator is uneven, the quality of the food it contains is damaged.

PASTRY BRUSHES

The reason for using a good pastry brush rather than a paper towel to grease a baking pan is that it needs to be done thoroughly and evenly to prevent sticking. Paper towels and other makeshift applicators almost always do an uneven job. Another important chore for a pastry brush is the removal of excess flour after dough has been rolled. This is hard without a brush. Blowing it off works, but to do that you have to have a certain disregard for your kitchen.

The brushes that do these jobs so well come in a variety of shapes and sizes. Flat ones that look like paint brushes are the most versatile. Their heads range from 1 to 4 inches in width. The wide one is especially good for working with large expanses of dough, such as puff paste, but for most work the smaller ones, 1½ or 2 inches in width, are at least adequate. Round-headed brushes, with diameters of 1 inch or 1½ inches, are designed to grease the curved walls. The bristles of all these brushes can be a synthetic, such as nylon, or the genuine article, pig's hair. The genuine bristles are superior because they will not melt if used on hot surfaces or if accidentally left on a warm stove. The bristles are bound to the handle of the brush either by a metal band or a leather one. The leather lasts longer and is handsome besides.

One factor I never considered before talking to Fred Bridge of the Bridge Kitchenware Corp. was the color of the bristles. It is an annoying truth that once in a while a bristle will come loose, lodge in the dough and ultimately find its way into the dental interstices of a guest's mouth. A way to cut down on this possibility, as Mr. Bridge pointed out, is to use pastry brushes with black rather than the commoner light bristles, so the loose bristle can be spotted in the dough.

The care of these brushes requires some attention. Don't throw them into the dishwasher. Instead, wash them individually in detergent and water, then press them dry with a paper towel.

1. *Use a pastry brush to butter a baking sheet, because you can cover the whole area with a thin, even coating of softened butter.* **2.** *A pastry brush also lets you spread softened butter into the crevices of a springform pan, which is important to ensure that the crumbs adhere evenly.*

PASTRY BAGS

I don't know for sure why so many home cooks seem leery of pastry bags and tubes. Maybe the glossy decorated cakes produced in bakeries with the help of pastry bags appear to grow out of some arcane skill best left to bakers. Maybe the process of decorating seems too unforgiving of a little clumsiness. Whatever the reason, I suspect it is not well founded. True, an unpracticed hand will not do quite the job of a practiced one. But by leaving the decoration of cakes to bakers one is leaving the baking to them, too, and for the good home cook that is a matter of surrender.

Moreover, pastry bags and tubes are useful for chores far beyond the decoration of party cakes. They efficiently fill éclairs, cornets and cream puffs. They can be used to make petals of butter on a smoked salmon canapé, or to stuff eggs with a professional-looking swirl. And they are extraordinarily helpful in forming meringues and the French version of gnocchi.

For cake decoration it does help if you have just the slightest artistic bent because much of the job is trial-and-error creativity. The best way to decide on a particular pattern of, say, butter-cream flowers (perhaps tinted by vegetable coloring) and a heavy scrolled border of whipped cream is to experiment on a plate before approaching the cake; use a small bag and tube for the more ornate work with butter cream and a large bag and tube for the sweeping work with whipped cream.

At the start you will need at least two bags — a 10-inch one and a 14-inch one, along with perhaps eight or ten inexpensive tubes of different sizes and shapes, which are sometimes sold in sets. The tubes simply drop into the bag from the top before the bag is filled. Some of these nozzles are flattened to make ribbons, others are jagged and rounded to make swirls, and still others are specifically designed to produce petals and leaves.

When you begin your practice run, try a variety of rhythms and motions. To give a ribbon on the periphery of a cake some character, rock your hands back and forth, producing waves as you move along.

1. *Push the desired tip into a pastry bag and fold the top over your hand. Spoon the filling in until bag is three-quarters full.* **2.** *For meringues, force out a small oval by pulling the tip toward you, then lifting and pushing it forward to cut it off. Smooth the meringues with a damp towel held taut in both hands.*

3. *A pastry bag is also handy for making small quenelles. Twist the top of the bag over simmering stock or water and cut off the quenelle with a paring knife when it is about 1½ inches long.*

STUFFED EGGS

6 **hard-cooked eggs, chilled and halved**
6 **tablespoons butter**
1 **teaspoon curry powder**
2 **teaspoons red wine vinegar**
   Salt to taste
3 **tablespoons vegetable oil**
¼ **teaspoon Worcestershire sauce**
   Dash of Tabasco
1 **sprig fresh coriander for garnish**

1. Remove the yolks and with fingers press them through a coarse-meshed strainer into a small, heavy mixing bowl (a ceramic bowl will be more stable in this procedure than a stainless steel one).
2. With a wooden spoon or stiff rubber spatula, blend the yolks with remaining ingredients except coriander until a smooth paste is produced.
3. Arrange the egg white shells on a platter.
4. Equip a pastry bag with a star tube (number 4). Fill the bag with egg mixture and pipe it into the egg hollows, filling each one and then creating a decorative swirl rising above the shell by at least ½ inch.
5. Garnish with a leaf of coriander on each.
   Yield: 12 stuffed eggs.

MERINGUES

1 **tablespoon butter**
2 **tablespoons flour**
4 **egg whites**
½ **cup plus 3 tablespoons superfine sugar**
⅓ **cup confectioners' sugar**

1. Preheat the oven to 200 degrees.
2. With wide pastry brush, butter a cookie sheet. Using sifter, sprinkle flour over sheet. Tap sheet on its edge to remove excess flour. The result should be an even, thin layer of flour coating the sheet entirely.
3. In a heavy, stable mixing bowl (Pyrex works well) beat whites at medium speed with electric hand mixer for about 10 seconds. Add 3 tablespoons of superfine sugar while beating and continue to beat until whites are stiff. Combine remaining sugars in sifter. Add sugar to the whites, continuing to beat all the while. Beat for another 20 seconds. The consistency should be such that when the beater is removed from the whites they hang like thick drapes.
4. With a large rubber spatula, place all the beaten whites into a pastry bag equipped with a number 7 tube. On the cookie sheet form about a dozen meringues of about 3½ inches in length and 1¾ inches in width.
5. Place in oven for 2 hours. The slow cooking should keep them white but make them crisp.
6. Serve 2 to a person, with ice cream and sauce or crème anglaise (see recipe, page 58). If kept in a dry place at room temperature in a covered canister the meringues will keep for a week.
   Yield: 6 servings.

DOUGH CUTTERS

Every day as I methodically ready my kitchen for another sortie into the business of cooking I make sure that all the required tools will be at hand. And every day I take out my dough scraper — even when I'm not planning to do any baking. The reason for that is the broad expanse of its metal blade, which makes it marvelous for picking up shallots or parsley from the cutting board and transporting them to pot or platter. The wooden handle and blade form a rectangle that is about 6 by 5 inches.

In its primary use — dough preparation — it is perfect for that quick thrust through a large ball of pasta dough, converting it into smaller, more manageable units that can be fed into a pasta machine. It divides bread dough into even quantities for the desired number of loaves. It also helps in the manipulation of dough and is effective in scraping the board clean when you're done. Were a knife used for many of these jobs, it would almost certainly be dulled by the contact with the pastry board. But this scraper is not a knife; its blade starts out dull. The handle of the dough scraper should be firmly riveted — two rivets will do — to the blade, to give you the same sturdiness you'd expect in a good knife. The best metal for this purpose is stainless steel.

A related tool is the wheel-shaped pastry cutter. As you know if you've tried to cut pizza with a knife, you don't do it as well as the man at the pizza shop who uses his big wheel. The knife meets too much resistance. I own one of those pizza cutters and use it for cutting pizza as well as uncooked dough. An extraordinarily useful variation on the theme is the double-wheeled pastry cutter, which I also use in making ravioli. One of the wheels has a jagged edge, which cuts dough while leaving a pointed pattern along the sides. It leaves the appearance of cloth cut with pinking shears. The other wheel is a smooth blade. Both cut dough quickly without any of that nettlesome tugging.

1. *Use a pastry scraper to cut bread or pasta dough into the desired number of portions. The wide blade is also useful for scraping dough into a ball, for scraping the board clean and for transferring chopped vegetables from the cutting board to the stove.*

BREAD PANS

Under the best of circumstances, it is difficult to make a perfect loaf of French bread. Its creation, after all, is an exercise in extremes: The dough must be induced to form a thin crust so crisp it threatens to shatter on impact, while the interior that the crust surrounds remains as airy as a down pillow.

And even after you've taken all necessary steps to ensure that textural duality — allowed your dough to rise properly, thrown ice cubes into the oven or placed a pan of water there to produce the steam that will aid the formation of a thin crust, baked the dough until the loaf is a rich color — even after all that, the loaf may defy you by assuming some strange, idiosyncratic shape during the baking process.

There's nothing wrong with idiosyncracy, if what you like is a freeform look — and very often that is exactly what I like — but if you have in mind the replication of some baguette of bread remembered from Paris, freeform doesn't quite make it.

A device useful both in developing a worthy crust and in creating the classic shape is the double French bread pan, which was a novelty some years back but is now common. It looks like a section of pipe split open.

For one thing, this pan allows you to simulate what old-time professional bakers did: They would place the dough, during its last rising stage, in a long and narrow woven basket to persuade the dough to keep its shape. Then they would remove it from the basket and slide it into the oven. That last rising stage can be done in one of these pans, and then the pan can be moved directly into the oven, where it maintains the loaf's shape.

Each pan produces two loaves. Since the process takes several hours, it makes sense to bake a few loaves at once. They do turn stale quickly, but freeze well.

The pans, 16 inches long or so, now come in triple as well as double configurations. I found that if I employed a double and a triple at the same time they fit my oven perfectly. They also come in a number of materials. What I use most is black steel, which distributes and intensifies the heat superbly. (I also use black steel for rectangular loaf pans.) White aluminum is not terribly inferior to black steel, however, and if it is all that is available, don't hesitate to use it. I've also used stoneware loaf pans, which provide a delightful crust, but they are somewhat more fragile and are heavier than the metal pans.

Incidentally, when you serve the bread, an attractive vessel is a straw basket the same shape as the loaf and lined with a checkered napkin. I know that that's a cliché in a restaurant, but I think it's a warm thing to do at home. In cutting the bread, remember to use a serrated slicing knife (see page 22), so that you can't flatten it or shatter the crust (or you can ignore the slicing completely and tear at the loaf with your hands, which is actually the traditional approach).

1. *After the dough has risen the second time, turn it out onto a lightly floured board and cut it into desired number of portions. Shape each portion roughly.* **2.** *Roll and stretch each portion by moving the palms of your hands from the center out to ends until bread is a long cylinder.*

3. *Lay the cylinders in the bread pan and let rise. When they are almost proofed, use a razor blade or sharp knife to make diagonal slits about ½ inch deep, which will open up in baking. If the bread is overproofed, it will collapse when slit because the yeast is no longer working.* **4.** *The cooked bread.*

FRENCH BREAD

1½ envelopes yeast
¼ cup warm water (90 degrees)
2 cups unbleached flour
2 cups all-purpose flour
1 tablespoon salt
1¼ cups cool water
2 ice cubes

1. Place the chopping blade in the food processor bowl. Add yeast and warm water. Mix by turning the chopping blade by hand. Add all the flour. Blend for 5 seconds. Add salt and blend for 5 seconds. While blade continues to turn, gradually add cool water. Blend until batter begins to form a large ball, 20 to 25 seconds more.
2. Flour a board and knead the dough, forming it into a ball. Flour a large mixing bowl and place the ball of dough in it. Sprinkle its top with flour. Cover with a kitchen towel. Let dough rise in a warm place until it doubles in bulk. (The time required varies with environmental factors, but at room temperature of about 75 degrees it will take at least an hour.)
3. Turn dough out onto a lightly floured board and punch it down. Make a new ball and put it back in the mixing bowl. Sprinkle with flour; cover and let rest again for 45 minutes to an hour.
4. When the dough rises about double again, remove it from the bowl, punch it down and shape it into the loaf desired. This quantity is sufficient for three or four baguettes of 18 inches in length, each stretched along the length of a tubular French bread pan. But it is also handsome shaped as a single ring on a baking sheet or pizza peel (see following discussion). Let it continue to rise to 50 percent additional volume.
5. Meanwhile preheat the oven to 425 degrees.
6. With a razor blade, diagonally score the surface of the loaves several times, each incision about ½ inch deep.
7. Place loaves in the oven and throw ice cubes onto the oven floor. (The ice cubes add steam to produce a thin, crisp crust.) Bake for 30 minutes. Reduce the heat to 400 degrees and bake an additional 10 minutes. Transfer the bread to a rack and let cool.
Yield: 3 or 4 long loaves.

PIZZA STONE & PEEL

Failure in bread-baking, common though it may be, just doesn't have to happen. That black metal French loaf pan in the preceding discussion is an excellent aid in baking bread well and ensuring that it will hold its shape. Another remarkable aid is a stoneware platform that sits on the oven floor.

The stoneware is intended to mimic the brick ovens of professional bakers. The stoneware being sold these days is usually called a pizza brick or pizza stone because the manufacturers evidently think of pizza baking as its main purpose, and it is indeed fine for that assignment. When I baked a pizza on one, its crust was far crisper than that from the more common home device, the metal pizza pan.

But it is for baking bread that I use it most.

An important team-mate in baking bread as well as pizza is the traditional wooden pizza paddle, called a peel, 12 by 14 inches in size. The peel is used to place the pizza on the hot stone and to remove it later.

In baking bread it comes into play for the third rising of the dough. The recipe often calls for you to allow the dough to rise once in a bowl, punch it down and let it rise again, and then shape it before it rises the third time. If you are shaping the dough into a ring, it can be done on a pizza peel sprinkled with semolina to prevent sticking.

Meantime the oven should be preheating to 425 degrees with the stoneware tray in it. After the dough has risen and the stoneware has heated for at least 15 minutes, slide the loaf from the pizza peel onto the hot stone. At that point it is also wise to throw two or three ice cubes into the oven to get a momentary burst of steam. The steam helps form a thin skin that will become a thin crust later.

At the same time the stoneware will be doing its job on the bottom of the loaf, producing a dry, intense, extraordinarily even heat that will brown the bottom deeply.

1. *For pizza, roll the dough around a rolling pin and unroll it onto the pizza paddle, which has been sprinkled with semolina.* **2.** *Pat the dough into a neat round.*

3. *Spoon a small amount of sauce into the center of the pizza dough and spread it with the back of the spoon.* **4.** *Keep adding spoonfuls of sauce and spreading it to within ¾ inch of the edge, which will rise in the baking. Sprinkle with cheese.*

5. *Slide the pizza off the paddle onto the hot stone on the bottom shelf of a preheated oven.* **6.** *Remove the cooked pizza by sliding the paddle under it. Cut into wedges with a pizza cutter.*

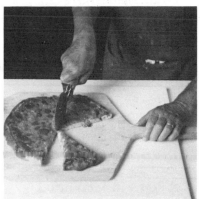

DOUGH FOR ONE 12-INCH PIZZA

1 **envelope dry yeast**
¾ **cup warm water (100 degrees)**
2 **cups plus 2 tablespoons flour**
    Salt to taste
1½ **tablespoons olive oil**

1. Dissolve the yeast in ¼ cup of the warm water. Place in food processor bowl and add the 2 cups of flour, salt and olive oil. Turn on and off three times.
2. Add ½ cup water and mix for about 10 seconds, until the dough begins to form a ball. Remove the dough from processor bowl onto a floured board. Knead it and form into a neatly rounded ball. Wrap dough in a towel (or cover with plastic wrap in a bowl) and let rise in a warm place for about 30 minutes.
3. Flour the ball of dough lightly and press it down into a circle of 12 inches, about ¼ inch thick.

CHEESE AND TOMATO PIZZA

1 tablespoon semolina
  Dough for 1 12-inch
  pizza
1 cup basic tomato sauce
  (see following recipe)
1 cup mozarella cheese,
  grated coarsely
2 tablespoons grated
  Parmesan cheese
1 tablespoon olive oil,
  optional

1. With stoneware pizza tray placed in oven, preheat to 500 degrees.
2. Sprinkle semolina onto the pizza peel and place formed round of dough on it. Spoon sauce over the dough. Sprinkle mozarella over the sauce. Sprinkle with Parmesan.
3. Pour olive oil over the cheese. (This is optional because some cooks feel it makes the pizza too oily.) Slide pizza from peel onto stoneware.
4. Bake for 10 to 12 minutes, rotating once or twice with pizza paddle to diminish hot spot problems. When the rim is dark brown but not burned, remove the pizza with peel. Cut into wedges to serve, a task most easily accomplished with a circular-blade knife.
   Yield: 2 to 4 servings.
   Note: The same pizza can be made satisfactorily in a metal pizza tray, although it will lack some of the crispness. To do that press the dough into the oiled tray, top it with sauce and cheese and place the tray on the floor of the preheated oven.

BASIC TOMATO SAUCE

2 tablespoons olive oil
½ cup chopped onion
1 teaspoon finely chopped
  garlic
  28-ounce can Italian
  whole tomatoes in thick
  purée
2 teaspoons dried oregano
  Freshly ground pepper to
  taste

1. Heat the oil in a wide, shallow saucepan (ideally, one that is 9 inches or so in diameter to allow sauce to reduce somewhat) and sauté onion gently for about 2 minutes, or until translucent. Add garlic and cook gently so garlic and onion remain white. Add tomatoes, oregano and pepper and stir.
2. Simmer uncovered for 10 minutes, stirring occasionally.
   Yield: 3 cups.
   Note: If only one pizza is made, requiring just 1 cup of sauce, the remainder can be saved for future pizzas or for pasta.
   Variation: For meat loaf, delete the oregano and add ½ teaspoon of rosemary and ½ teaspoon of basil.

FLAN RING

The flan ring is a more capable piece of equipment than you might imagine. That's because when you first look at one it's hard to imagine it does anything at all. It is nothing more than a metal ring, usually tinned or stainless steel, several inches in diameter and ⅝ of an inch deep. It looks like something that might hold together a small barrel, but what can it do in cooking?

Quite a lot, actually. What it does is supply one of the best and simplest methods for preparing tarts and quiches. Tarts and quiches are lovely when served unmolded; they are easier to cut that way and they look better. But to do that you need a mold that will slide off easily. The flan ring is the traditional one for the purpose.

The ring works in tandem with a baking sheet. (The baking sheets I prefer are made of black steel — the dark color intensifies the heat — and they are rigid enough to prevent the warping that can result in uneven cooking; see page 172.) When you are creating the shell it's important to build up the dough along the wall so that it will be somewhat thicker than the bottom and thus will be sturdy enough to stand unsupported once the mold is removed. The wall of dough should be created a bit higher than the sides of the mold for any decorative fluting.

It makes sense to do the fluting in such a way as to incline the rim of the shell toward the center. The reason is that the quiche or tart will be unmolded by lifting the flan form straight up and you don't want to knock off the decoration. After the shell is unmolded, slide it onto a serving platter or a cooling rack.

Quiches and tarts most often require partial baking of the shell before the ingredients are placed inside to cook. Some recipes for tarts call for fully baked shells because the ingredients are already cooked before they're placed inside, or because the filling is one of fresh fruit.

The problem in this process, which is known as baking "blind," is in keeping the bottom of the shell from rising. The cleverest way to do that is to use small metal pie weights (reminiscent of the dried beans used for the same purpose) spread over wax paper or kitchen parchment paper that has been pushed down onto the dough. Because the weights absorb heat they aid in the baking while helping the shell keep its shape.

I have three flan rings at the ready, 10 inches, 8 inches and 6 inches in diameter. The variation in size, of course, means that it is possible to make just precisely the amount of quiche required by the moment: An 8-inch shell, for instance, serves four to six.

1. *Place flan ring on an unbuttered baking sheet. Roll the pastry around a rolling pin to transfer it and lay it loosely over the ring.* **2.** *Press the dough into the ring without stretching it. Use your thumb and forefinger to build up the sides of the pastry. Cut off excess dough, leaving a ½-inch rim.*

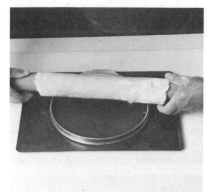

3. *Press the back of a fork all around the inside edge of the ring, which makes the dough of even thickness and creates a decorative rim. Press the fork around the outside of the pastry to flute it and incline the rim slightly toward the center.* **4.** *Lay a large piece of wax paper inside the refrigerated shell and fill with aluminum pellets or dried beans. Spread them evenly to keep the crust from rising as it bakes.*

5. *When shell is baked, lift out pellets with wax paper. Spoon the filling into the partly cooked shell and finish baking.* **6.** *When the tart is cooked, place the baking sheet on a rack to cool and lift off the metal rim. Serve the tart warm.*

CHEESE AND ZUCCHINI TART

TART SHELL

1½ cups flour
8 tablespoons butter, cut into small pieces
1 egg yolk
½ teaspoon salt
2 tablespoons ice water

FILLING

1 tablespoon butter
½ cup thinly sliced onion
1 pound small zucchini, sliced very thin (3 cups)
Salt and freshly ground pepper to taste
3 egg yolks
1 whole egg
½ cup cream
½ cup milk
⅛ teaspoon nutmeg
Dash cayenne pepper
1 cup Gruyère in ¼-inch cubes
¼ cup chopped fresh basil (optional)
2 tablespoons grated Parmesan cheese

1. Place all the ingredients for the tart shell, except water, in bowl of food processor and blend for 5 seconds. Add water and blend just until pastry pulls away from sides of bowl and begins to form a ball. On a floured board, shape the dough into a ball. Wrap it in wax paper and let rest in refrigerator for 30 minutes.
2. Preheat the oven to 375 degrees.
3. Roll out dough on a floured board until it is slightly larger than a 9-inch flan ring. Place ring on a black steel baking tray.
4. Roll dough onto the rolling pin and unroll it over the ring. Press dough against the wall of the ring. Cut away most of excess dough, leaving only enough to create a thickened rim with fingers. Press a kitchen fork lightly along the rim to create a crimped design.
5. Line the shell with wax paper or kitchen parchment and weight down with aluminum weights or dried beans. Bake for 10 minutes. Remove weights and paper and bake 5 more minutes.
6. To prepare filling, melt the butter in a shallow skillet. Sauté the onion and zucchini for about 5 minutes. (Do not let the vegetables brown.) Sprinkle with salt and pepper to taste. Drain in a colander.
7. In a mixing bowl, use a wire whisk to beat the yolks, whole egg, cream, milk, salt and pepper, nutmeg and cayenne until well blended. With a slotted spoon, place zucchini and onions in shell. Cover with Gruyère. Ladle the batter over the cheese and zucchini. Sprinkle with basil and Parmesan. Bake in a 375-degree oven for 45 minutes.
8. Let cool on a rack, unmold and serve warm.
   Yield: 6 servings.

TART PANS

An alternative to using the flan ring for making tarts and quiches is the very clever and good looking fluted tart pan with a removable bottom. The bottom here is the part of the design that allows you to serve the quiche or tart unmolded, just as you would with a flan ring. And it has exactly the same purpose as the baking tray does under the flan ring. It needs to be able to give the crust an even, deep brown color. So with this pan I again want to argue for dark steel.

Dark tart pans absorb and distribute heat with far more alacrity than do glistening stainless steel or aluminum ones and certainly better than anything made of glass. Failure to achieve a well-cooked crust can result in a quiche or tart whose shell has the taste of raw butter and the texture of moist clay.

It might seem that an antidote to the undercooked crust is more cooking, but there is a peril in that approach. The danger proved palpable when an acquaintance of mine cooked an apple tart in a light-colored, tinned-steel pan. After baking the tart, which was topped with a neat array of painstakingly arranged apple slices, for the prescribed time and at the appropriate heat, he noticed that the crust was still undercooked, so he kept baking, and the dough did crispen somewhat — but the apples blackened beyond redemption.

The false-bottom pans that seem to be the most satisfactory are made for Isabel Marique in Belgium and distributed here under her name. Their fluted walls add an attractive touch to the tart or quiche. The bottoms, which are disks that can be pushed up and out of the pan, make the removal of a tart an easy, almost foolproof maneuver. The Isabel Marique pans come in two sizes: 9 inches or 11 inches in diameter, both 1⅜ inches deep.

1. *Peel the apple, cut in half through the stem and then into quarters. Remove the core and cut the apple into ⅛-inch slices.*
2. *Place apple slices overlapping around the uncooked tart shell and mound slices decoratively in the center. Dot with butter and sugar.*

3. *When the tart is cooked, put it on a rack to cool. Brush all over with glaze. Push up removable bottom so tart stands free for serving.* **4.** *For individual tarts, put a small piece of dough in a fluted pan.*

5. *Using your thumbs, press the dough into the bottom and sides of the pan.* **6.** *The tart will have a decorative fluted edge.*

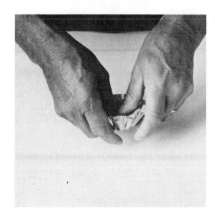

TARTE AUX POMMES (French apple tart)

Pastry for a 9-inch tart (see following recipe)

6 or 7 firm, unblemished apples, about 2½ pounds

2 tablespoons butter
Grated rind of 1 lemon

½ cup sugar

1 tablespoon Calvados, rum or brandy, optional

½ cup apricot preserves

1. Preheat the oven to 400 degrees.
2. Line a 9-inch pie tin, preferably a quiche pan with a removable bottom, with pastry. Refrigerate or place in the freezer.
3. Core and peel 3 of the apples. Cut them into eighths. Cut these pieces into thin slices. There should be about 2 cups.
4. Heat 1 tablespoon of butter in a small skillet and add the apple slices. Sprinkle with lemon rind and ¼ cup of sugar. Cook, shaking the skillet and stirring, for about 10 minutes. Add Calvados. Mash the apples lightly with a fork. Chill.
5. Core, peel and neatly slice the remaining apples.
6. Spoon the cooked apples over the bottom of the prepared pie tin. Arrange the fresh apple slices in a circular pattern over the cooked pulp. Sprinkle with remaining sugar and dot with remaining butter.
7. Bake for 40 to 45 minutes, or until pastry is browned.
8. Heat the preserves and put through a sieve. Brush this over the tart. Cool and serve.

Yield: 6 to 8 servings.

PASTRY FOR FRENCH TART

1½ cups flour

8 tablespoons butter

2 teaspoons sugar

3 to 4 tablespoons ice water

1. This is much more easily done in a food processor than by hand, but either method is acceptable. If the processor is used, put the flour into the container of the processor. Cut in the butter and the sugar. Start processing while adding the water a little at a time. Add only enough water so that the dough holds together and can be shaped into a ball.
2. Alternatively, put the flour into a mixing bowl. Cut the butter into small pieces and put on top of the flour. Sprinkle with sugar. Using a pastry cutter, cut the butter into the flour. Using the hands, start working the mixture while adding the water one teaspoon or so at a time. Add only enough water so that the dough can be gathered and shaped into a ball.
3. Flatten the dough into a round patty about 1½ inches thick. Wrap tightly in foil or wax paper. Refrigerate for 30 minutes or longer.

Yield: Pastry for a 9-inch tart.

SPRINGFORM PAN

When I was young I regarded making a cheesecake as a riskier business than it seems to me now. The primary source of the relative calm I feel today is the springform pan, a tool whose acquaintance I made for the first time when I became a chef in this country.

A cheesecake, like an ice cream cake and some other kinds of pastry, does not give you the opportunity to cover up mistakes with a delicate glaze or a dense frosting. The walls of the cake remain unadorned, so if the cake has adhered to the side of the pan because of inadequate preparation before the batter was poured into the mold, the cheesecake will emerge blotched, perhaps torn, and will stand there on its pedestal as if the elevation were meant as a mockery.

The extrication of a cheesecake from its mold is made the harder by the fact that cheesecake is not meant to be placed upside down as are cakes that take an icing, so it can't be turned out of a pan in one motion. The springform pan greatly diminishes the amount of risky manipulation required. While the cake bakes, the pan wall is held tightly closed by a clip. When it is done, the clip is opened, allowing the walls of the mold to spring into an expanded position, pulling away from the cake. The wall is then lifted up and away.

Although this is simple to do, the springform still requires diligent preparation. The wall and the bottom should be well greased. The best way to do that is to melt butter and chill the pan at the same time. Then brush the warm butter onto the cold metal with a pastry brush.

If a recipe calls for putting crumbs into the mold, that should be done uniformly, too. Don't sprinkle the crumbs on. Rather place all of them in the pan and toss them around until they have adhered everywhere on the surface, then turn the pan upside down and strike it gently to remove the excess.

1. *Chill the springform pan and brush it all over with softened butter. Be sure to coat the sides well.*
2. *Put in crumbs and tip the pan this way and that until it is evenly coated on the bottom and around the sides. Pour out excess crumbs.*

3. *Put the springform on a baking sheet and pour and scrape the batter into it with a rubber spatula.* **4.** *Put the cooked cheesecake on a rack to cool. Release the spring lock but do not remove the ring.*

5. *Spoon berries over the cooled cheesecake.* **6.** *When ready to serve, put the springform pan on a plate and lift off the ring.*

ROSE'S STRAWBERRY CHEESECAKE

1½ teaspoons butter
¼ cup graham cracker crumbs
2 packages (8 ounces each) cream cheese, cut into 8 pieces
4 large eggs, separated
1 cup sugar
2 tablespoons flour
1 teaspoon vanilla
Pinch of salt

1. Preheat the oven to 325 degrees.
2. Butter the bottom and wall of a 9-inch springform pan. Dust the inside with graham cracker crumbs, reserving 1 teaspoon. Shake out excess.
3. In the bowl of a KitchenAid or other tabletop mixer, blend the cream cheese at number 5 setting until smooth, about 40 seconds. Stop the machine and scrape down the side of the bowl as needed. Add the egg yolks and blend for 15 seconds. Add ¾ cup of the sugar along with the flour, vanilla and salt and blend for 15 seconds. With the mixer running, pour the cream into the bowl. Blend for 5 seconds.

1 cup heavy cream
  Strawberry glaze (see
  following recipe)

4. In a 2-quart mixing bowl, beat the egg whites with an electric mixer at medium speed until soft peaks form. Gradually add the remaining ¼ cup sugar and continue beating until stiff. Using a large rubber spatula fold the whites into the cream cheese mixture in the bowl of the mixer.
5. Place the springform pan on a black baking sheet and pour the mixture into it. Sprinkle the top with the remaining graham cracker crumbs. Bake for 1 hour. Turn off the oven but leave the cake in it, with door ajar, for 15 minutes. Close the door and leave the cake in the oven for an additional 45 minutes. Remove it from the oven and place on a rack to cool. Release the spring lock but do not remove the ring. Let it cool for at least 4 hours.
6. Brush the cheesecake with the glaze.
7. Just before serving, remove ring of the springform pan. Serve at room temperature or chilled.

Yield: 8 servings.

STRAWBERRY GLAZE

½ cup water
1 tablespoon cornstarch
1 pint fresh strawberries,
  washed, hulled and sliced
  in half
½ cup superfine sugar

Mix 2 tablespoons of the water with the cornstarch. Combine the remaining water with the strawberries and sugar in a saucepan. Bring to a boil, add the cornstarch, stirring well, and remove from the heat. Allow to cool to room temperature.

CHOCOLATE CAKE

10 eggs, separated and at
   room temperature
14 tablespoons sugar
3 ounces bittersweet or
   semisweet chocolate,
   melted slowly over hot
   water and cooled
2 cups finely chopped (not
   ground) pecans

1. Preheat the oven to 350 degrees.
2. Beat the egg yolks and sugar until very thick and lemon colored. Stir in the chocolate. Fold in the nuts.
3. Beat the egg whites until stiff but not dry and fold into the chocolate-nut mixture. Turn into a greased 10-inch spring-form pan and bake 1 hour, or until the center springs back when lightly touched with the fingertips. Cool in the pan.

Yield: 8 to 12 servings.

CHARLOTTE MOLD

Elegance often comes easy, created by a single well-placed flower or just a bit of garnish.

And it happens that some of the most elegant desserts I can think of also are among the simplest to prepare. I have in mind the charlottes, especially the classic charlotte aux pommes (apple charlotte) and the sumptuous charlotte russe, which was invented by the great Antonin Carême in the 19th century and has been relentlessly gorgeous ever since.

These pastries are prepared in a classic, slope-sided charlotte mold of, say, 6 inches in diameter and 3½ or 4 inches in depth.

The russe is merely a matter of lining the buttered mold with lady fingers, filling it with Bavarian cream, then chilling it and unmolding. There are countless variations; the cream can be flavored with raspberries, for instance, or chocolate.

The charlotte aux pommes involves lining the mold with thin slices of buttered white bread, filling the cavity with an apple compote and baking it. This charlotte can be served chilled or warm.

Once you've obtained one of these molds for its intended purpose, you'll quickly find that it also becomes one of those wonderful kitchen acquisitions that can be put to work in a variety of ways.

It is superb for a fish mousse (see recipe, page 208): Just butter the walls and fit a round piece of parchment paper into the bottom to aid in unmolding. Then fill the mold with the mousse and bake it. To be especially glorious about the whole thing, line the walls of the mold with some kind of white fish mousse and fill the center with, say, a salmon mousse. The result is like an ice cream bombe, the wedges revealing different colors.

The mousse is given yet another character if the mold is first lined with aspic that is then decorated with pimiento pieces or truffles.

Unmolding is rarely a problem for any dish that is to be served warm. The only time you have to be careful is when the mold contains a chilled mixture. Then the trick is to dip it into warm water just for a moment to partly liquefy the butter on the mold's walls.

The charlotte mold comes in a number of materials: copper, aluminum and tin-lined steel. I prefer the tinned steel more out of a sense of custom than anything else. All three materials would do the job well. My only concern is that the mold should be sturdily built so that it will not dent or warp. The shape of a mold is everything and a misshapen one has lost its use.

Some charlotte molds come with lids. These are nice for covering the mold while it is stored in the refrigerator, but they are unnecessary otherwise. In any event, I have almost always cooked and stored dishes made in a charlotte mold covering it only with waxed paper or foil, and that has sufficed.

1. *Butter a charlotte mold with a pastry brush and place bread slices next to each other around the mold, toasted side facing in. Place a slice on the bottom, toasted side up.*
2. *Spoon sautéed apples into the mold to within an inch of the top.*

3. *Cover the top with another piece of bread, toasted side down. Press the side slices down over the top.*
4. *Place the mold in a large pan (I'm using a gratin pan) and pour boiling water around it. Bake.*

5. *Hold a large plate over the mold and invert it onto the plate. Lift off the mold.* **6.** *Glaze the charlotte with a pastry brush while it is still hot.*

APPLE CHARLOTTE

½ cup white raisins
¼ cup Cognac
7 to 8 thin slices white bread
8 tablespoons butter
2½ pounds apples, peeled, cored and sliced
½ cup sugar
1 tablespoon lemon rind
Apricot sauce (see following recipe)

1. Preheat the oven to 400 degrees.
2. Soak the raisins in the Cognac.
3. Trim the crusts from the bread. Butter the slices on one side and toast only that side under the broiler.
4. Butter a 5-cup charlotte mold and line the wall with the toasted bread, pressing the untoasted side firmly against the wall of the mold so it follows the contour. Place some of the bread, untoasted side down, on the bottom of the mold. (The untoasted sides will brown when the charlotte is baked.)
5. Melt 4 tablespoons of butter in a large skillet and sauté the apples with sugar and lemon rind for about 10 minutes, or until tender. The idea is to remove much of the moisture in the apples. Turn the apples frequently.
6. Add the raisins and Cognac and keep cooking until the liquid has evaporated so the apple slices will brown lightly. Spoon the apples into the mold. Cover the top with a slice of bread, toasted side down. Seal the charlotte closed by pressing the tops of the slices lining the wall inward so they fold over the slice capping the charlotte.
7. Place the mold in a shallow pan in which there is enough water to rise about 1½ inches up the side. Bring to a boil on top of the stove, then bake uncovered in the oven for 45 minutes.
8. Unmold by placing a platter on top of the charlotte and turning the charlotte upside down. Brush completely with apricot sauce. Serve hot or warm.
Yield: 10 servings.

APRICOT SAUCE

1 12-ounce jar apricot preserves
¼ cup water

Heat the preserves and water in a small saucepan, whisking occasionally, until it reaches the boil. Pour sauce through a strainer, using a rubber spatula to force solids through completely.
Yield: 1 cup.

TIMBALE MOLDS

One of the most obvious charms of nouvelle cuisine is that each dish arrives as if it were a new, individual creation. Of course, elegant food preparation, whatever the style, tries to give that feeling of individuality. The intention is to show a flattering degree of care, without being ostentatious about it.

One way to arrive at that balance in home entertaining is to individualize dishes that otherwise might be large and ungainly in their presentation. A number of specialized molds with remarkable versatility help enormously. A favorite of mine is called a timbale mold. It comes in a range of sizes, but the most useful is 2 inches in diameter.

Its most common use is in the baking of crème caramel, sometimes called flan, a light and lovely custard dripping with caramel. Sugar is heated on the range and caramelized first, then poured into the bottom of each mold. The custard mixture follows and the timbales are then placed in a shallow pan with water, which is brought to a boil. After the custard is gently baked and cooled, it is unmolded. To unmold, I use a paring knife that I run around the periphery of each cup, thrusting it all the way to the bottom of the cup. The loosened custard will slide out easily when inverted.

But crème caramel aside, a timbale shows its versatility and usefulness in individualizing dishes when it is used for a mousse of chicken or fish, delicate, light dishes that, served this way, will seem to be somewhere between a quenelle and a mousse.

You can line the timbale's sides with cooked rice and fill it with chicken curry or seafood. As a matter of fact, just filling it with baked rice and unmolding the rice for each guest's plate lends the rice a dignified look. The versatility of this mold is further underlined by the fact that it bears another name: baba mold. It is also used to make babas au rhum, those little liquor-soaked cakes.

1. *Put timbale molds in a shallow pan and pour in about ¼ inch of caramel syrup to coat the bottoms. Fill almost to the top with custard. Pour boiling water around the molds and bake.* **2.** *When custard has cooled, run a paring knife around the upper edge where it has caramelized.*

3. *Hold a small plate over each mold, with thumbs holding the timbale, and turn it over.* **4.** *Lift off the mold.*

CRÈME CARAMEL

THE CARAMEL

¾　cup sugar
2　tablespoons water

THE CUSTARD

3　whole eggs
⅓　cup sugar
½　teaspoon vanilla
1½　cups milk
½　cup cream

1. Preheat the oven to 350 degrees.
2. Put six small timbale molds (⅔ cup in capacity) in a shallow pan.
3. Place sugar and water for caramel in a small straight-sided saucepan. Cook the sugar at medium flame, agitating the pan and stirring occasionally. Watch it carefully; the change of color to the required deep brown takes place all of a sudden. Just as it turns dark pour the caramel in even amounts into the timbales.
4. Combine the eggs and sugar for the custard, whisking until they turn lemon color. Add vanilla, milk and cream and blend with a whisk. Strain the custard through a fine-mesh sieve. Pour into each of the timbales.
5. Pour enough water into the pan holding the timbales to rise 1 inch around the walls of the molds. Bring to a boil on top of the range. Place in the oven for 30 minutes. Remove from the water and cool at room temperature for half an hour, then place in refrigerator. To serve, loosen the custard by running a paring knife between it and the wall of the timbale and invert the mold.
Yield: 6 servings.

SAVARIN MOLD

If it is possible to be both simple and sumptuous at the same time, the savarin is. It is a yeast-risen, kirsch-soaked, ring-shaped cake named in honor of the great chef Brillat-Savarin.

The hole in the center of the mold that is traditionally used to make a savarin is large, occupying proportionately more space than do the holes in other ring molds, such as those for a kugelhopf or a bundt. The reason for the size of the hole is that after the batter is prepared and the cake is glazed with sugar and then perhaps decorated with almonds and candied fruit, the center area is waiting to be filled with whipped cream or custard or fruit macerated in kirsch.

The savarin is a convenient cake for summer entertaining because the baking can be done as much as a couple of days in advance, then on the day it is to be served the cake can be heated briefly before the glaze is applied.

As you can probably tell from the sound of it, the cake has more than a little sybaritic potential and it alone would be reason for me to suggest that the purchase of one good-sized plated steel savarin mold (8½ inches in diameter) is not a waste of buying power.

But this mold does have many other uses. On occasion I have used it to prepare a cold avocado mousse and employed the strategically placed emptiness in the middle of the mold to encompass a crab meat salad. Once I produced a chicken mousse in this mold and then used the center for a very thick tomato sauce that was intentionally too dense to come pouring out as the mousse was cut.

It is terrific for a quick ice cream cake. Press the ice cream into the mold so that it takes on the ring shape. When you unmold the ice cream fill the center with mixed fruits that are in season — sliced strawberries, bananas or apples — then douse it with kirsch or some other richly flavored alcohol that pleases you.

With all these cold dishes, the knack is in the unmolding. The best thing to use is a hot wet towel to warm the mold. If it contains ice cream cake, a little warmth will, of course, help the ice cream slide out as it melts an infinitesimal amount of the cream. The same principle applies with a cold mousse, for which you always initially grease the mold. When it chills, the grease will congeal; a hot towel will cause it to return to a liquid state and allow the mousse to slide out undamaged.

An interesting advantage offered by such molds is that not only does the hole stand ready for a filling but it also provides the mold with more exposed surface than would a commoner shape. That means anything in it will chill more quickly. So the mold will help you if you've fallen behind schedule and want to freeze a chocolate mousse quickly.

SAVARIN WITH RUM

1 **package dry yeast**
¼ **cup lukewarm water**
1½ **cups sifted all-purpose flour**
1 **tablespoon sugar**
½ **teaspoon salt**
3 **medium eggs**
¼ **cup milk**
⅔ **cup butter, at room temperature**
2 **teaspoons grated lemon rind**
Rum syrup (see following recipe)

1. Soften the yeast in the water for 5 minutes, then stir until blended.
2. Combine the flour, sugar and salt in a mixing bowl. Stir in the yeast and eggs beaten slightly with the milk. Beat until the batter is smooth, about 100 strokes. Add the butter and lemon rind and beat until the butter is blended into the batter, about 50 strokes.
3. Spoon the batter into the 9-inch ring mold, filling it half full. Cover with a towel and let rise until the batter just fills the mold, about 1 hour.
4. Meanwhile, preheat the oven to 400 degrees. Bake the savarin 30 to 35 minutes, or until browned.
5. Carefully turn the savarin out of the mold and spoon hot rum syrup over it until the cake is saturated. Keep warm and serve filled with whipped cream. If desired, the savarin may be served blazing. To do this, pour ¼ cup warm rum over the warm savarin and set ablaze. Accompany with warm sabayon sauce (page 149).
   Yield: 8 to 10 servings.

RUM SYRUP

1½ **cups water**
1½ **cups sugar**
3 **slices lemon**
2 **slices orange**
1 **1-inch stick cinnamon**
1 **teaspoon vanilla**
1 **clove**
½ **cup rum**

1. Bring all the ingredients except the rum to a boil, stirring until the sugar has dissolved. Simmer 5 minutes.
2. Strain and add the rum.
   Yield: About 1½ cups.

MACHINES

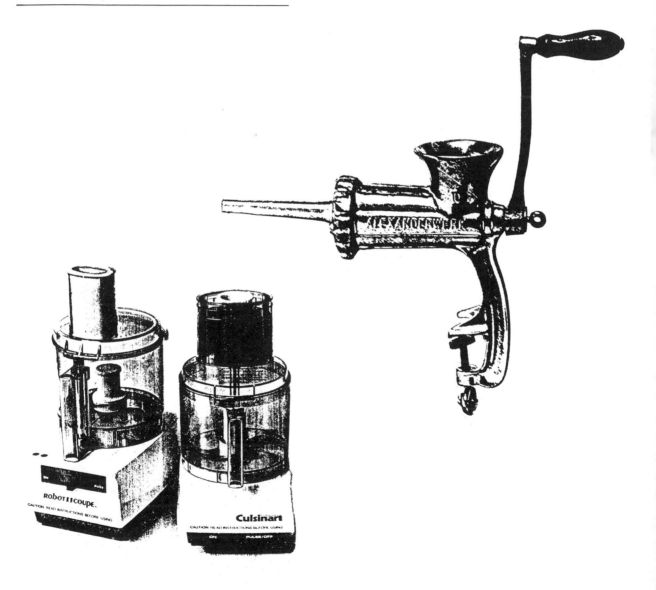

Even to this day, machines that assist in cooking in the home are rare in France. The Robot-Coupe, a French product that became so popular in the United States under the name of Cuisinart, is only now catching on in the country of its origin. As much as I have come to admire America and have come to feel I could never live for long periods anywhere else, the fact remains that in France the food one buys in stores is far better than it is here, and the French simply don't need machines for cooking at home as badly as we do in the United States. They go to the patisserie and order exquisite pastries for a party. Even in the town of Tonnerre, with its population of something like 4,000, there are six patisseries, each with some merit. The French can, of course, buy wonderful bread, as well, and the most marvelous sausages.

In the United States, especially anywhere distant from the ethnic riches of some big cities, the home cook will have only himself to rely upon. The machinery is making it possible for everyone to be a semiprofessional. Actually, many of the tools that have moved into the home are adaptations of commercial equipment.

The largest part of this section is devoted to the food processor, a machine that changed the world of cooking. As I note in that discussion, there was a time when great numbers of people in the United States were buying these machines and were at a loss as to what to do with them. That is still to some small degree true as young cooks, or those who simply want to grow in their ability, come to the food processor for the first time. What happens at once when you learn to use a food processor is that the amount of time spent in cooking some difficult dishes becomes much shorter. When I was considerably younger, very few amateur cooks would be ambitious enough to produce the light and lovely quenelles that are so easily — and quickly — done now. The same is true of making ice cream in the new ice cream machines, sausages with a good sausage stuffer and so on.

However, there is a danger of doing too many things by machine that ought to be done by hand. To see what you prefer doing by hand, it is a good idea to use the manual method before employing a machine. Certainly, don't turn to a machine for slicing and chopping until you've done it by hand with a chef's knife (see page 2). Don't whip cream or make a mayonnaise with an electric whip until you've given a whisk (page 53) a chance. You'll almost surely confirm for yourself a few things that no amount of proselytizing on my part will drive home. Whipping cream, for instance, is definitely better when it is done with a whisk (although the job is somewhat arduous). Making a heavy batter by machine, however, is immeasurably superior to doing it by hand.

FOOD PROCESSOR

 When the food processor, namely the French-made Cuisinart, first made an important impression on American cooks, an amusing period ensued. Clearly, everybody had to have one. And lots of people, at least those who could afford it, did buy one. But many of those people didn't have the foggiest idea of what to do with it once they had it. The Cuisinart looked for a while as if it were going to reside in the affluent kitchen as a motorized white elephant. That period was relatively brief, however, and it was followed by too many years during which everybody who had one began using the Cuisinart to the point of absurdity. Dinner parties would be overwhelmed by foods the Cuisinart had chopped to mush. They, naturally enough, became known to some observers of the food world as baby food parties. And in the meantime there was a rush of manufacturers that wanted to turn out something like the Cuisinart, albeit cheaper. And they did. They turned out rough approximations that were in fact cheaper and didn't work nearly so well. The only American rival that I can remember even coming close was the Farberware food processor.

Soon, the food processor really had established itself in the kitchen, not in a faddish sort of way, but rather the way the chef's knife had, or the colander. The time had arrived when it could reasonably be said that no kitchen ought to be without one. No kitchen, that is, dominated by a cook of any aspirations (and some money, of course; good food processors have always cost a pretty penny, and it is surely possible to live and cook well without one, if you have to). The making of a mousse, or even the chopping of meat, or the shredding of cabbage for cole slaw, all of these things had suddenly become much, much easier and faster than they ever had been before.

The processor had some limitations: It could not whip cream, for instance, the way other machines or a whisk could because it had little ability to incorporate air into any food. It was also too big for many jobs, such as chopping small amounts of food or grinding spices.

These machines were, essentially, a collection of whirring blades that could, each as required, be placed in the machine's plastic bowl. A chopping blade could be placed on the bottom of the bowl and it would blend or purée as well as chop. Then there were a number of slicing and shredding blades that stood high in the bowl. The food to be transformed was pushed through a funnel and processed in an operation that rarely took more than a few seconds.

The Cuisinart brand was really unmatched by any other for many years. But then in 1981 a fascinating dispute broke into public view in advertisements and news stories. It had all the passion of a marriage gone sour. And that, of course, is precisely what it was.

Here was a food processor called Robot-Coupe (few people in this country had ever heard of it) attacking the noble Cuisinart, pioneer and leader in the field. There were claims and counterclaims.

Robot-Coupe tried to tell buyers that it was the first, true Cuisinart. Cuisinart accused Robot-Coupe of a "commercial vendetta" in which it was trying to cash in on the Cuisinart reputation. Prices fell; at one point a Robot-Coupe advertisement offered a second machine for a dollar with the purchase of the first.

The two companies had indeed been happily mated once. The early Cuisinarts were French-made Robot-Coupes sold in the United States and distributed by Cuisinarts Inc. of Greenwich, Conn.

After Cuisinarts decided to manufacture its own machines in Japan — bigger, more powerful ones than the original — it left Robot-Coupe sitting quietly behind the scenes. But it didn't stay there for long. The French company broke cleanly away from Cuisinarts and came charging back, using its maiden name and trying to show it was gorgeous in its own right.

Was Robot-Coupe as good as a Cuisinart? Or had Cuisinart, having grown too big and sophisticated for its French partner, left it behind in deserved obscurity?

I set about looking for answers to those questions with rigorous testing of four machines: the two newest large ones at the time in both lines (the DLC7E Cuisinart and the Robot-Coupe RC3500) and two of the very popular small ones (the DLC10E and RC2000).

They were compared in the chopping of meat, onions, parsley and mushrooms; slicing of zucchini; blending of the ingredients for a fish mousse; shredding of carrots, and mixing of bread dough (using the metal chopping blade, which I prefer to the plastic blades provided for bread dough).

Both machines rated just about evenly — that is to say they were excellent — in all realms but one: slicing. The two Cuisinart models did a more uniform, generally better-looking job. This was partly attributable to Cuisinarts' development of the new larger feed tube, which allows bigger vegetables to pass through than did the earlier versions, and which holds them in position better. In addition, it may have been a reflection of a superior Cuisinart slicing blade (although those in the Robot-Coupe are made by the usually estimable Sabatier).

But when Cuisinarts developed the wider feed tube, which became standard equipment on its new models, large and small, it eliminated what I considered to be a significant annoyance for anyone using the machines for slicing: Originally, many vegetables had to be shaped with a knife first so they would fit the smaller tube. That annoyance still existed, at the time of my testing, with both Robot-Coupe models, and the zucchini that were sliced had to be shaved along the sides so they would fit into the processor.

However, slicing is among the least of a processor's virtues. Many cooks rarely use one for slicing, since a good chef's knife is the rival of any such machine. And the mandoline (see page 30) is a lot better in my opinion. A knife or a mandoline, it should be noted, allows for an infinite variety of thicknesses. Processor slicing blades can't do that.

I concluded that if the slicing ability of the two machines was not crucial to a buyer, then it was virtually a toss-up. There were some small advantages in the Robot-Coupe. Its bowl on the larger model was a bit bigger than the Cuisinart's (12 cups to 11 cups) and, I felt, a shade more sturdy. Both smaller models had bowls of 7-cup capacity. And, also in the large model, Robot-Coupe had cleverly introduced a removable shaft for the blades that meant each blade could be stored flat, whereas the Cuisinart blades, each with its own rod, are more awkward to store. (Since I made my comparison of the machines, however, Cuisinart too has gone to the detachable stem design.)

Every food processor company supplies its supporters with an array of accessories: slicers providing several different thicknesses, french-fry cutters, juicers and so on. I find the profusion of accessories somewhat bewildering, but I have no doubt that they prove valuable in some kitchens. Cuisinarts is especially proud of its julienne slicer, for instance. And the Robot-Coupe dome for expanding the amount of dough that can be mixed in the smaller models is a good idea.

I am not sure how effectively Robot-Coupe was challenging Cuisinarts during all this. Even as the dispute was going on, I had the sense that Cuisinarts were simply more available then the Robot-Coupes. And meanwhile Cuisinarts was cleverly and effectively playing on and extending the public awareness of its name with a very good line of stainless steel pots and a less good (but still worthy) line of knives.

Anyway, that dispute between the two companies was not, in retrospect, nearly so interesting as the basic machine the participants in the dispute had given to life in the United States.

The good food processor is one of the few great additions to the home kitchen to come along in decades. It improved amateur cooking forever.

1. When puréeing meat, fish or vegetables in a food processor, add only 2 or 3 cups at a time. The food should be cut into small pieces.
2. The food processor produces pastry or bread dough quickly. Add all the ingredients and process until the dough comes together in a ball around the metal chopping blade.

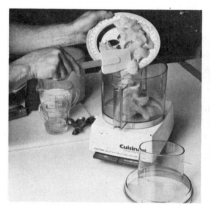 

MEAT LOAF

1	**pound pork**
1½	**pounds beef**
¾	**pound veal, trimmed of gristle**
1	**tablespoon butter**
2	**cups finely chopped onion**
½	**pound mushrooms, coarsely chopped (2 cups)**
⅓	**cup coarsely chopped parsley**

1. Preheat the oven to 400 degrees.
2. Cut the meat into 1½-inch cubes and combine them. Place the cubes in a food processor and chop for 10 or 12 seconds, so that the job is thoroughly done but the meat is not mushy. Chop only some of the meat at a time (exactly how much depends on your processor's size) so as not to overload the bowl.
3. Heat the butter in a skillet and add the onion. Cook briefly, stirring. Add mushrooms and cook until they release their liquid, then cook until the liquid evaporates, about 5 minutes, stirring frequently. Let mixture cool.

5 slices white bread
chopped in food
processor (1½ cups
crumbs)
2 eggs
Salt and freshly ground
pepper to taste
2 bay leaves

4. Combine the meat, parsley, onion-mushroom mixture, bread crumbs, eggs, salt and pepper to taste. Mix gently with moistened hands.
5. Divide mixture into two portions and press into two 6-cup loaf pans, adding a little at a time and patting it down as you go so that there are no air bubbles. Place a bay leaf on top of each loaf.
6. Bake for about 1 hour, or until internal temperature is 160 degrees.
7. Unmold and serve with basic tomato sauce variation (see recipe page 184).
    Yield: 8 to 10 servings.

LEEK AND POTATO SOUP

5 large leeks, white part
only
1 pound potatoes
2 tablespoons butter
1½ cups coarsley chopped
onion
4 cups chicken stock
2 cups water
Salt and freshly ground
pepper to taste
1 cup milk
½ cup cream

1. Cut leeks into pieces about 1½ inches in length. There should be about 7 cups. Wash thoroughly and drain. Peel potatoes and cut into ½-inch cubes (about 2½ cups).
2. Melt the butter in a large saucepan. Add the leeks and onion, and sauté for 5 minutes, but do not brown.
3. Add the potatoes, stock, water, salt and pepper, and bring to a boil. Simmer for ½ hour.
4. Ladle soup into the bowl of a food processor with chopping blade in place. Don't fill higher than one quarter of the way up the processor bowl to avoid leaking through lid as soup purées. Process for 2 minutes and pour the purée back into the saucepan.
5. Add the milk and cream. Bring to a boil, stirring, and serve immediately.
    Yield: 6 to 8 servings.
    Note: For vichyssoise, cool the puréed soup. Stir in 1 cup of milk, 2 cups cream and 2 tablespoons of Worcestershire sauce. Just before serving, add 1½ cups chopped chives, reserving a small amount of chives as garnish.

FISH MOUSSE WITH SAUCE DANTIN

1 pound very cold fillet of
nonoily fish (fluke,
flounder, pike, salmon,
striped bass, scallops)
⅛ teaspoon freshly ground
nutmeg
Dash cayenne pepper
Salt and freshly ground
pepper to taste
1 egg
1½ cups heavy cream
1 teaspoon butter
Sauce dantin (see
following recipe)

1. Preheat the oven to 375 degrees.
2. Remove all bones from fish (many fillets of flatfish have a bone remaining toward the head of fillet; it can be removed with a v-shaped incision). Cut fish into 2-inch pieces.
3. Place fish in bowl of processor and add nutmeg, cayenne, salt and pepper. Using chopping blade, blend for about 15 seconds. As blade turns, gradually add egg and then cream through funnel of processor. Blend for a few seconds more until smooth.
4. With pastry brush, butter a chilled 4-cup mold (a charlotte mold or savarin or baba or any of the fluted molds) and press mixture evenly into it, smoothing with rubber spatula.
5. Seal the mold tightly with aluminum foil and place it in a metal-handled saucepan containing enough water to rise 1½ inches up the mousse mold.
6. Bring water to boil on top of stove and then place saucepan in oven to bake for about 45 minutes, or until internal temperature is about 140 degrees, as measured by an instant thermometer with which you pierce the foil to the heart of the mousse at about the time you imagine it is done.
7. Invert mold to remove the mousse, and then slice it into wedges and serve with sauce dantin.

Yield: 4 to 6 servings.

ZUCCHINI AU GRATIN

6 zucchini (2 pounds),
sliced
½ cup sliced onions
1 small clove garlic, sliced
10 leaves fresh basil, or ½
teaspoon dried
Salt to taste
Dash cayenne pepper
⅛ teaspoon nutmeg
1 pint ricotta cheese
3 eggs
¼ cup grated Parmesan

1. Preheat the oven to 400 degrees.
2. With chopping blade of food processor in position, place zucchini in bowl and then all other ingredients except the Parmesan cheese. Blend for 10 seconds. (Depending on size of processor bowl, this may have to be done in two evenly divided batches.) Use a rubber spatula to scrape down the wall of the bowl. Process another 10 seconds, or until the whole mixture is revolving.
3. Transfer the mixture to a 6-cup gratin dish. Sprinkle with cheese. Cook on the bottom rack of the oven for about 40 minutes, or until nicely browned. Be careful not to overcook, which will cause the bottom to be watery.

Yield: 6 to 8 servings.

SAUCE DANTIN

3 tablespoons butter
2 tablespoons flour
1 cup fish stock (or clam juice)
2 tablespoons chopped shallots
½ pound mushrooms, sliced
1 cup peeled and chopped tomatoes (or ¾ cup whole canned tomatoes in thick purée)
¼ cup white wine
Salt and freshly ground pepper to taste
¼ cup cream
1 tablespoon chopped parsley

1. In a small saucepan, prepare the velouté base: Melt 1 tablespoon of the butter and add flour, cooking for about a minute at low flame. Whisk to prevent burning. Add stock, whisking thoroughly, and let simmer.
2. In a medium saucepan, melt 1 tablespoon of butter and sauté the shallots for about 1 minute, or until translucent. Add the mushrooms and sauté for 2 more minutes.
3. Add the tomatoes, wine, salt and pepper to taste. At a rapid boil, reduce by half, stirring with a wooden spatula.
4. Pour the tomato mixture into velouté and add cream. Simmer for 5 minutes and remove from heat.
5. Swirl in 1 tablespoon of butter and then stir in the parsley.
   Yield: About 2 cups of sauce.

PURÉE OF BROCCOLI

1½ pounds broccoli
¼ pound potatoes, cut into ¼-inch slices (1 cup)
4 cups salted water
2 tablespoons butter
2 tablespoons cream, optional
Nutmeg
Salt and freshly ground pepper to taste

1. Cut broccoli into flowerets; peel the stalks and cut into ¼-inch slices.
2. Place the stalks and potatoes in a saucepan and cover with water; bring to a boil and cook for 5 minutes, uncovered (the broccoli won't stay green if covered).
3. Add the broccoli flowerets and cook 9 more minutes, uncovered. Drain.
4. Place the broccoli and potatoes in bowl of food processor with chopping blade and process until it is a fine purée, a procedure that should take about 45 seconds. It may be necessary to use a rubber spatula to scrape the ingredients down the side of the bowl during the puréeing.
5. In a skillet or saucepan, warm the butter and cream and add the purée. Season with several gratings of nutmeg, salt and pepper to taste. Warm the mixture over a medium flame, mixing well, and serve.
   Yield: 5 to 6 servings.

COUNTERTOP MIXER

In 1948, my wife and I bought our first KitchenAid mixer (manufactured by the Hobart company). I recently acquired a new one, but not because the old one had failed. It had been moved to my summer house, where we now leave it permanently. It is working fine, thank you, and I have the suspicion it will be willed to the next generation.

I know that the modern kitchen is quickly filling up with machines of greater and lesser substance and with gadgets of all kinds. The reason the mixer is an important one to have even in a crowded kitchen is that it prepares cake batter like nothing else can. (In my experience, other mixers either lack its power or, if they have it, are too noisy as they do the job).

I was reminded of how good it was one day when my wife prepared two of her admirable cheesecakes a few days apart, the first using the mixer and the second with a food processor. The one made in the processor was not nearly so good as the other, although all the ingredients were the same. That's because this powerful machine uses all its strength to incorporate air into a heavy batter and thus make it lighter. No food processor does that acceptably well. The mixer does it better than a hand-held electric mixer, too.

Not only is the machine powerful, but also it is ingeniously designed (a design that has changed over the years, but surprisingly little). The beating action is done with what is called a planetary motion. As the beater spins, the machine moves it around the entire mixing bowl so that all the batter is processed.

In addition to preparing cakes, the mixer is excellent for whipping large quantities of cream or preparing a big batch of mayonnaise. The machine comes with a variety of beaters, each designed for a particular use. And these days, it is possible to buy a great many other accessories as well. To my mind, some of them are silly. I would not use this noble and powerful machine for a trivial job like the opening of cans (and thus would not buy the can opener attachment), and I certainly wouldn't call all its strength into play to operate a citrus juicer.

But the tried-and-true meat grinder is a good one. There are a number of slicers and shredders available. One of them is splendid for cole slaw.

What I believe is a relatively new design, the pouring shield, makes a lot of sense to me, too. This is a collar that fits around the mixing bowl. On the front of it is a chute for pouring ingredients into the bowl while the mixer is whirring. The chute prevents splattering. It is especially useful if you are preparing a mayonnaise and need to pour a steady stream of oil into the fragile emulsion.

As for cleaning, the new models remain as easy to deal with as the old ones. Most of the attachments can be placed in a dish washer. The main stand must never be immersed in water, however. The only way to clean it is with a damp cloth.

MARBLE CHEESECAKE

½ cup graham cracker
  crumbs
2 pounds cream cheese, at
  room temperature
4 eggs
1¾ cups sugar
¼ teaspoon almond extract
2 ounces unsweetened
  chocolate

1. Preheat the oven to 325 degrees.
2. Butter the inside of a metal cake pan measuring 8 inches wide and 3 inches deep. Do not use a springform pan. Sprinkle the inside with the crumbs, enough to coat the bottom and sides. Shake out excess crumbs, reserving about 1 teaspoon.
3. Place the cream cheese, eggs, sugar and almond extract into the bowl of a KitchenAid or other electric mixer. Start beating at low speed and, as the ingredients blend, increase the speed to high. Continue beating until thoroughly blended.
4. Melt the chocolate in a saucepan placed in a larger pan of boiling water, or use a flame-control device. Remove from heat to cool.
5. Place about one third of the cheesecake batter in the small bowl of the electric mixer. Add melted chocolate. Mix until smooth. Place plain batter and chocolate batter alternately, a large spoonful at a time, into the cake pan. Rotate pan briskly back and forth several times to level the top and slightly marbleize the two batters.
6. Place the pan inside a larger pan. The larger pan must not touch the sides of the cake pan and it must not be deeper than the cake pan. Pour hot water into the larger pan until it is about 1½ inches deep. Place in the oven and bake for 1½ hours. The top of the cake should be a rich golden brown and feel dry to the touch, but the cake will still be soft inside. Turn off the oven heat. Leave the cake in the oven for 30 minutes, then remove from the oven.
7. Remove the cheesecake from the water and place it on a cake rack for a few hours until it is completely cool. Do not cool the cake in the refrigerator because it will harden the butter and the cake will stick.
8. When the bottom of the cake pan has reached room temperature, place a flat plate or a board on top and invert. Remove the cake pan. Sprinkle the bottom of the cake evenly with a few more graham cracker crumbs. Refrigerate the cake for at least 5 hours, or preferably overnight. Or freeze it. Serve very cold. When cutting the cake, always dip the knife in hot water before each cut to prevent the cake from sticking to the knife.
   Yield: 12 or more servings.

HAND MIXER

There was a time when I looked on hand-held electric mixers with something not very short of disdain. After so many years with my nonmotorized whisks, I viewed those small electrical mixers with all the appreciation of a bicycle racer beholding a moped.

The day came, of course, when I was coaxed into using one. On that occasion I set the mixer to "beat" and almost instantly overbeat my egg whites — turning them into an ugly, granular substance — and left them for dead.

In recent years I, as well as many other serious cooks, have come to acknowledge that the hand-held mixer does have its strengths. It does not yield whipped cream that is as smooth as that achieved by skillful hand beating, nor does it beat egg whites as well. But for both jobs it is certainly better than merely adequate and relies less on individual strength and experience than does the whisk. The electric mixer does not allow the cook to feel the consistency of a food as well as a whisk does, but it is faster and requires much less effort.

When there is a lot of work to be done rapidly, I do turn to an electric portable every now and then. I've learned to use such mixers cautiously, however.

In beating cream or egg whites, I generally prefer to use the lower settings, regardless of what the dial on the mixer says. The slow beating incorporates the air with the cream or whites more gently, resulting in greater smoothness. Toward the end of most procedures one needs to increase the machine speed. But great watchfulness is required at all times. With cream, if you beat just a little too long and fast, heaviness sets in. With unsweetened egg whites — intended, say, for a spinach or cheese soufflé — overbeating will cause the whites to break down, leaving them with the look of watery rice cereal. (Egg whites that have had sugar added, as in the case of a meringue, resist breaking down.)

Whatever the chore, be careful not to leave the mixer spinning in one place for long; continuously move it clockwise and then counterclockwise to ensure evenness. You'll get better results with cream, by the way, if you make certain that the bowl and cream are well chilled.

The portability of these mixers means that they are excellent for working over the stovetop — to mix the yolks and sugar of a frosting in a double boiler, for instance, or to make a hollandaise sauce.

I like hand mixers that have many settings. One with six settings, for instance, is capable of going slower than those with fewer, and it can be increased in speed less abruptly as the cream or eggs thicken.

1. *An electric mixer makes a fine mayonnaise in not much more than a minute. (Those accomplished with a whisk can do it just as fast.) Beat all the ingredients except the oil on medium speed. Gradually add oil in a steady stream, moving the mixer all around the bowl. Turn speed to high for a few seconds to finish it off.*

MAYONNAISE

1 egg yolk
1 tablespoon Dijon
   mustard
1 tablespoon white wine
   vinegar
   Dash of Tabasco
¼ teaspoon Worcestershire
   sauce
   Salt and white pepper to
   taste
1 cup vegetable oil

With electric hand mixer (or a whisk) blend all ingredients but the oil for a few seconds. Continue to blend at medium speed while pouring oil in slowly. When mayonnaise is almost done, turn to high speed to finish it off.

Yield: About 1 cup.

Variations: For mayonnaise with herbs, add 1 tablespoon parsley, 1 tablespoon chives, 1 tablespoon tarragon.

PASTA MAKER

Some of the same people who have nothing but scorn for the dehydrated powder called instant coffee readily dine on reconstituted pasta. Yet the dried pasta that turns up in most kitchens is as far from the fresh variety as instant coffee is from the home-brewed.

Although there are many variations, the basic preparation of fresh pasta involves a large egg for each cup of flour (with a little water, if necessary, to help bind the two). The ingredients are blended into dough that is kneaded, rolled thin, cut and then boiled for about 3 minutes. Granted, the rolling and cutting are tedious if done without any specially designed equipment. That equipment does exist, however, and in profusion. With good machinery one is capable of producing a batch of flawless pasta — from raw ingredients to steaming noodles on a platter — in 15 minutes or so.

There are essentially two approaches. One kind of machine employs rollers that knead and roll the dough and cutters that render it into the desired shape. The other is the extrusion system; the ingredients are fed into the machine, forced through it and out holes of a given shape, producing a wide variety of pastas, since you choose a particular plastic cap with particular holes the way you would choose a particular tube for a pastry bag.

The first type of machine — the one with rollers — can be bought in manual and electric models. Some of the electric models come with a compartment that mechanically blends the flour and egg. The manual does not. The advantage of the electric models is that they are faster and leave both hands free to feed the rollers. With the manual version, one hand has to crank.

However, my own preference in all this is for the crank-operated machine that I've had for years. (I do ask for some electrical assistance, however, using my food processor to blend the dough and egg.) The extrusion machines, at least the newest ones I've seen, work marvelously but cost hundreds of dollars. The sturdy, reliable manual costs a fraction of that. And while the electrically powered rollers and cutters are nice to have, I really can't justify what is a considerable extra cost.

The slowest part with a manual is in the rolling. With two rollers set to offer the widest gap between them, a ball of dough is forced through so that it is flattened, then it is folded and run through several more times.

That done, the rollers are moved closer together in progressive stages until the machine turns out a thin band of dough. The band can be sliced with a knife to produce lasagna. But for thin pasta, another set of rollers, with cutting grooves, is used to slice the dough into long streams.

The machine I have, an Atlas, stands 5½ inches high on a 7-by-5-inch base. I love the feel of it. It is a chromed-steel, hand-cranked example of fine Italian engineering.

1. *Secure the machine firmly to the counter top and set the kneading rollers at 7. Flatten a ball of dough into a ½-inch-thick circle and feed it into the machine while turning the handle.* **2.** *Pull the dough out.*

3. *Fold the dough over and put it through the same setting. Repeat the folding and kneading at progressively lower settings until the dough is paper thin.* **4.** *Feed the thin sheet of dough through the noodle cutter.*

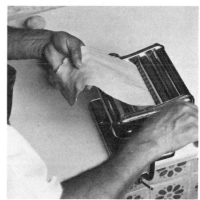

5. *Turn the crank to get long strands of fresh noodles.*

FRESH NOODLES

2¼ cups flour
3 large eggs

1. With the chopping blade in place, put flour and eggs in the bowl of a food processor and blend for about 20 seconds, or until well mixed. Press the dough with your hands into six balls.
2. Flatten each ball into a circle about ½ inch thick. Set the kneading rollers of a pasta machine at 7 (the highest level of most machines) and begin pushing the dough through the rollers as you crank. Fold dough over and put it through again. Repeat the folding and kneading at the 7 setting twice. Now begin pushing it through each successively lower number until it has been made paper thin at the number 1 setting.
3. Crank the dough through the noodle cutters of the machine.
   Yield: 1 pound fresh noodles.

PESTO (Basil and nut sauce) FOR PASTA

2 cups fresh basil
½ cup olive oil
2 tablespoon pine nuts (pignoli)
2 cloves garlic, peeled
Salt to taste
½ cup grated Parmesan cheese
2 tablespoons grated Romano pecorino cheese (or increase the quantity of Parmesan by this amount)
3 tablespoons butter at room temperature

1. Remove all tough stems from the basil. To measure, pack the leaves gently but somewhat firmly in a measuring cup without crushing the leaves.
2. Empty the basil into the container of a food processor or electric blender. Add the olive oil, pine nuts, garlic and salt and blend on high speed. Using a rubber spatula, scrape the sides down occasionally so that it blends evenly. Pour the mixture into a bowl and beat in the grated cheeses by hand. Beat in the softened butter.
3. Let stand until the pesto is at room temperature. When the pasta is cooked, and before draining, quickly add 1 or 2 tablespoons of the hot pasta water to the pesto and stir. Toss with the hot drained pasta and serve.
   Yield: Enough sauce for 1 pound pasta.

SAUSAGE MAKER

The Government allows up to 50 percent fat in a sausage, which makes for a lot of waste, let alone cholesterol. And that bit of knowledge alone might provide some motivation for making your own sausages. In addition to being less fatty, they also will taste a lot better than anything bought in a store.

Sausage is simply a combination of ground meat — generally pork — spices and herbs and it is most often stuffed into a casing. A good sausage should not be too lean, but it needn't be too fat either. About 35 percent fat suits my taste. In homemade sausage, I try for a mixture that is close to two parts lean pork to one part fatty pork.

There are many ways to grind the meat and stuff a casing. The method I find the most sensible is provided by a combination grinder-stuffer. With one of these contraptions, you force a length of casing (from a pig for larger sausages, or from a sheep for very small ones) onto a funnel in front, then feed the cubed-meat mixture into a chimney at the top. The casing should first be tested for holes by pouring water directly from the spigot through it.

As you grind, the meat is forced into the casing. The machines come with a variety of plates, which are blades that provide a fine or coarser grind, depending on the sausage. (Italian sausage or salami, for example, is far coarser than a frankfurter or bratwurst.)

Some suggestions about the machine's use: When the sausage reaches the desired length (which happens in seconds), twist the casing to seal off that link and start another. Each time you twist a link closed, do it in the direction opposite from the previous one; if all the twisting were done in the same direction, you would create the rubber-band-propeller effect — the whole works might spin itself open.

As the casing fills, try to put gentle pressure on it to prevent the formation of air pockets. If one does form, puncture it with a slender needle. Too much pressure on the casing will cause it to burst, although that is actually no catastrophe (you seal off the ends with string and continue).

The sausages can be made easily enough by one person, but it's faster with two: one feeding the mixture into the machine and controlling the casing, while the other turns the crank to grind. It's also the kind of thing that promotes kitchen camaraderie — if you're the kind of cook who can laugh when a sausage bursts and if you and your co-worker are likely to share a wave of elation when you have produced a mountain of sausages.

1. *After soaking and testing the sausage casing for holes, fit one end on the nozzle. Carefully pull the whole length of casing onto the nozzle.*
2. *When you reach the end, leave 2 to 3 inches of casing hanging.*

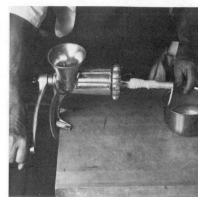

3. *Put the meat mixture into the grinder and turn the crank, guiding the sausage casing with the other hand as it is filled. Tie a knot at the end of the first sausage, then twist 3 times between each sausage, first one way then another.* **4.** *When all the sausages are made, tie a knot at the end.*

COUNTRY SAUSAGE

2 **pounds lean pork, cut into 1-inch cubes**
1 **pound cubed pork fat (from the shoulder)**
2 **tablespoons salt**
1 **teaspoon freshly ground black pepper**
1 **teaspoon marjoram**
⅛ **teaspoon chopped garlic**
4 **yards sheep casing**

1. Assemble meat grinder, with coarse blade and sausage extension in place.
2. Combine meat and fat in a large mixing bowl and toss with seasonings.
3. Place casing in a basin of cold water and let stand. Drain and return to basin of cold water. Check for holes by running a stream of water through extended casing. If a hole is found, cut away that part of the casing.
4. Pull the casing over the extension tube until the whole piece is coiled onto tube. Place some meat in the machine's funnel and begin cranking, holding the casing with one hand to permit free entry of the meat. Add more meat to the funnel as necessary. At first there may be air pockets forming at the end of the casing. Pinch off the meat until the air has stopped coming out (return the pinched-off meat to the funnel of the machine). Then keep cranking.
5. When each sausage has reached the desired length, twist the casing closed (with three turns) at the point where the meat enters. Resume cranking to form the next sausage, which should be twisted closed in the opposite direction from the preceding one.
6. Continue, alternating twisting directions, until ingredients are used. If sausage bursts at any point, tie a knot where it broke and resume. Tie the last sausage closed with a knot.

Yield: About 16 sausages of 4 inches in length.

Note: All of this can be done by one person but it is far easier if two people do it, one cranking and feeding the machine while the other manages the casing.

ICE CREAM MAKERS

Among my many jobs in the food world, ranging from an apprentice in France to a chef at Le Pavillon in New York City, one was as an executive at Howard Johnson's. This fact matters for the purposes of the discussion at hand because I have in my life dipped into so much ice cream that I can feel the amount of air in it with precision; I can taste the additives that a company uses; I know if one machine being used for a particular flavor has been poorly cleaned and has been contaminated with another flavor. I have a true and burning passion for ice cream, and I understand it all the way to its essence.

I also know how much Americans adore ice cream: Children, adults, the elderly crave it, sometimes feeling greatly satisfied, sometimes feeling disappointed, often feeling sinful in their excess.

Some manufacturers do a good job in making ice cream and others do not. But by far the best ice cream produced in America can be made by the home cook, who can eat it free of additives and absolutely fresh before it has started to deteriorate. The best, most elegant and the simplest of ices — the sorbets, as the French call them — can be produced in the home kitchen, too, with the same machines.

A good ice cream machine is a superb investment, although it will produce a costly dessert (the cream and milk and eggs being more expensive than many an additive).

Of the many ice cream makers I have tried, several are very unsatisfactory, too small, or awkward or slow. The one that I used for the longest time and liked the most until recently was the trusty White Mountain, a traditional ice cream maker that consists of a container within a bucket that holds ice and rock salt to intensify the cold. As the container turns (powered by electricity or by hand, depending on the model), it binds the ingredients, introducing some air for lightness, and freezes the mixture. I have always liked the look of this machine: It's reminiscent of the way ice cream was made generations ago.

I compared it to a new machine, the Il Gelataio manufactured by Simac, a crisp new piece of equipment that I knew little about at the time. This new machine cost about twice what the White Mountain did and had, I felt, an obligation to perform well. In fact it did do its job with great efficiency. It looks something like a large food processor and isn't any harder to use.

The Simac's cooling is done electrically, its bowl and churner housed in a white plastic-enclosed refrigeration unit that sits on the tabletop. What you get from it is not a better ice cream, but a neater procedure: There is, of course, no rock salt or ice to worry about, and the machine cleans easily.

The container can make only one quart of ice cream at a time (compared with a gallon or so in the White Mountain), but that is much less a fault here than in some other machines. The whole process takes only about 20 minutes and it is a simple matter to prepare several batches when needed. The clear plastic lid on top allows you to watch the progress of the mix.

Unquestionably, this is an impressive machine. I wondered as I used it that first time whether it would supplant the White Mountain in my heart. And ultimately, although my traditional self wanted me to deny it, the Simac did win out. Certainly, some traditionalists and others who simply don't want to spend the extra money will still opt for the White Mountain, and I am glad of that, rather the way a divorced husband feels when he knows that his once beloved first wife will surely find other suitors.

As for the ice cream and sorbets that these machines can produce, the accompanying recipes make, I hope, an important point. Simplicity is the secret. That, and a sense of creativity. Once you understand that there are bases on which you can build whatever dessert you desire, the way is clear for the making of ice creams and sorbets to become a kind of artistry. Add a liqueur. Try a different fruit. But first try the recipes as presented until the procedure and the machinery become familiar to you.

1. *Beat egg yolks and sugar together with a stiff wire whisk until they are a bright lemon color. Stir in the milk.* **2.** *Cook the mixture in a wide saucepan until it registers 175 degrees. When removed from the heat, it will continue to cook to 180 degrees.*

3. *Strain the custard mixture through a chinois or other fine-meshed sieve into a metal bowl, which will facilitate cooling.*
4. *When the custard is chilled, pour and scrape it into the container of an ice cream machine. Freeze according to the manufacturer's instructions.*

5. *The finished ice cream should be smooth and not runny.* **6.** *If you are using the Simac machine, pour the cooked custard directly into the machine, which is self-refrigerated, then proceed according to the manufacturer's instructions.*

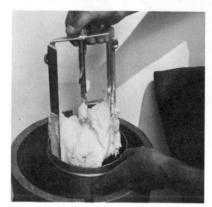

BASIC SORBET SYRUP

3 cups sugar
3 cups water

Mix sugar and water thoroughly in a saucepan. Bring mixture to a boil, stirring. Simmer for 5 minutes and remove to a stainless steel bowl to cool. Stir occasionally. Syrup will cool faster if placed over ice in a second mixing bowl. When syrup is no longer steaming, chill in refrigerator. Once under refrigeration the mixture will last for at least two weeks.

Yield: About 3½ cups or enough for 2 quarts sorbet.

STRAWBERRY SORBET

2 pints hulled fresh
   strawberries (or
   raspberries)
1¾ cup basic sorbet syrup
2 tablespoons lemon juice

Using chopping blade, purée the berries in a food processor for 20 seconds. Pour into a medium mixing bowl. Add the sorbet syrup and stir. Add the lemon juice. Pour into ice cream machine and freeze, following manufacturer's instructions.

Yield: About 1 quart.

Variation: For an extraordinarily light sherbet, gently beat 1 egg white with a fork and add it just as mixture starts to freeze (after 10 or 15 minutes). A nice idea is to serve the two sherbets in layers to alternate textures.

ORANGE SORBET

1 quart fresh orange juice
½ cup sugar
2 tablespoons lemon juice
1 teaspoon grated orange
rind
1 egg white, slightly beaten

Combine all the ingredients except egg white and pour into ice cream machine. Start to freeze following manufacturer's instructions. As mixture begins to thicken add egg white and resume freezing.

Yield: About 1 quart.

STRAWBERRY SORBET WITH FRAMBOISE

2 pints cold fresh
strawberries
Sugar to taste
Lemon juice to taste
2 tablespoons framboise
brandy

1. Purée the strawberries in a food processor until very fine and pour into a mixing bowl. Taste the purée and add ½ to 1 cup sugar, depending on natural sweetness of the fruit. Add 2 tablespoons to ¼ cup or more lemon juice, depending on how pronounced the strawberry flavor is (lemon juice enhances the strawberry's own flavor).
2. Pour mixture into ice cream freezer and follow manufacturer's instructions.
3. As mixture thickens add the framboise
   Yield: 1¼ quarts.

GRAPEFRUIT SORBET

2¼ cups fresh grapefruit
juice
1¾ cups basic sorbet syrup
1 tablespoon grated
grapefruit rind
2 tablespoons lemon juice

Combine all the ingredients in a mixing bowl. Pour into ice cream machine and freeze according to manufacturer's instructions.

Yield: About 1 quart.

ORANGE SHERBET WITH GRAND MARNIER

5 egg yolks
¾ cup sugar
1½ cups milk
1 cup cream
1 tablespoon grated orange rind
4 cups orange juice
2 tablespoons grand marnier

1. In a heavy mixing bowl, blend the yolks and sugar with a wire whisk until lemon colored. Add milk and cream and stir. Add orange rind and stir. Bring mixture to 180 degrees, as measured with instant thermometer, stirring constantly with a wooden spatula. Pour into a stainless steel bowl and let cool at room temperature.
2. Pour orange juice and grand marnier into mixture. Place in ice cream maker and follow instructions for the machine.

CUSTARD BASE FOR FRENCH ICE CREAM

¾ cup sugar
5 egg yolks
2 cups milk
2 cups cream

1. In a heavy 1-quart bowl, beat the sugar and yolks with a small, stiff whisk until yolks are a bright lemon color. Add 1 cup of the milk and stir.
2. In a wide saucepan, combine the egg mixture with the cream and remaining milk. Stirring constantly, bring mixture to 180 degrees, as measured by a rapid-reading thermometer. If you allow mixture to boil, it will take on an undesirable cooked flavor. Strain the mixture into a stainless steel bowl and use as directed in specific recipes.
Yield: About 1 quart.

VANILLA ICE CREAM

Using the custard base recipe, add 2 teaspoons vanilla extract or 1 split vanilla bean to the saucepan. Cook and strain as described and then chill the mixture, stirring occasionally, before placing it in ice cream machine. Follow the manufacturer's instructions.

PEACH ICE CREAM

When the ice cream base is cooked and cooled, add 1 cup finely chopped, skinned peaches (to remove the skin, drop peach in boiling water for 12 seconds and then peel with paring knife and fingers). Place in ice cream machine, following manufacturer's instructions.

CHOCOLATE ICE CREAM

Melt 4 ounces semisweet chocolate and 1 ounce unsweetened chocolate in a double boiler. Add to ice cream base while it is still warm. Chill, stirring occasionally, and place in ice cream machine, following manufacturer's instructions.

ESPRESSO ICE CREAM

Dissolve 4 tablespoons instant espresso in 4 tablespoons of warm water. Add to basic mixture while it is still hot. Chill, stirring occasionally, and place in ice cream machine, following manufacturer's instructions.

MAPLE PECAN ICE CREAM

Add 1 cup pure maple syrup and 1 cup coarsely chopped pecans to the basic mixture. Cool and place in ice cream machine, following manufacturer's instructions. This is a very sweet concoction. To make it less so use only ½ cup sugar in the base.

PERNOD ICE CREAM

Follow recipe for vanilla ice cream, stirring in 2 or more tablespoons of Pernod (depending on how pronounced you want the flavor to be) and a dash of green vegetable coloring while the mixture is still warm.

CITRUS JUICER

Despite claims coming from the direction of Madison Avenue, we all know full well that freshly squeezed orange juice does not taste at all like any of the other products called orange juice, whether frozen, powdered, canned or containerized.

For people who enjoy good orange juice, all those commercials have to be put out of mind. The only real question is how to squeeze fresh citrus fruit fast and with the least effort. The most common devices use conical reamers that dig into the fruit. This is done manually (the orange is forced down over the reamer and is rotated while the reamer remains still), or it is done mechanically — the reamer spins while the fruit is pressed over it.

I don't especially care for either method. Both are slow — even electric juicers seem to me to take much more time than they ought to. And the reamer can cut into the rind, resulting in a bitter taste.

I much prefer juicers that work on the principle of the manual press. The press is an expensive — approaching $200 as of this writing — but magnificent piece of machinery that is often used in restaurants or by sidewalk vendors. The one I have in mind is made by Hamilton Beach.

It works this way: A glass is placed beneath the device (as that is done a plastic, spring-operated cup is pushed aside; it will swing back into position to catch drips as soon as the glass is removed); half an orange or grapefruit is placed on a pyramidal strainer positioned above the glass. By turning the machine's handle, a caplike unit is lowered onto the fruit, pressing out its juice, while the pulp and pits stay behind. The engineering of this juicer is so exquisite that virtually no effort is necessary. The juicer is simply cleaned. The strainer and funnel under it pop out and rinse clean. The cap that lowers over them can be unscrewed for washing or it can be wiped dry where it is.

1. *When you want fresh citrus juice to drink or in quantity for a recipe, there is nothing easier than a manual press. Just put the halved fruit on the metal strainer and pull down on the handle.* **2.** *If you need just a small amount of juice, use a citrus reamer placed over a cup.*

OUTDOOR EQUIPMENT

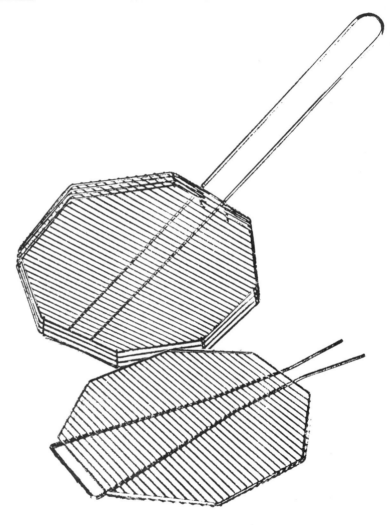

When the days grow hot, I move to my summer place, more a cabin than a house, on Gardiners Bay at the eastern end of Long Island. It is my seasonal tradeoff. I pay for the expansive view of placid water and deep sky by accepting the burden of a kitchen so constricting that it is difficult to wash dishes in it, let alone cook.

I wanted cooking equipment that would allow for some ambitious work, the poaching of fish, for instance. But it would have to be portable enough to be carried in and out of the house or in and out of my car's trunk. None of the campers' equipment I saw — designed as such things are for backpacking and the like — was adequate. Too flimsy. Hibachis were too limited in their uses. And, anyway, I prefer to light my fire not in some metal container but right on the beaches of the bay, where the rocks that abuse the feet of bathers turn benign as they intensify the heat of a wood-fueled flame.

What I ultimately did was design my own devices. There are two that especially please me. I had them built at a local ironworks, but it is my impression that similar pieces of equipment could be made by any resourceful welding shop, of which there are many.

I also acquired a splendid grilling basket, which holds on to food over a fire better than anything else I've seen. As for special utensils, I have never been one to worry much about a grilling batterie de cuisine (I don't wear my chef's toque while I hover over the flame; actually, I only rarely wear a shirt). Ordinary tongs of the scissor-action type seem adequate to me. And I use my long-pronged fork to pop a grilling steak free of the hot rods beneath it, always careful not to pierce the meat.

When autumn comes around and I move away from the beach, I store the various grills, but I still have work to do outdoors. My smokehouse is my pride and joy in the fall. It is home made, too.

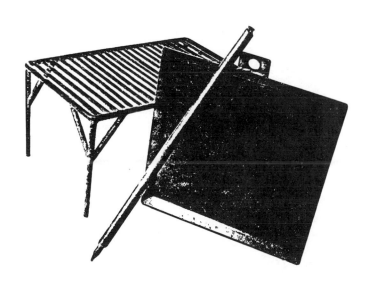

GRILLS

Since I couldn't find anything else like it, I designed and had built for me at the local ironworks a massive frying pan made of rolled steel. The pan is ⅛ inch thick and is supported by a single pole driven into the ground. It is 15½ inches square, large enough to accommodate one cut-up chicken, a couple of pounds of sliced potatoes and a mound of sliced onions. It is excellent for pan-frying several trout or for any large sautéeing job.

The lip along its rim is 1¼ inches high and is sloped, which makes for easier access with a spatula than do perpendicular sides, but the latter should work, too. At the top of the rim on one side is a ¼-inch-thick appendage, angled upward, with a hole ⅞ of an inch in diameter. Through that hole goes the pointed pole, just barely narrow enough to fit (mine measures 1/64th of an inch less than seven-eighths). When the pole is angled just a bit away from the fire, the weight of this pan creates enough tension to hold it at any given level, so it can be adjusted to sit lower to the coals or farther from them. The astonishing thing is how sturdy it is.

Another device I designed and had made is a 20-inch-long grill that, when it settles onto the beach, provides an extremely solid surface for cooking meat directly over coals or for supporting a kettle of bouillabaisse. Its sturdiness comes from the thickness of the steel, ½ inch in the legs and in the supports and the rim, ⅜ of an inch in each of the traverse rods.

The care of these two grills involves no more than a good wire brushing, similar to what one does with the gas grill described in a later discussion.

1. *When I want to fry or sauté anything outdoors, I use the iron pan I had made. Pound the rod firmly into the sand or ground at an angle, which allows the grill to rest on it at any level and to swivel away from the heat.* **2.** *Heat the grill over the coals and use it as you would a frying pan.*

3. *For steaks or chicken, I use a 20-inch-long grill that sits directly over the coals. Grease the grill well and be sure to turn the meat with tongs so you don't release the juices.*

4. *This same grill is good for supporting large pans — in this case sautéed zucchini and broiled swordfish in a butter sauce.*

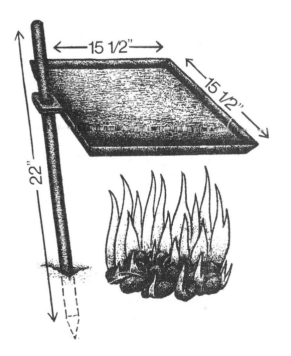

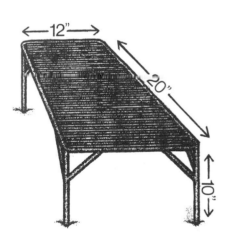

Illustrations by Chuck Albano

GRILLING BASKET

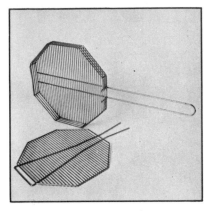

My outdoor repertoire was enhanced nicely the day I acquired a remarkable stainless steel grill that is a clever improvement on the grill for steaks and chops that one commonly sees. Those are usually two square wire surfaces hinged at one end with a long handle at the other. They work, of course, for steaks and chops, allowing you to turn the meat easily. They are hazardous, however, for more slippery fare, slender bits of fish, for instance, which are likely to slide out the side when you flip them. The new grill I brought home was an octagon made of stainless steel rods.

It is 13½ inches across, and the base has a wall (of steel rods) that rises about 1½ inches. Then there is a lid, which is adjustable at four different levels both at its handle and at its head. What it all amounts to is an extremely stable cooking area from which few morsels will ever slip. The lid holds food tightly; the sides prevent anything that does manage to slide from slipping out, and the corners provided by the octagonal shape also help keep things in place.

Because of the security offered by this grill, I was able to grill on the same surface at the same time the following: four marinated fillets of bluefish, twelve marinated shrimp (split open but left in their shells), and eight marinated slices of zucchini, cut lengthwise. The test was in the turning, and the whole meal, arranged so neatly, slid not at all. It also proved to be the best utensil I ever used for grilling a swordfish steak. But I would favor this grill for many other foods as well.

A word or two about care if you wish to grill fish: Grills constructed as this one is, with rods of wire, require that you scour them clean with soap and water. A mere wire-brushing of the surface will not do. The reason is that the surface must have absolutely no particles adhering to it. It takes very little to cause a fish to stick and for its looks to be irreparably ruined.

1. *For small or large pieces of fish, the octagonal stainless steel grill is the best I've ever found.* **2.** *Brush the grill with oil and hold it about 1 inch above the flame. When the grill is turned over, the fish doesn't slide and it can't fall out because of the wire sides.*

BROILED SWORDFISH IN BUTTER SAUCE

1 **2-pound swordfish steak**
  Salt and freshly ground
  pepper to taste
2 **tablespoons vegetable oil**
10 **leaves fresh basil, if**
  available
  Butter sauce or beurre
  blanc (see following
  recipes)

1. Sprinkle the fish with salt and pepper and rub with oil. Let marinate for 10 or 15 minutes, turning the fish a couple of times.
2. Place a grill about 1 inch from the coals. Brush it with some oil from the marinade. Place fish on the grill and cook 3 or 4 minutes on each side so that it has a seared appearance, but don't overcook the fish.
3. Transfer to a serving platter. If fresh basil is available, place about 10 leaves on top of the fish and spoon some of the butter sauce over it, or serve with beurre blanc spooned over it and alongside.
Yield: 4 servings.

BUTTER SAUCE

½ **cup melted butter**
  Juice of ½ lemon
2 **tablespoons chopped**
  parsley
  Salt and freshly ground
  pepper to taste

Combine all the ingredients and mix well.

BEURRE BLANC

3 **shallots, finely chopped**
2 **tablespoons finely**
  chopped ginger
⅓ **cup red wine vinegar**
½ **bay leaf**
12 **tablespoons softened**
  butter, cut into 12 pieces
  Salt and freshly ground
  pepper to taste

1. Just before the fish is cooked, place shallots, ginger, vinegar and bay leaf in a slant-sided fait-tout saucepan. Bring to a boil and reduce by two thirds, stirring occasionally.
2. Add the butter a tablespoon at a time while mixture is boiling, whisking rapidly. When all the butter is incorporated, the sauce should be very thick. Add salt and pepper to taste. Remove from heat and keep warm until fish is cooked.

GAS GRILLS

There are some days when the homemade grills I love so dearly seem not to fit the moment very well. When I want to do my outdoor cooking fast and cleanly, almost as if it were being done indoors, I turn to a gas grill, a hybrid device that first gained popularity more than a decade ago in California.

Gas is especially quick because it is ready after a preheating period of only 10 or 15 minutes. (The reason for even that much preparation is that the grill's volcanic rocks or ceramic blocks must be hot enough to cause dripping fat to flare and sizzle so they can flavor food much the way charcoal does.) The heat is infinitely variable, giving the cook much more control than an open fire does. And gas grills come with lids that can be closed for baking or roasting.

Manufacturers suggest that high-heat grilling also ought to be done with the lid closed to smoke the food more thoroughly and to cook it rapidly. Generally, I ignore that suggestion. Smoking by design is one thing. But smoking inadvertently doesn't make sense. I don't like steak that tastes too conspicuously of smoke. What I do instead is preheat the closed grill to 400 degrees, as indicated by a thermometer built into the lid, then grill with the lid raised at least part way.

Gas grills have improved over the last few years. The common cast iron construction, which left the grills vulnerable to the weather, has given way to cast aluminum, which is more durable.

The grills employ two kinds of gas supply: They can be permanently attached to a home's main gas line (the installation requires a plumber), or they can be hooked up to a bottle of propane gas. The latter option, combined with the lighter aluminum construction, makes these grills far more portable than they were before. A 20-pound bottle of gas will provide 20 hours or more of cooking.

Of course, gas grills still don't approach the portability of the standard hibachi and they are many times more expensive. The gas grill I am most familiar with is the G3TX model in Warm Morning's Broilmaster line. It is large and elaborate (too elaborate, if you expect to use it only rarely; others in the same line are simpler). This one has two independent burners, and it is 26½ inches wide with three adjustable grilling racks.

1. *Although I always clean the grill after using it, just to be certain I run a brush and a cloth over it immediately before I cook on it to remove any particles that might remain.*
2. *When cooking the barbecued duck, brush it frequently with the marinade and move and turn the pieces with tongs.*

BARBECUED DUCK

1 **4½ pound duck (Muscovy duck is preferable because it is low in fat)**
2 **tablespoons soy sauce**
¼ **cup dry sherry or marsala**
1 **tablespoon chopped ginger**
2 **teaspoons chopped garlic**
1 **tablespoon chopped fresh coriander**

1. Cut the duck into serving pieces, as with chicken (see page 7). Trim away excess fat.
2. Prepare a marinade of soy sauce, sherry, ginger and garlic in a shallow pan (a gratin pan is perfect) and place the duck pieces in the pan. Marinate for 2 hours or more in the refrigerator, turning the pieces occasionally.
3. Preheat a gas grill and cook the duck for about 25 minutes at low heat, basting frequently with the marinade. The duck will have a charred look when it is done.
4. Top with chopped fresh coriander and let rest about 10 minutes before serving.
   Yield: 4 servings.

SMOKEHOUSE

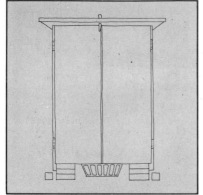

I have trouble describing the feeling I had about the smokehouse when I finally finished building it. Glee. That's close, anyway. I had done some smoking of food before, but I had never had my own roomy smokehouse to do it in. And now I felt like a scientist given a grant for a whole new project.

The three pheasant I brought back from a hunting trip in the Catskills had been hung for a week, then soaked in a honeyed brine for 24 hours. They were then smoked for most of a day as I kept touch with the smokehouse, adding wood, pulling some away, worrying about whether the heat was excessive or too gentle. The results were excellent.

I was also delighted with the sausage that came from the house and the smoked bluefish was a great success. The smokehouse was a splendid repository for sturgeon, mackerel or porgy, too.

As I write this, my smokehouse is limited so far to hot smoking. That is, the fire is contained inside. I expect, one of these days, to adapt it for cold smoking, with an external stove that pipes in smoke.

In hot smoking the objective is the production of a great volume of flavorful smoke — from hickory, cherry or apple wood — without intense heat. The fish, for instance, was smoked for 3½ hours at only about 160 degrees, the pheasant were mostly at 200 degrees. To measure the heat I used a simple kitchen thermometer thrust through a hole at the top of the smokehouse.

The heat within the house is regulated by opening the doors when necessary. But more subtly it is controlled by small manipulations of the amount of air that reaches the smoldering wood.

The house is 51 inches high and 48 wide and deep, made of marine plywood that will not warp in the rain. It contains three racks, two of which cost me dearly. I had a local craftsman make them from sturdy grating for $36 each. The third rack I found in a junkyard, a vestige of a refrigerator. The smoldering wood inside the house is held by an iron basket that is common for holding logs in fireplaces. I found it, too. Rods at the top of the house allow for the hanging of eel or sausage.

The fire is vented through six ½-inch holes drilled on each side just under the roof. It is fed through the house's simple cinder block foundation. To ensure that some air could get through, one of the blocks supporting each wall is positioned on its side so that the openings these blocks are designed with would face outward rather than upward. To control the airflow through those holes from outside the house, I slide a piece of two-by-four in front of the holes, covering them completely or just part way. Crude, but it works. To ensure that no flame touches the food, a perforated piece of sheet metal is propped over the fire, allowing smoke through and around the food but shielding away more intense heat.

The total cost of the house was about $150, given my willingness to salvage. Obviously, depending on the vagaries of inflation and luck, a similar one might cost a good deal more. It is certainly possible to buy small, commercial smokehouses for home use. All the ready-made alternatives undoubtedly require less work than my house does. But they don't have its capacity or its character.

A — Meat thermometer for temperature
B — Ventilation holes
C — Three firebricks
D — Cinder blocks placed as shown to provide ventilation or draft on side
E — Plywood sides overhang to cover one-half of cinder block holes
F — Board to block or regulate draft

G — Closure
H — Pole for hanging sausage
I — Shelves
J — Sheet metal to guide smoke/heat
K — Grate for fire
L — Front view of firebricks — overhanging plywood sides and board to block draft on side

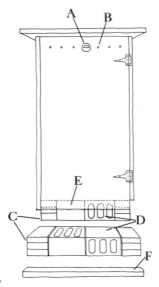

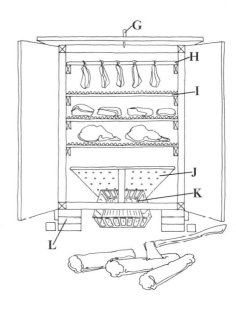

Illustrations by Lauren Jarrett

Preparing the Smokehouse

Place two handfuls of cherry wood, apple or hickory twigs in the base of the smokehouse along with about a cup of hickory chips, which can be purchased commercially. Start the fire with paper. With the doors of the smokehouse open, let the flame die down and then close the doors. What you want is a steady temperature of about 160 degrees for the initial stage of smoking fish and 200 for poultry or sausage. If the temperature is too low, add more wood. If it is too high, leave the doors slightly ajar until it has fallen.

HOT-SMOKED BLUEFISH

4 tablespoons kosher salt
4 tablespoons brown sugar
¼ teaspoon paprika
4 large bluefish fillets
   (about 1¼ pounds each)
   with skin and scales still
   on
¼ cup vegetable oil
   Freshly ground pepper to
   taste

1. Remove smokehouse racks and prepare fire (see page 237).
2. In a mixing bowl, combine the salt, sugar and paprika.
3. Brush rack lightly with oil and place fish on the rack, skin side down. (The skin and scales must be left on because they will help hold the fish together, but they are not to be eaten.) Sprinkle fillets liberally with seasoning mixture, about 2 tablespoons each fillet. Using a soft-bristled brush, apply the oil to each fillet, thoroughly moistening fish and seasonings. Sprinkle generously with freshly ground pepper.
4. Place fish in smokehouse at 160 degrees. After about ½ hour allow temperature to drop to 150 degrees, and then check smokehouse regularly to be sure that the temperature is maintained, at least within the range of 140 to 160 degrees. Smoke for 3 hours. Then add wood to the fire and bring temperature up to about 200 degrees. Smoke ½ hour longer.
5. Serve chilled, sprinkled with lemon juice or accompanied by a mixture of sour cream, horseradish and a dash of Tabasco.
   Yield: 4 to 6 servings per fillet.
   Note: Other fish that can be prepared this way include sturgeon, mackerel, porgy, brook trout and lake trout. Small fish can be smoked whole. They can be stored for 2 or 3 weeks in the refrigerator.

HOT-SMOKED PHEASANT

3 2½-pound pheasant that have been hung for at least a week
18 cups water
1¾ cups salt
½ cup honey
¼ teaspoon allspice
1 teaspoon freshly ground black pepper
Bay leaf
¼ cup vegetable oil
¾ teaspoon paprika

1. Truss the pheasant. Combine the water, salt, honey, allspice, pepper and bay leaf, and soak the pheasant for 24 hours.
2. Prepare the smokehouse (see directions).
3. Pat each pheasant dry and brush with oil. Sprinkle liberally with paprika and, using a brush, spread it over the birds.
4. Place pheasant in smokehouse at 200 degrees and maintain the heat in a range of 180 to 200 degrees for about 6 hours. Raise the temperature in the smokehouse to 220 to 240 degrees for 1 hour. Remove the pheasant and allow to cool. Serve chilled with fresh lemon juice or cranberry sauce.

Yield: Each pheasant serves 4 to 6.

Note: Smoked pheasant stores extremely well, at least a month under refrigeration. The same procedure can be used for turkey or chicken (without, of course, the necessity for hanging), but the smoking time would have to be increased depending on the bird's size.

ODDS & ENDS

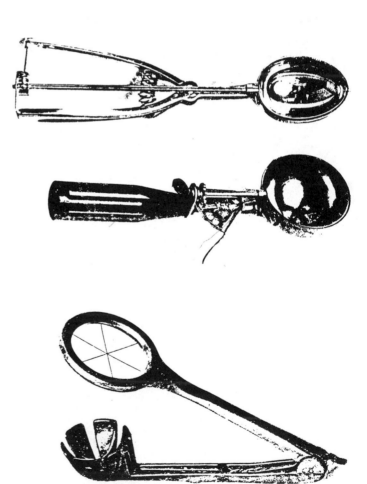

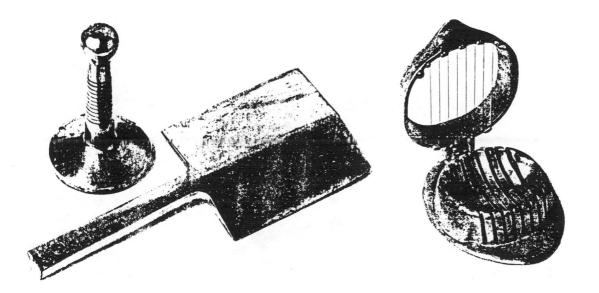

SHRIMP DEVEINER

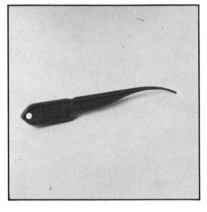

During the days when my son Jacques was well on the way to becoming a cook in his own right, he would tell me about a new technique he learned or a new gadget he'd been using in some local restaurant. I am grateful for the day he reported to me on a bizarre looking plastic tool called a Zipout, which shells and cleans shrimp with one quick thrust.

The shelling and deveining of shrimp has always struck me as a tedious procedure, the price one paid for the fact that the shrimp cook so quickly once they are prepared. Although I was skeptical about this long (10½ inches) curved tool, I was in a hurry to try it, and I found that the thing does work well. You insert the point into the wide end of the shrimp just under the shell where a hole has been formed by the dark strand of the digestive tract. Holding the shrimp straight with one hand, you force the tool through with the other hand. When the point has gone all the way through the shrimp and about 4 inches beyond it has almost invariably pulled the shell away from the shrimp while scraping it clean. It does this in most cases without significantly damaging the flesh, although to do this maneuver fast and without fail one must practice for a few minutes. I've tried the tool on very large shrimp as well as on those somewhat smaller and it works nearly as well on both.

It is a relief to be able to say that this delightful gadget, manufactured by Zipout International (P.O. Box 1972, Cedar Rapids, Iowa) is as inexpensive as a vegetable peeler. If you're interested in buying this gadget, and find it unavailable in local stores, my suggestion is that you write to the company for current availability and price.

1. *Push the deveiner into the black hole at the top of the shrimp, and then all the way through and out the other end, which breaks the shell.*
2. *Pull the shrimp away from the shell.*

SHRIMP PROVENÇALE

1½ pounds shrimp
4 to 6 medium-size tomatoes, about 1½ pounds
3 tablespoons olive oil
Salt and freshly ground pepper to taste
4 tablespoons butter
1 whole chili pepper, optional
1 tablespoon finely minced garlic
2 tablespoons chopped fresh basil, optional
2 tablespoons chopped parsley

1. Shell and devein the shrimp.
2. Peel and core the tomatoes. Cut them in half crosswise. Squeeze the tomatoes to remove seeds. Cut them into ½-inch cubes. There should be about 1½ cups.
3. Heat 2 tablespoons of the oil in a skillet and add the tomatoes, salt and pepper. Sauté for about 5 minutes, to remove most of the liquid, and place on serving platter.
4. In a black steel frying pan, heat the remaining tablespoon of oil and the butter. Add the shrimp and salt and pepper. Cook, shaking and stirring, for about 3 minutes. Do not overcook. Add chili pepper and garlic. Sauté quickly so garlic does not brown. Place over tomatoes. Garnish with basil and parsley.

Yield: 4 servings.

NEW ORLEANS SHRIMP

1½ pounds fresh shrimp
3 tablespoons butter
¾ cup chopped onion
3 small ribs celery, chopped
1 green pepper, cored, seeded and chopped
3 cloves garlic, minced
2 cups canned tomatoes
2 sprigs fresh thyme, or ½ teaspoon dried
1 bay leaf
Tabasco sauce to taste
½ teaspoon grated lemon rind
Salt and pepper
2 tablespoons finely chopped parsley
Juice of half a lemon

1. Shell and devein the shrimp. Rinse and pat dry. Set aside.
2. Melt the butter in a saucepan and add the onion. Cook, stirring, until onion is wilted and add the celery, green pepper and garlic. Cook briefly, stirring. The vegetables must remain crisp.
3. Add the tomatoes, thyme, bay leaf, Tabasco, lemon rind, salt and pepper. Simmer 10 minutes uncovered.
4. Add the shrimp and cover. Cook 3 to 5 minutes, no longer. Add the chopped parsley, lemon juice and, if desired, more Tabasco sauce to taste.

Yield: 4 servings.

EGG SLICER

If ever there was justification for gadgetry in the kitchen, it is the egg slicer. Egg slicing is an annoyance by hand, but it is instantaneous as well as almost always perfect when done by a gadget designed for the purpose.

There are two designs that interest me most. One has parallel wires that deliver the uniform thin slices that are especially good for sandwiches. It is by far the commonest variety of egg slicer. But, the shape it yields is not the ideal one for an antipasto or for what I like to think of as an egg salad (I try never to think of the mush of mayonnaise and eggs most often described by that term; when I make egg salad I use wedges of egg along with various sliced vegetables adorned by a dressing).

A particularly good slicer is one that produces the desired wedges rather than slices and is sold under the Westmark Columbus brand. The little device consists of two limbs joined like a nut cracker at one end. At the open end, one limb has a cup to hold the egg and the other has a circular cutting area with crisscrossed wires. When the device is shut over an egg, six uniform wedges emerge. It is simple and fast and, at first, it makes you giggle a little bit, as if it were a toy.

TOMATO AND EGG SALAD

4 medium tomatoes, cut into ¼-inch slices
4 hard-cooked eggs cut into wedges with egg slicer
1 can anchovies
4 slices red onion
  Salt and freshly ground pepper to taste
4 tablespoons olive oil
2 tablespoons vinegar
1 tablespoon chopped fresh basil, or 2 tablespoons chopped parsley

1. Alternate the tomato and egg slices around the periphery of a serving platter.
2. Place remaining egg slices in the center. Arrange anchovies over the egg and tomato. Separate onion slices into rings and place attractively over other ingredients. Pour oil of anchovies over all. Season with salt and pepper.
3. Blend the oil and vinegar and pour over platter.
4. Garnish with basil or parsley.
   Yield: 4 to 5 servings.

SALAD SPINNER

Once the drying of salad greens was a more athletic enterprise than it generally is now. I can remember placing the greens in a wire basket and firmly holding the basket's handle while whirling it through the air like a lasso. The centrifugal force would propel the water out of the leaves — and, incidentally, onto everything in the immediate environment.

Messy and tiring though it was, the effort was absolutely necessary. A salad must be cold, crisp and, most especially, it must be dry so that it will not repel the oil of a dressing.

A number of improvements on the drying procedure, all using the centrifugal principal, have been made in recent years.

The most common device these days is a plastic design comprised of a basket inside a covered bowl; the basket is turned by vigorous manipulation of a crank on the cover. As the basket spins, the expelled water settles in the bowl. It's less exhausting and neater than the original wire salad basket by far, and it is what I use most frequently. It's not necessarily the most efficient design, but I am content with it.

A good, perhaps better design for drying salad greens is one that is a lot like the crank-top models but varying in a significant way: It is operated by a cord attached to a flywheel. Just a single pull on the cord will set the basket inside the bowl spinning rapidly and smoothly. I have used one version of this design from time to time. A minor problem with some of these is that they come with no cover and have an annoying proclivity for hurling lettuce out of the basket.

Another spinner is a truly clever adaptation of the same mechanism. It is a covered flywheel dryer (the flywheel is in the lid and not in the base, as it is in uncovered models). The one I tried had a basket that is 4 inches deep and 9¾ inches in diameter, which is about the size of most of these. If the cord fails to rewind after it is pulled, the device is not broken — the mechanism is simply acting like a yo-yo that has refused to return, and the cord needs to be rewound. To do that, rotate the plastic plate that is screwed to the inside of the cover.

There are some tricks to using any salad spinner. Don't fill the basket too full; the greens will not dry as thoroughly if you do, and delicate leaves, such as those of the silken Boston lettuce, will be bruised in the crush.

No spin-dryer removes every single droplet of moisture from the leaves. Thus a number of methods have been devised for the final touch. One is to lay the leaves on paper towels and then put the whole batch — greens and towels — into a plastic bag or pillowcase in the refrigerator. After they have been dried, greens can be stored in a plastic bag in the refrigerator for one or two days.

MIXED GREEN SALAD VINAIGRETTE

4 cups mixed greens
(romaine, escarole, Bibb,
Boston, endive, arugula,
watercress)
Vinaigrette dressing (see
following recipe)

1. Purchase a sufficient number of the above greens to provide a salad of varied textures. Wash four cups of greens and dry thoroughly in a salad spinner. Tear the leaves with the hands. If leaves are small use them whole.
2. Toss with vinaigrette dressing. Usually, 1 tablespoon of vinaigrette is adequate for each cup of greens.
Yield: 4 servings.

VINAIGRETTE DRESSING

1 egg yolk
2 tablespoons Dijon
mustard
4 tablespoons red wine
vinegar
¼ teaspoon freshly ground
pepper
Salt to taste
1 cup vegetable oil
1 whole clove garlic

1. In a ceramic mixing bowl, place all ingredients except oil and garlic and blend well with a wire whisk.
2. Pour in oil in a steady thin stream, whisking all the while. Since vinegars vary greatly in strength, taste to see if the vinaigrette has enough punch. Add more vinegar if necessary.
3. Place the clove of garlic in the sauce and simply leave it there. The vinaigrette will store well in the refrigerator for several weeks.
Yield: 1½ cups.

Note: Use of the yolk makes the dressing creamier and prevents it from breaking up. However, it can be omitted to produce a lighter vinaigrette, if desired.

ZESTERS & STRIPPERS

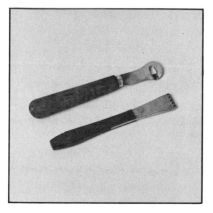

Routinely, one peels an orange or squeezes a lemon and throws away the skin, as if it were just so much kitchen detritus. That kind of disregard is sometimes misplaced, however. Citrus skins can be born again as candy, as the enhancement of a sauce or as decorations at the table.

The tools in this particular business are delightfully called peelers, strippers and zesters.

The zester is often used in serious cooking. This tool, which is reminiscent of a rake, is designed to cut into only the orange part of an orange's skin and not the white. The reason is that the skin's oils reside in the orange part, and that's all you want for a duck à l'orange sauce or any other orange sauce; the white part of the skin is too bitter. These shavings can also be used with cakes and can be candied by boiling them in sugar.

A variation of the same tool — it is called a scorer or a stripper or a lemon peeler — has a rounded head with a single cutting area. This device is drawn down the length of a lemon, making a deep, even excision. The shaving that results can also be candied, or it can be applied to a martini or coffee. The scoring of a lemon is often done not to obtain shavings but to enhance the appearance of a lemon slice. A single thin slice of scored lemon (the scoring gives it a fluted look) is placed on every piece of sole or trout meunière. Sometimes a lemon is meticulously scored and then carved into the semblance of a straw basket to prettify a dish.

These tools are generally equipped with stainless steel blades and like all other utensils ought to be sturdy. The fact is that you will use them only infrequently. They should last a lifetime; I've had the same ones for as long as I can remember.

1. *Pull a zester over citrus fruit when you want fine shavings of the peel for sauces and cakes.* **2.** *Pull the stripper over a lemon, with your thumb pushing against the fruit, when you want larger pieces of peel for drinks or candied peel. If you then slice the lemon, it will make a decorative garnish for fish.*

PARCHMENT

You may never have heard of bakers' parchment. But you've touched it often enough, peeling it off the bottom of a store-bought pound cake, for instance. In the sometimes risky business of baking, parchment can make a big difference. A cake pan with its bottom lined with greased parchment will always relinquish its cake intact (at least I've never heard of an instance when the paper failed to work). The paper is fitted to the pan by placing the pan over it, drawing an outline and then cutting out the shape.

When the cake is finished, the paper readily peels off the bottom. There is generally little need to line the sides of a pan because the cake will tend to pull inward and away from the sides as it cooks and thus should not stick.

1. *To cut paper for quenelles (see page 61), cut a large square and fold it in half. Fold in quarters, then eighths and continue folding as if you were making a paper airplane. Hold the paper over the pan with the tip in the center; cut at the inside edge and cut the tip.* **2.** *Open the circle of paper.*

DREDGER

As I have said time and again, an important part of good cooking is to have your act down to the point where you can move quickly and effectively. What may seem like an inconsequential piece of equipment — but I wouldn't do without it — is something called an all-purpose dredger. This aluminum dredger is the size and shape of a mug with a perforated cap that screws on top of it. I keep it on a shelf just under the worktable.

It could hold flour or a mixture of sugar and cinammon or even salt. Mine holds confectioners' sugar largely because of my affection for strawberry soufflés (see recipe, page 157). If I am entertaining at home, at the appropriate moment I excuse myself from the table and, with the practice of many years, quickly put together what almost always proves to be a satisfying and handsome group of individual soufflés. Timing and presentation are, of course, at the core of soufflé-making. As these little soufflés emerge from the oven, I reach down below the worktable, grasp the dredger, dust the tops with sugar almost in the same motion, and march the soufflés toward the table. In my orderly kitchen, the dredger has always been there. If it weren't, I think I would suspect sabotage.

1. *I use the dredger to sprinkle confectioners' sugar over soufflés, cakes or pastries, when I want a fine garnish without any lumps. But you could also use it for flour and granulated sugar. The dredger should always be near at hand so you can rapidly dust soufflés evenly just before serving.*

ICE CREAM SCOOPS

Like most kitchen tools, the ice cream scoop has its secrets. The novice will take one or another of these utensils and, not quite knowing the rules that apply, will make the kind of small mistake that is hard to pinpoint in retrospect.

For instance, most cooks know that they need to dip a scoop in water before each use, or else the ice cream will not come loose. But you also have to remove the excess water from the scoop before dipping it into the ice cream. If this is not done, you will introduce droplets of water into the ice cream, the water will freeze and crystals will form, destroying the texture. The way to remove the excess water is to hold a folded towel in one hand and strike the scoop against the towel sharply once or twice before dipping.

Also, the water should be warm, but not hot. Hot water will melt part of the ice cream; it will refreeze in the container, but will have lost its consistency.

And always begin scooping along the wall of the container, working your way inward in a circular fashion. Failing to do that results in a thin layer of ice cream adhering to the sides where, if it is returned to the freezer, it will deteriorate more rapidly than the rest. Incidentally, ice cream keeps best at 0 degrees or below; its best scooping temperature is 10 to 15 degrees.

Of the scoops available, there are a few good options. The Zerol scoop is a nonmechanical tool (that is, it has no movable parts) that is able to create a perfect ball. The scoop is pushed forward into the ice cream or sherbet and as it goes it causes the dessert to roll over on itself until it is a complete ball. Interrupting this process midway allows the scoop to produce a curved ribbon for decoration.

As for the mechanical scoops, they pop out the ice cream very cleanly because of a movable scraper, often spring-operated, inside the bowl of the tool. The common circular version of this type is perfect for ice cream cones. One side of the scoop is relatively flat with what people in the ice cream business call a lip, which is a rim of ice cream at the scoop's base, securing it on the cone.

The oblong-shaped mechanical scoop is a good way of producing quenelles, if you find your skills uncertain in the traditional wet-spoon method.

Mechanical scoops are good for apportioning food, too. If you are making stuffed cabbage and want to quickly allot 3 ounces for each serving, a 3-ounce scoop will do it. That apportioning ability works with muffins, too, allowing you to deposit equivalent amounts of dough in each form.

The scoops come in a variety of metals as well as sizes. Stainless steel is not the most expensive, but it is more than adequate. A scoop about 2 inches in diameter will give you 20 servings per quart, each serving being the size that one is accustomed to in ice cream stores.

MEAT POUNDERS

When a recipe instructs you to pound a piece of meat until it is flat, be careful. A fine cut of veal does not call for a sledgehammer approach; it requires an appropriate meat pounder and enough sensitivity to flatten the meat without pulverizing it.

The reason you pound meat is to make it thin, smooth and yielding, while leaving its fibers intact. Pounding is indispensable in the preparation of veal scaloppine and works magic on a chicken breast.

Pounders come in several designs. All of the useful ones weigh at least a pound and are made of metal (wood is too light and is prone to splintering). With each of them you will have to use a certain amount of force, emanating largely from your wrist, but mostly you will want to allow the weight of the head to do the work for you. It is best to place the meat between the sides of a plastic storage bag cut open at the seams.

One design familiar to French cooks has a head that is 4 or 5 inches square and a straight handle. It has a thick center that tapers to honed edges that can be used for cleaving. Its broad, flat surface makes it excellent for dealing with large cuts of meat as well as smaller ones. The disadvantage is that the handle is level with the surface of the pounder, so you must be able to work on meat near the edge of a counter to prevent rapping your knuckles while striking the meat.

An Italian design is small and round with a little handle that springs straight up from its center and it is thus easier to use in tight spaces.

As you shop for a pounder, I suggest you try the various designs on an imaginary piece of meat to see which suits you best. It is possible to buy pounders at a wide variety of prices and in many different metals. So long as it is sturdy, heavy enough and comfortable, one pounder is as good as another.

Don't confuse a pounder with one of the hammerlike tenderizers that have metal studs on the surface; they are for breaking the fibers of, say, a tough Swiss steak, but a tender slice of meat will be brutalized by one of those things.

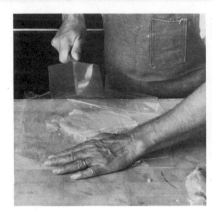

1. *Pound each side of the chicken breast, slowly working from the middle out to the edges.* 2. *Finished breasts should be about ¼ inch thick.*

CHICKEN BREASTS FRANCESE

2 **pounds chilled chicken breast (8 whole breasts, split), boneless, skinless and trimmed of excess fat and gristle**
3 **eggs**
 Salt and freshly ground pepper to taste
1 **cup flour**
3 **tablespoons oil**
7 **tablespoons butter**
8 **slices lemon**
 Juice of ½ lemon
¼ **cup chopped parsley**

1. Place chicken between layers of wax paper or, better yet, cut a plastic storage bag open and place the chicken in it (it is far stronger than paper). Pound on each side until ¼ inch thick. Start slowly, striking toward the middle of the breast and pulling toward the periphery. Repeat with each breast.
2. Crack eggs onto a platter. Add salt and pepper and whisk together. Place flour on another platter.
3. Heat the oil and 3 tablespoons of butter in a large skillet.
4. Sprinkle the chicken with salt and pepper. When butter is bubbling begin to dredge chicken in flour and then in egg and place in pan. Cook each piece about 2 minutes on each side until lightly browned and remove to a platter. If the pan is large enough, it should accommodate about three pieces at a time.
5. Place lemon slices over chicken. Pour lemon juice evenly over chicken. Pour off oil from the pan and wipe with toweling. Place remaining butter in pan over medium heat and swirl it around until it bubbles and begins to brown (this is beurre noisette). Pour over the chicken and sprinkle with parsley.
 Yield: 8 servings.

VEAL SCALOPPINE

1¼ pounds veal scaloppine
Salt and freshly ground
pepper to taste
¼ cup flour
4 tablespoons vegetable oil
5 tablespoons butter
1 slice peeled lemon for
each scaloppine
Juice of ½ lemon
2 tablespoons chopped
parsley

1. Place each scaloppine between two sheets of plastic wrap (or between halves of a cut-up storage bag) and flatten with metal meat pounder, taking care not to break the meat but at the same time striving for a thickness of only 1/16 inch.
2. Sprinkle scaloppines with salt and pepper.
3. Place flour on a flat plate and pat each scaloppine in flour to coat both sides.
4. Heat the oil and 1 tablespoon of butter in a shallow skillet until bubbling hot. Sauté the veal quickly, perhaps a minute on each side, turning with a long, narrow spatula. Remove to a serving platter.
5. Place 1 slice of lemon on each scaloppine. Pour lemon juice over the veal. Pour off fat and place 4 tablespoons of butter in the still-warm pan. Melt and pour over scaloppine. Sprinkle with parsley.
Yield: 4 servings.

CHEESECLOTH

The bouquet garni, basically a mixture of herbs, owes much of its usefulness to its package, which is porous and allows the flavor of the herbs to spread. The bouquet can contain ingredients in countless combinations, but generally consists of parsley, thyme and bay leaf wrapped in cheesecloth.

The wrapping of cheesecloth is vital, for it holds the packet together as a single unit but does not hold in the flavor. The cloth is necessary because in many preparations such as stocks and soups you do not want pieces of the parsley, thyme and bay leaf to infiltrate the liquid. Only their flavor is supposed to escape before they are removed as a unit from the pot.

Cheesecloth — which got its name because it was used to separate the curds and whey in cheese making — has a great many other uses, too. A frequent one in my kitchen is for straining consommé. It is also useful in poaching fish, because the fish can be wrapped in the cloth, set into liquid and then lifted out whole by grasping the cloth firmly and gently transporting it to a serving dish.

For any preparation, good quality cheesecloth makes sense. Cheesecloth that is too flimsy will not hold a shape (if you are using it to wrap a galantine of chicken, to take one elegant use) or will have to be used in many layers. If it is too coarse, it will allow the bouquet garni to slip through its pores.

The way to recognize the good from the bad is to give the cloth a little lateral tug. Cheesecloth is almost always loosely woven cotton, but the inferior kinds will seem so loose in weave that they will lose all their strength in the face of the slight tug.

The best cloth I know about is available through the Voice of the Mountains catalogue of the Vermont Country Store, Weston, Vt. 05161. It is a very fine weave that has never failed.

1. A bouquet garni is just one of the many uses for cheesecloth. Cut a square of the cloth and place fresh and dried herbs in the center. 2. Pull up the sides to form a pouch and tie it securely so that nothing can escape into the cooking liquid except the flavor.

SOURCES APPENDIX

Good equipment can be found almost anywhere in the country. Specialty stores, once scarce, are now remarkably common. The cities have their commercial supply houses, which are especially useful for large pieces of equipment. Department stores in recent years have shown that they know a decent pan when they see one.

Among the department stores that I've found to be most useful are: Macy's, Gimbels, Bloomingdale's, Neiman-Marcus, Henri Bendel, Foley's, Sangor Harris, G. Fox, J.L. Hudson's, Rich's and, in Canada, Simpson's and Eaton's.

Among the other sources that I know to be extraordinarily helpful if you drop in (or write) are:

Bridge Kitchenware Corporation, 214 East 52d Street, New York, N.Y. 10022. The gruff, eccentric proprietor is offensive to some, endearing to others, but, regardless, Fred Bridge knows more about kitchen equipment and keeps a better stock than any other store owner I know.

The Chef's Catalog, 725 County Line Road, Deerfield, Ill. 60015. An attractive display purveying a number of items described herein.

Dean & Deluca, 121 Prince Street, New York, N.Y. 10012. This store in New York's SoHo opened primarily as a food shop, but it quickly became clear that these people knew a great deal about selecting and selling equipment. The New York store and the East Hampton, Long Island branch are especially strong in molds, pans and small utensils.

Kitchen Bazaar, 4455 Connecticut Avenue, N.W., Washington, D.C. 20008. For years we've received this shop's cheerful mail-order catalogue, and at one time or another it has included a majority of the items in this book.

Kitchen Kaboodle, 2260 N.E. 28th Avenue, Portland, Ore. 97212. A widespread chain of these stores in the Northwest, each of them competent, is a reminder to me of how pervasive attempts at good cooking have become.

The Professional Kitchen, 18 Cooper Square, New York, N.Y. 10012. A good supply of knives, pans and some machinery, as well as other important pieces of equipment.

Sur La Table, 84 Pine, Pike Place Farmers' Market, Seattle, Wash. 98101. This place never fails to remind me of Bridge because of its wide range of equipment.

Williams-Sonoma, 576 Sutter Street, San Francisco, Calif. 94102. Another chain of excellent equipment stores. This one happens to have an attractive and full mail-order catalogue.

Zabar's, 2245 Broadway, New York, N.Y. 10024. Like Dean & Deluca, this place was primarily a food store that just kept expanding its equipment merchandising. Most notable, perhaps, is the fact that it offers the best prices we've seen on many of the tabletop electric utensils.

The large equipment mentioned in the kitchen design section will not be as readily found as everything else in this book. Here are some specific addresses:

The Delfield Company (also Foodservice Equipment), 980 South Isabella Road, Mount Pleasant, Mich. 48858.

Sub-Zero Freezer Company, Inc., P.O. Box 4130, Madison, Wisc. 53711.

Thermador Division of Norris Industries, 5119 District Boulevard, Los Angeles, Calif. 90040.

Wolf Range Company, 19600 South Alameda Street, Compton, Calif. 90221.

EQUIPMENT INDEX

RECIPE INDEX